A Handbook on
International
Wilderness Law and Policy

A Handbook on
International
Wilderness Law and Policy

Cyril F. Kormos, Editor

Fulcrum Publishing
Golden, Colorado

Library of Congress Cataloging-in-Publication Data

A handbook on international wilderness law and policy / Cyril F. Kormos, editor.
    p. cm.
  Includes bibliographical references and index.
  ISBN 978-1-55591-680-0 (alk. paper)
  1. Wilderness areas--Law and legislation. 2. Nature conservation--Law and legislation. 3. Wilderness areas--Management. 4. Conservation of natural resources--Law and legislation. I. Kormos, Cyril F.
  K3478.H357 2007
  346.04'6782--dc22
                                2007039780

Printed in the United States of America by Malloy Incorporated
0 9 8 7 6 5 4 3 2 1

Design by Patty Maher

Fulcrum Publishing
4690 Table Mountain Drive, Suite 100
Golden, Colorado 80403
800-992-2908 • 303-277-1623
www.fulcrumbooks.com

Table of Contents

Part III—Non-Statutory Wilderness Designations

Part IV—New Directions for Wilderness Law and Policy and Conclusions

Preface

The wilderness idea—that the force of law can protect an area in its natural and undisturbed state—is a powerful one. This book reveals the global reach of that concept and its enduring pull. By providing cutting-edge information on wilderness laws and policies, this volume portrays the current state of wilderness management around the world.

For practitioners in countries that already have a wilderness preservation system in place, this book will bring fresh perspective and a broader understanding of the wilderness concept. For conservationists in countries that have no such formal program, it will prove an invaluable guide to adapting the wilderness idea.

The Interagency Wilderness Policy Council (WPC) is pleased to have contributed to the development of this book. Based in Washington, D.C., the U.S. Government's WPC brings together all four wilderness management agencies—the National Park Service, the U.S. Fish and Wildlife Service, the Bureau of Land Management, and the U.S. Forest Service—as well as the U.S. Geological Survey to streamline discussions on policy, research, and management. In 2004, the WPC sponsored the International Roundtable on Wilderness Law and Policy to commemorate the fortieth anniversary of the 1964 Wilderness Act, the landmark law that led to the designation of the world's first wilderness areas. Organized and chaired by the editor of this volume, the roundtable brought together representatives from seven countries and the Confederated Salish and Kootenai tribes to present differing approaches to wilderness law and policy. Out of this gathering came the idea for a book that would lay out various ways of managing wilderness throughout the world.

The need to adopt a broad approach to wilderness has become increasingly apparent. Over the last few decades, it has become clear that conservation is more difficult—and in some cases impossible— if it is practiced with an exclusively national focus. Ecosystems and migratory species cross national boundaries. Loss of habitat in far-away places such as the Amazon basin can affect rainfall in North America. Just as important, technical cooperation and professional exchange can benefit all parties concerned, saving precious time, money, and effort. Given the scale and scope of these challenges and opportunities, leveraging resources and working with international partners has become a necessity.

This is particularly true in the wilderness arena. Saving large wild areas is a challenge for any country, and benefiting from the experience of others is especially valuable. The fact that wilderness is a multidimensional concept, with both social and biological components, makes it all the more important to be open to innovative management solutions from around the world. Since each nation has a big stake in the success of the efforts of other countries to protect the planet's biodiversity and ecosystem services, cooperation becomes even more essential.

As chair and vice-chair of the WPC, we are proud to sponsor this book.

Karen Taylor-Goodrich

Chair, Interagency
Wilderness Policy Council

Associate director, visitor, and
resource protection,
National Park Service

Elena C. Daly

Vice-chair, Interagency
Wilderness Policy Council

Director, National Landscape
Conservation System
Bureau of Land Management

Foreword

The WILD Foundation and our colleagues have worked for decades through our World Wilderness Congresses, the World Conservation Union (IUCN), and numerous other venues to establish the concept of wilderness as the bedrock for a healthy, sane, peaceful, and prosperous human society. We have attempted to communicate this fundamental message using every means at our disposal—through the arts, policy publications, photography, wilderness experiential programs, and by providing an open and constructive forum for public discourse and free expression. We have found over the years that because we all have wilderness deep within us, the wilderness message can be conveyed in almost any language or form of expression, and, indeed, that using multiple avenues of communication is often most effective.

While motivating and inspiring people to act to protect wilderness will always be one of our principal objectives, The WILD Foundation has also long recognized its obligation to generate conservation results on the ground. One way we work toward this vital objective is the development of practical and widely applicable conservation tools for the international wilderness conservation community. Among these tools is, of course, the textbook written by Hendee and Dawson and published by WILD and Fulcrum Publishing—*Wilderness Management: Stewardship and Protection of Resources and Values.* First published in 2002, this landmark publication is now in its third edition, with a fourth soon to follow. It has become a standard reference in the wilderness community.

This law and policy handbook is another such tool, and an important milestone in WILD's ongoing campaign to champion the cause of wilderness internationally. There have been repeated calls over the years for a handbook of this kind by government representatives and other delegates at World Wilderness Congresses, inspired by the wilderness cause and looking for comprehensive and up-to-date guidance in developing laws and policies in their own countries. This book is an answer to those calls. It is a proactive and highly useful publication for policymakers and activists—in fact, for anyone committed to a livable world in which wildness is not just a concept, but a vibrant reality that resides and thrives within wilderness areas.

Though laws alone cannot protect wildness, wilderness is certainly as worthy of legal protection as is any treasured natural resource. Without laws, we will surely fail in our task of providing lasting protection to our planet's remaining wilderness and its many services to human communities. In the end, dedicated, inspired people empowered by effective legislation will ensure that the spirit and services of wilderness will thrive and permeate our society, preserving a world that we are proud to hand over to those who come after us. We hope this book will help accomplish this urgent and essential task.

Vance G. Martin

President,
The WILD Foundation

Ian Player

Founder,
The WILD Foundation

Part I

Introducing the Wilderness Concept

Black bear in the El Carmen Complex in Northern Mexico,
site of the first designated wilderness area in Latin America.
Photo by Patricio Robles Gil.

Wilderness Zone in Serengeti National Park.
Photo by Boyd Norton.

CHAPTER 1

Introduction

Cyril F. Kormos[1] & Harvey Locke[2]

Overview

Wilderness laws and policies give effect to one of humanity's noblest and most prudent impulses: the desire to leave some parts of the planet to function on their own terms, rather than managing all lands intensively and exclusively for the short-term benefit of the human species. This handbook reviews the different wilderness laws and policies currently in use around the world. Specifically, we focus on those laws and policies that create an explicit wilderness protected area classification corresponding to Category 1b-Wilderness in the World Conservation Union's (IUCN) protected areas classification system. We do not thoroughly review those laws and policies that protect wilderness *de facto* in large protected areas, which would be a much larger undertaking.

This handbook is intended for two principal audiences. The first includes conservationists who might be interested in developing a wilderness protected area classification in their own countries. A small but growing number of countries have a protected-area classification explicitly dedicated to wilderness conservation. For many others, establishing new wilderness laws and policies could represent an important untapped source of conservation benefits. We hope this handbook will be a useful tool to help guide countries in developing their own wilderness protection laws and policies. The second audience consists of conservation professionals in countries that have already established wilderness protection laws and policies, but are interested in learning from the wide range of experiences internationally.

In this introductory chapter we provide an overview of the broader concept of wilderness. We briefly review the history of the concept, discuss the contextual nature of the term *wilderness*, and summarize what, in our view, are the three essential and universally recognizable dimensions of the wilderness concept. We then consider how the wilderness term has been applied more narrowly in a protected areas context, provide a review of the key elements of wilderness laws and policies, and compare several legal definitions of wilderness for illustrative purposes.

Chapter 2 consists of a matrix that provides a more detailed overview and comparison of the different legal definitions of wilderness around the world. Chapters 3–14 in Part II are case studies summarizing wilderness legislation approaches in eleven countries, as well as one tribal government in the United States. These chapters cover Australia, Canada, the Confederated Salish and Kootenai Tribes of the Flathead Nation, Finland, Iceland, Japan, Mexico, New Zealand, Russia, South Africa, Sri Lanka, and the United States. All of these governments either have (a) laws establishing wilderness areas as a protected areas category, and requiring an act of the legislature to establish wilderness areas, or (b) laws creating wilderness zones within existing protected areas. As such, they correspond to Class I and Class II countries respectively under The WILD Foundation's (WILD) classification scheme.[3]

Chapters 15–17 in Part III cover a range of additional countries that do not have any form of wilderness legislation, but nonetheless recognize wilderness as a type of protected area classification–usually through zoning mechanisms established as a result of government policy statements or guidelines, and implemented through management plans or other administrative mechanisms. These countries correspond to Class III under WILD's classification scheme.[4]

Chapters 18 and 19 in Part IV consist of a brief summary of new directions in wilderness conservation, including conservation initiatives by indigenous groups and the private sector, and the emerging wilderness concept in a marine context. The conclusion provides some thoughts on the key characteristics of wilderness legislation and how wilderness legislation might evolve in the future.

Understanding the Wilderness Concept

In essence, *wilderness* refers broadly to the most intact, undisturbed, wild, natural areas—those last truly wild places that humans do not control and have not developed with roads or other industrial infrastructure. But *wilderness* is a word used in a wide variety of ways: sometimes very loosely, in a colloquial or metaphorical sense, and sometimes very precisely, for example as a biological descriptor or as a protected-area classification in land-use statutes. This handbook is concerned specifically with this last usage. However, coming to an understanding of wilderness law and policy first requires an understanding of the wilderness concept: its origins, how it has evolved throughout human history, and the multiple dimensions of the term as it is used today.

The Origins and Evolution of the Wilderness Concept

Humans began as hunter-gatherers, a wilderness species like all others. For most of our history and prehistory, we evolved with wilderness all around us. Wilderness was both a dangerous and a deeply nurturing place, but most importantly, it was not a thing apart—it was the matrix in which our hunter-gatherer lives unfolded.

Human perspective on wilderness underwent its first fundamental shift roughly 10,000 years ago when we developed the ability to cultivate plants. Humans had already begun domesticating and breeding certain plant species, using wild grasslands for the primary benefit of some species, and eliminating predators that threatened domestic animals. As a result, we had already begun to alter our surrounding ecosystems. But through the innovation of cultivation—particularly manipulating grasses and converting biologically diverse areas to mono-cultures through crop planting—this process of alteration accelerated.[5]

Over time, as agriculture intensified, communities developed around clusters of farms. As agriculture enabled human-population growth, we eventually moved beyond grasslands and began to clear forests to create additional cropland. This process of conversion and urbanization began in earnest with the expansion of European popula-tions around the globe in the sixteenth century, though in some places it occurred earlier, such as in the Mediterranean Basin[6] and the Yucatan Peninsula.[7] Inexorably, we began reducing the global wilderness estate, becoming more conscious of the difference between cultivated land that we controlled on the one hand, and self-willed land where wild species lived on the other. The concept of *wilderness* eventually entered our lan-guage to capture that difference. As human settlements in Europe expanded, *wilderness* took on an additional meaning, describing those lands that were not just wild, but also far from human civilization.

The word *wilderness* is derived from northern European lan-guages and originally referred to the "place of wild animals," or, more generally, wild nature not subject to human control.[8] The term for many centuries had negative implications—wilderness was a myste-rious and hostile place, a place to be feared. The implications were not entirely negative, however, because wilderness was also the place to which religious figures such as Moses, Jesus, or Saint Augustine retreated in order to obtain spiritual insights for the enlightenment of humanity.

As human populations grew, hunting increased and the abun-dance of game species declined. The need arose to manage the use of wild places near large settlements to protect wildlife resources. The first wilderness areas were set aside by kings in Europe as game reserves through forest laws.[9] These include the New Forest in England established shortly after the Norman conquest and the Doñana reserve in southern Spain established 700 years ago (now a national park, and which still retained wilderness qualities when it was designated a World Heritage Site in 1994).[10] These enabled rulers to control access to ensure they could always go hunting. The iMfolozi Game Reserve was established by King Shaka in Zululand (in what is now the Republic of South Africa) in the early nineteenth century as his hunting reserve, and would later play a pivotal role in the recovery of white rhinoceros from the edge of extinction.[11] These royal decrees from Europe and Africa can be considered some of the earliest wilderness laws, though they had a very private dimension.

Industrialization during the mid-nineteenth century exponentially accelerated the process of wilderness transformation. Large cities began to form, reducing some humans' contact with wild nature and increasing the demand for resources. Wild forests were cut down for wood, even if the area was not well-suited for cropland. The oceans and their seemingly limitless bounty were subjected to heavy exploitation. Intensive mining began—for energy sources such as coal, and then oil and natural gas, and also for precious minerals or minerals used in industrial products. Wild rivers were dammed for irrigation or hydropower, or used as sewers for industrial effluent.

On trail above the iMfolozi river.
Photo by the Wilderness Leadership School, Durban, South Africa.

Vast amounts of waste were sent into the atmosphere, as gas or particulates, or dumped into the oceans.

By the end of the twentieth century, whether through direct impact, particulates falling from the sky, or as a result of human-induced climate change, very few if any wild places on earth were untouched by our activities.[12] The Millennium Ecosystem Assessment Synthesis Report stated that:

> Humans have changed ecosystems more rapidly and exten-
> sively in the last 50 years than in any other period. This was
> done largely to meet rapidly growing demands for food, fresh
> water, timber, fiber and fuel. More land was converted to
> cropland in the 30 years after 1950 than in the 150 years
> between 1700 and 1850.[13]

At some point in the industrialization process came a recognition that transforming wilderness for the utilitarian purposes of industrial civilization was not always good for society.[14] This recognition corresponded with a rise in democracy in the Western world. Wilderness laws were a public reaction to that industrial destruction. Watershed protection areas were established and strictly protected from exploitation and unsanitary recreation. These laws or binding customs to protect water are a longstanding form of wilderness law designed to protect ecosystem services.

But there were other social motivations as well. The late-eighteenth- and early-nineteenth-century Romantic movement extolled nature for its own sake and for the spiritual inspiration it gave humans. Wilderness's role as spiritual refuge expanded from the domain of prophets to include the middle class. It provided a place to escape from the stress of industrialized modern society and big cities and to experience spiritual renewal through solitude. This led to wilderness laws enacted for the psychological and spiritual benefit of the public.

In the late nineteenth century, support began to grow for laws to set aside lands to protect their wilderness values. The first such enactment covering a large area was the Yellowstone National Park Act of 1872. Many other English-speaking cultures followed suit, so that by the end of the nineteenth century there were wilderness reserves in Canada, New Zealand, South Africa, and Australia. At about the same time, the massive slaughter of large mammals for meat was leading to an extinction crisis. Game-protection laws of universal application to both public and private lands were enacted and specific wildlife parks were established as breeding sanctuaries.[15] The Thelon Game Sanctuary in Canada's Northwest Territories and Nunavut was set up to prevent the extinction of musk oxen in the 1920s and remains one of the most remote and wild places on earth. These wildlife parks are examples of legislated wilderness areas for biological purposes.

In the twentieth century, many other governments around the world enacted wilderness protection laws. Increasingly, these laws began explicitly to use words directly associated with wilderness, starting with New York State's 1895 constitutional amendment to ensure that lands included in Adirondack Park would be "forever kept wild as forest lands." These laws are reviewed in subsequent chapters.

Today, at the start of the twenty-first century, wilderness laws are a significant part of many countries' legal systems. They protect substantial areas of land and, in a small but growing number of cases, marine and freshwater systems as well.

The Contextual Nature of Defining Wilderness

Because the word *wilderness* refers to a set of qualities, including wildness, intactness, and remoteness from urban and industrial civilization, and because these qualities are to some extent contextual and subject to interpretation, the term can be difficult to define in generic terms that can be applied uniformly around the world.

For example, someone from an urban setting without much experience with wild nature might apply the word *wilderness* loosely to a small, protected area that is close to an urban center, surrounded by development, and that has been significantly degraded through species loss and invasion of exotic plants, yet still provides a degree of solitude and contact with wild nature (such as the Chicago Wilderness in the greater-Chicago area of the United States[16]). At the other extreme, outdoors enthusiasts or conservation biologists might apply a very narrow standard, using the term only in connection with the very largest, most biologically pristine, and most inaccessible places on the planet (such as Antarctica or the most remote parts of the Amazon basin). The fact that the term *wilderness* is frequently used colloquially in casual conversation contributes to this lack of absolute uniformity.

An additional element of complexity was added during the 1990s, when it became fashionable in some circles to deconstruct the word *wilderness* using techniques of analysis designed to reveal cultural biases.[17] For postmodern critics, all knowledge was suspect,[18] and all words, including *wilderness*, could be analyzed and shown to be instruments used by elites to control power or exclude others. Critics pointed to the fact that the word *wilderness* does not exist in all cultures as further evidence that wilderness was, in essence, a social construct. Some asserted there is no such thing as wilderness on the basis of evidence that aboriginal people had once cultivated areas that are now seen as wilderness, extrapolating from this to argue that all areas must have been thus managed by people at one time or another.[19] Others argued that the wilderness ideal is so powerful that it devalues conservation or stewardship efforts for other areas that are not in a wilderness state.[20] One critic has even gone so far as to call wilderness a discredited concept.[21]

These postmodern criticisms are of limited value because they are based on an overly restrictive interpretation of the term *wilderness*, a meaning that critics construct in order to deconstruct. In particular, the criticism often focuses on a part of the U.S. Wilderness Act of 1964—which speaks of wilderness as a place where "man is a visitor who does not remain"—as *the* definition of wilderness. This is problematic on several counts. First, it ignores the many other wilderness laws that have been passed around the world and the fact that wilderness is interpreted in a variety of ways internationally. Second, this analysis is highly selective: the 1964 Act is often described as enshrining an exclusionary and elitist approach to wilderness resources despite the fact that it has allowed for subsistence use in Alaska, where, unlike the rest of the United States, a significant percentage of the population still depends on the land for subsistence.[22]

Postmodern criticism also fails to address the biological component of the word *wilderness*, nor does it fully address wilderness as a description of land that is wild.[23] Biological intactness is something that can be measured scientifically, and wilderness has been inventoried by scientists who have found it throughout the planet (see box on page 15). The limited evidence of aboriginal agricultural use in areas that are now considered wilderness does not justify ignoring the many parts of the world that have never been suitable for agriculture and thus have always been in an uncultivated state. And as discussed below, the wilderness concept is any case robust even for areas that have some form of human presence because the standard for wilderness is not whether an area is completely pristine, but rather whether it can be characterized as having a high degree of biological intactness. Thus, wilderness areas can include areas once cultivated or logged that have since reverted to a wild state, or areas with subsistence use.

However, postmodern analysis has had one notable benefit: it did cause wilderness proponents to think more carefully about the role of humans, particularly aboriginal peoples, in wilderness.

Though wilderness is a wide-ranging concept, the term *wilderness* is not so elusive as to defy any definition. It is possible to establish some clear scientific and social parameters for the term that provide fairly firm and universally recognizable boundaries. There will always be some variation in the definition of wilderness because different societies have different standards and because the condition of their lands will vary. However, the three dimensions of wilderness described below are an effort to ensure that these variations in meaning are not extreme and that the term can be used with adequate precision and mutual understanding, despite differences in approaches.

Wilderness Areas Are a Three-Dimensional Concept

Wilderness areas generally have three essential characteristics: biological, social, and iconic value.

The first and core dimension is *biological*. *Wilderness* refers to land that is mostly intact (or the most intact in its context) in terms of natural habitat, faunal and floral assemblages, and biological processes, including evolutionary processes and ecosystem services. As these criteria suggest, wilderness areas tend to be large, undisturbed areas. Exactly how big and how intact depends on a range of determinants: the particular ecosystem type, how sensitive it is to disturbance, its inherent biological productivity, whether the faunal assemblages include wide-ranging large predators and so forth. A biological approach to identifying wilderness was taken by Mittermeier et al. (2002)[24] (see the box on page 15). There may not always be

The Guayana Shield region of northern South America contains some of the most intact forests in the world.
Photo by Russell A. Mittermeier.

agreement regarding how large an area must be to qualify. However, as a rule, wilderness areas need to be as large and as undisturbed as possible because they provide an essential foundation for biodiversity conservation.

The second key characteristic of wilderness is *social*, and has to do with its role in sustaining human communities. Although *wilderness* refers to land that is wild and biologically intact, wilderness is also in many ways a social concept—capturing human relationships with wild nature. Given the many different relationships between humans and wild nature around the world, the concept of wilderness necessarily has multiple social dimensions. For indigenous cultures, wilderness is not something apart from civilization, but, in the most literal sense, is their home. Wilderness is essential to their traditional lifestyles and often to their very survival. For many cultures that are not, strictly speaking, leading traditional lifestyles, wilderness nonetheless often has religious or spiritual significance. For industrial societies, wilderness is also a source of spiritual renewal, a place for recreation, and a place to escape the stress of modern life. In this last context, the term *wilderness* is sometimes used for areas that would not easily meet the biological parameters outlined above. All of these approaches are equally valid so long as they are predicated on a fundamental respect for the integrity of wild nature, and, just as importantly, for each other.

Wilderness areas around the world also have an economic dimension. They are a key ingredient in the sustainable livelihoods of local communities through a range of ecosystem services—for example, erosion control or reliable supplies of fresh water. Wilderness areas are also vital for traditional peoples whose cultural survival depends on a degree of isolation in remote, intact areas, or for mobile peoples that have traditionally migrated over large distances in pursuit of subsistence hunting and gathering. They support a wilderness-tourism economy in many places. And perhaps most importantly, they provide globally important ecosystem services—such as carbon sequestration—that benefit all of humankind. Wilderness areas are critical cornerstones for sustaining human communities at all scales.

The third characteristic of wilderness is more abstract and has to do with the strong *iconic* quality of wilderness areas. Wilderness areas are often the most wild and beautiful landscapes left on earth, and, as a result, people around the world identify with these areas at a fundamental level, even if they never see them in person. In recognition of this special significance, many areas with wilderness qualities are awarded special status—not only at a local or national level as protected areas, but also internationally, such as through UNESCO World Heritage status or through peace parks and trans-boundary protected areas. And wilderness areas may hold deep religious significance as sacred sites important to indigenous cultures, in many cases retaining their wildness precisely as a result of their religious significance. They are also often important places for recreation.

Although there are many pragmatic and urgent biological and socioeconomic justifications for protecting wilderness, for many people, wilderness is more about spectacular landscapes, awe-inspiring wildlife, and especially spiritual renewal, than it is about pragmatism. For these individuals, the best justification for protecting

Wollemi Wilderness, Wollemi National Park, Greater Blue Mountains World Heritage Area. Photo by Ian Brown.

wilderness is the visceral satisfaction of knowing that the planet retains a strong, wild soul.[25] Indeed, the continued existence of wilderness is a confirmation of the un-extinguished wild element within ourselves, which is an essential dimension of our humanity.[26]

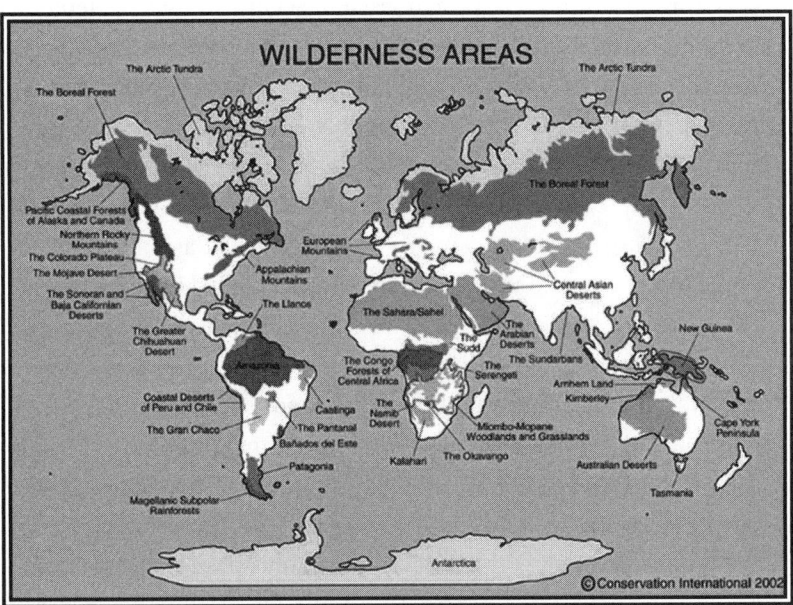

Figure 1—From Mittermeir, et al., 2003

Wilderness at the Global Scale:
How Much Is Left?

The wilderness concept is best understood as a multidimensional concept, consisting of both biological and social elements. However, it is important to recognize that wilderness is often used essentially as a biological descriptor, without reference to protected area status or other social or legal characteristics. In this context, four global inventories have been conducted to assess how much wilderness remains on earth at the continental scale. Each of these assessments used a different threshold to determine what qualified as wilderness. Some used biological criteria to measure an area's intactness; others used surrogates, such as the absence of roads and other infrastructure. Although each assessment used different methodologies, they all attempted to define how much of the world is in an indisputably wild condition. Taken together, these assessments indicate that very roughly one-third of the planet remains undisturbed in large areas of wilderness.

A few caveats are in order regarding these assessments. Because these global assessments were conducted at such a large scale, and because some of these assessments relied on surrogates to assess the wildness of particular areas, each is likely to have excluded smaller areas that nonetheless have good wilderness qualities. It is also important to understand that these are assessments of *de facto* wilderness areas, and that the actual area protected by wilderness laws and policies is much smaller. Finally, none of these assessments dealt with marine wilderness, which, at the time of writing, is still a developing concept in the protected areas field (see Barr, Chapter 16). Nonetheless, they provide a useful global overview, and offer good insight into various methodologically rigorous approaches to defining wilderness.

The four inventories are summarized briefly below.

A Reconnaissance-Level Inventory of World Wilderness Areas

McCloskey, M. J. and Spaulding, H. 1988. A reconnaissance-level inventory of the wilderness remaining in the world. In *For the conservation of the earth: proceedings of the 4th world wilderness congress,* eds. V. Martin and P. Sarathy. Golden, CO: Fulcrum Publishing, 18–41.

The first global wilderness assessment was a 1987 Sierra Club survey conducted in preparation for the 4th World Wilderness

Congress, entitled *A Reconnaissance-Level Inventory of World Wilderness Areas.* This analysis was conducted exclusively using jet navigation charts to identify areas of 400,000 hectares (988,000 acres) or more with no permanent human infrastructure and identified roughly one-third of the planet's surface area as wilderness.

A Preliminary Inventory of Human Disturbance of World Ecosystems

Hannah, L., et al. 1994. A preliminary inventory of human disturbance of world ecosystems. *Ambio* 23 (4–5): 246–250.

This study, published in *Ambio*, produced a Geographic Information System map of global human disturbance in natural ecosystems. The study produced a habitat index and used a three-category scale of undisturbed, partially disturbed, and human-dominated to map results. Undisturbed areas retained primary vegetation and had population densities of fewer than ten people per square kilometer (roughly four people per square mile). The map was produced using units of 40,000 hectares (98,800 acres) and found that approximately 52 percent of the planet was undisturbed. Of this 52 percent, approximately half was desert, ice, or rock, leaving 27 percent as undisturbed, potentially productive land.

The Human Footprint and the Last of the Wild

Sanderson E., et al. 2002. The human footprint and the last of the wild. *Bioscience* 52 (10): 891–904.

The Wildlife Conservation Society (WCS) used four criteria: population density, land transformation, human access points, and electric power infrastructure. These factors were individually scored, then combined to generate a Human Influence Index rating. The results were then mapped. WCS found that 17 percent of the planet remained wild, though that assessment was conducted without including Antarctica, which would raise the amount to about 27 percent.

Wilderness and Biodiversity Conservation
Mittermeier, R., et al. 2003. Wilderness and biodiversity conservation. *PNAS*, 100 (18) September 2, 2003.

This study used three criteria: a size threshold of one million hectares (2.47 million acres); 70 percent habitat intactness with intact faunal assemblages of mammals, birds, and large predators; and a population density of fewer than five people per square kilometer. This assessment found that 46 percent of the planet was wilderness, though, with Antarctica and the Sahara removed, that number is reduced. Using a population density of fewer than one person per square kilometer, the percentage of wilderness decreased to 38 percent.

Law and Policy Approaches to Defining Wilderness
The following section provides an overview of how the wilderness concept is translated into laws and policies, creating wilderness protected areas. However, before looking at the main elements, we first examine why special wilderness laws and policies are even necessary, given the existence of other more widely used protected area classifications such as national parks, wildlife refuges, or strict nature reserves.

Why the Need for Wilderness Law and Policy?
Wilderness is protected *de facto* in large protected areas around the world, and sometimes through land-management guidelines designed to protect ecosystem services such as valuable watersheds. Many countries and cultures have therefore enacted some form of wilderness law, whether or not they explicitly refer to them as such.

However, a small number of countries have taken the additional step of developing wilderness legislation. These laws explicitly establish a separate protected area classification corresponding to Category 1b (Wilderness) in the World Conservation Union's (IUCN) protected area classification system, and require an act of the legislature to create individual wilderness protected areas. Why this additional step? Is a separate, protected classification truly necessary if wilderness can be protected *de facto* through other mechanisms, such as national parks?

Although the essence of wilderness protection obviously lies in the result—a functioning, healthy, wild ecosystem—and not the name or the particular mechanism used, there are nonetheless a number of important advantages to using the term *wilderness* explicitly and creating a separate wilderness, protected-area classification. Indeed, the term *wilderness* as a label for a particular kind of protected area seems to resonate with an ever-wider audience. A growing number of countries with very different cultures—from Japan to the Ukraine, and Iceland to Mexico—are choosing to create a special protected-area classification for wilderness.

One explanation for this trend is the recognition that protected wilderness areas have special characteristics that sometimes need to be addressed separately from other types of protected areas. Protecting large, intact wild areas presents distinct management challenges, and at the same time generates exceptional opportunities and benefits. For example, the wilderness label signals that there will be very limited infrastructure for visitors. These unique characteristics are sometimes more easily addressed through a separate protected-area classification than by a patchwork of zoning mechanisms or management-plan guidelines.

A second factor has to do with the disturbing reports on the state of the planet's health. The United Nation's *Millennium Ecosystem Assessment*, published in 2005, contains some troubling statistics: six of the planet's fourteen major biomes have been converted by 50 percent or more. We have converted more forest land in the three decades between 1950 and 1980 than we did in the 150 years between 1700 and 1850, and we will likely reduce forest lands and grasslands by another 20 percent between 2000 and 2050 unless we change our behavior.

Reports on global climate change are also alarming: 2005 was not only the warmest year on record, but there is now more carbon dioxide in our atmosphere than at any point in the last 650,000 years. As a result of these pressures, we are experiencing extinction rates of 100–1000 times higher than background extinction rates found in the geological record.[27]

Against this backdrop of environmental destruction, two things are becoming apparent. Conservation must occur at a larger scale, and the strongest legal protection, such as that offered by wilderness legislation, is necessary to ensure that conservation gains are not quickly eroded or even overturned completely. For example, if Alaska's Arctic National Wildlife Refuge had an additional layer of protection from the 1964 Wilderness Act, it would have obviated much of the debate over drilling for oil that has dominated conservation in the United States for almost six years at the beginning of this century. And although a large national park may contain designated wilderness zones via its management plan, unless that management plan is accompanied by very strong legal protections, it will likely be easier to change than it would be to remove a wilderness protected area established by law. (See for example Canada National Parks Act, Chapter 4, and Chapter 14 on the importance of statutory protection.)

A third factor is the term *wilderness* itself. The planet's remaining wild places have strong iconic value. They are refuges from the stresses of modern civilization and places where one can experience spiritual renewal and the thrill and challenge of meeting wild nature on its own terms. Few words describe this visceral response to wild nature as well as the word *wilderness*.

A number of aboriginal cultures also embrace wilderness as a good concept for their deep relationship with the lands they have long used and want to protect. Finland's wilderness law, for example, is centered around protecting Lapp culture (see Chapter 6). The Confederated Salish and Kootenai Tribes of the Flathead Nation in the United States have a wilderness designation on their land (see Chapter 5), and numerous other tribes in the United States have included wilderness protection zones in tribal land management ordinances (see Chapter 18). More than 100 indigenous people from around the world met to form a caucus at the 8th World Wilderness Congress in Alaska in 2005.

As the planet's wilderness estate shrinks, the term *wilderness* seems to be growing in its appeal—even, and in some cases especially, in countries where it has no obvious linguistic equivalent.

Legal Parameters of Wilderness

The challenge for policymakers drafting a wilderness statute is to combine the biological, social, and iconic dimensions of wilderness into laws that will protect the wild character, wild animals, and natural processes of a specific place: for their own sake, for the inspiration they provide to humans, and to ensure a continuous outward flow of ecosystem services.

In practical terms this means that a wilderness statute must do two things. It must (1) define which lands would be wild enough to qualify as wilderness (or could be restored to such a state), and (2) define which uses would be permissible on those lands to ensure that the wilderness resource is preserved. The resulting statute provides a legal and political definition of the concept of wilderness.

It is essential to emphasize that the term *wilderness* exists outside such statutory definitions, just as the concept of *real property*, for example, can exist with or without land title legislation. It is pointless, and even counterproductive, to look for the true meaning of wilderness in any one law that has been enacted; the law is simply a legal and political expression of wilderness values, involving numerous political compromises, and as a result, necessarily imperfect. These varying definitions are summarized in Chapter 2. We will consider only a few here to demonstrate the variety of wilderness laws and policies.

Wilderness Definitions

Listed below are some policy and statutory expressions of *wilderness* from around the world:

IUCN Protected Areas Classification System: Category 1b—Wilderness
"A large area of unmodified or slightly modified land, and/or sea, retaining its natural character and influence, without permanent or significant habitation, which is protected and managed so as to preserve its natural condition."

U.S. Wilderness Act of 1964
"A wilderness, in contrast with those areas where man and his works dominate the landscape, is hereby recognized as an area where the earth and its community of life are untrammelled by man, where man himself is a visitor who does not remain. An area of wilderness is further defined to mean in this Act an area of undeveloped federal land retaining its primeval character and influence, without permanent improvements or human habitation, which is protected and managed so as to preserve its natural conditions and which (1) generally appears to have been affected primarily by the forces of nature, with the imprint of man's work substantially unnoticeable; (2) has outstanding opportunities for solitude or a primitive and unconfined type of recreation; (3) has at least two thousand hectares (five thousand acres) of land or is of sufficient size as to make practicable its preservation and use in an unimpaired condition; and (4) may also contain ecological, geological, or other features of scientific, educational, scenic, or historical value."

Finland—Act on Wilderness Reserves (1991)
Wilderness reserves are established to preserve wild areas, to safeguard Lapp culture and indigenous livelihoods, and to develop the potential for diversified use of nature.

New Zealand—Conservation Act 1987
    1. the following provisions apply to every wilderness area:
        a. Its indigenous natural resources shall be preserved;
        b. No building or machinery shall be erected on it;
        c. No building, machinery, or apparatus shall be constructed or maintained on it;

    d. No livestock, vehicles, or motorized vessels (including hovercraft or jet boats) shall be allowed to be taken into or used in it and no helicopter or other motorized aircraft shall land or take off or hover for the purpose of embarking or disembarking passengers or goods in it;

    e. No roads, tracks, or trails shall be constructed on it.

2. If—

    a. The doing of anything on a wilderness area is in conformity with the conservation management strategy or conservation management plan for the area;

    b. The minister is satisfied that its doing is desirable or necessary for the preservation of the area's indigenous natural resources,

    The minister may authorize it.

3. If satisfied that the undertaking of any scientific test or study in a wilderness area is necessary or desirable for the preservation of indigenous natural resources, the Minister may authorize it.

4. Nothing in subsection (1) of this section prevents the doing of any thing for any person's protection, or because of some emergency involving any person's property.

Although all of the examples listed above use the term *wilderness*, a law need not use the word *wilderness* to protect wilderness values. It is the substance, not the form, that matters most.

    A wilderness law is a statutory, contractual, or other demonstrably binding designation that applies to a discrete area of land to protect it and the living things in it from human activity destructive to its wild character, or to the benefits that area provides, such as ecosystem services. Thus, wilderness protected by law is not a place whose reason for being is to exclude people, but rather a formally designated place where only certain human uses are allowed in order to maintain its wild character. To be effective, a wilderness law must specify which uses it permits and which it excludes.

Uses of Wilderness Areas Allowed by Law

The most important function of a wilderness law is probably to specify uses and prohibitions, rather than to define the term *wilderness*. The wide range of human uses allowed in legislated wilderness around the world reflects local cultures, attitudes, and political pragmatism. But at some point, whether the statute that governs it is called a wilderness law or not, an area that is too heavily exploited simply cannot qualify as true wilderness. Policy makers must therefore make careful choices when deciding what activities are compatible with wilderness protected areas. Legal wilderness designations range from *zapovedniks* in Russia, which preclude almost all human use except tightly controlled access for research scientists and some tourism; to federal wilderness areas in the United States, which allow hunting, fishing, grazing of domestic livestock, and exploitation of mines that preexist their designation; to wilderness areas in Finland that embrace reindeer herders living permanently within them.

There is no one model or ideal wilderness law that policy makers can resort to in making those choices. However, it is possible to articulate some general principles. The following section provides an assessment of the categories of use that are most consistent with the purpose of a wilderness law, and provides some sense of the compromises that may be permitted in a wilderness law without undermining the wilderness values of the protected area.

Broadly speaking, the spectrum of human land uses includes the following, not all of which are compatible with wilderness:

Compatible

Wildlife sanctuary—Humans restrain their own activity, providing an area in which other species are free from human predation.

Hunting and gathering—Humans hunt wild animals and harvest plants that have grown without human intervention or cultivation.

Fishing—Humans take species from fresh or salt water for food or recreation.

Primitive recreation—Humans use their own legs, canoes, or domestic
  animals to spend time in places they enjoy.
Benchmark study—Humans use an area to learn more about the
  world's natural processes by observing natural conditions.
Restoration—Humans restore natural processes and conditions to an
  area they have previously converted to other use.

Rarely compatible

Grazing of domestic animals—Humans domesticate animals and
  concentrate their grazing activity. They may use an area permanently or move through it temporarily.

Incompatible

Farming—Humans change the species composition of an area for
  their own nutritional benefit by altering the land or seabed and
  planting one or several species.
Mechanical recreation—Humans use vehicles for recreational activities,
  including bicycles, automobiles, off-road vehicles, motorboats,
  and snowmobiles.
Transportation corridors and infrastructure—Humans build highways,
  railways, airports, harbors, shipping lanes, irrigation canals, or
  straightened river channels for navigation.
Permanent dwellings—Humans build structures that provide permanent human habitation in a fixed place.
Towns and cities—Humans build large collections of permanent
  dwellings and other infrastructure.
Industrial activity—Humans refine or reassemble primary products
  from the earth on a large scale for human use or obtain such
  primary products by clearing forests for lumber; damming
  rivers for hydroelectricity or diverting them for irrigation;
  mining; or oil and gas exploration and exploitation.

In a wilderness law, any of the uses listed under the *compatible*
category are appropriate uses of wilderness, provided that they are

managed not to impair the overriding wilderness purpose. Choices can be made among the first three categories of compatible use (is the goal a pure wildlife sanctuary or not) or even within a category. For example, hunting, gathering, or fishing can be restricted to a class of people—such as traditional aboriginal inhabitants—or to particular zones in the wilderness area.

The incompatible uses of wilderness should be expressly excluded in any wilderness law. Most of them are obviously inappropriate: farming, mechanized recreation, transportation corridors and infrastructure, permanent dwellings, towns and cities, and industrial activity. But judging by the number of countries that permit it, grazing is often seen as a compatible use and thus requires further discussion.

The justification for allowing grazing is that it is a nonindustrial harvesting activity similar to hunting or fishing. This is understandable in certain contexts, such as herding native reindeer in Finland. Seasonal grazing or transhumance may also be compatible with wilderness. But the reality is that unless grazing is practiced very lightly and transitorily, it can transform a wilderness ecosystem by removing some vegetation altogether, creating conditions amenable to nonnative species, reducing the amount of forage available for native species, eroding stream banks, and silting up creeks. Grazing also very often leads to wild-predator control to protect livestock. Only the most ecologically benign form of grazing could be compatible with the purpose of a wilderness law.

What of the anomalies like the mines and water diversions that are grandfathered in the U.S. Wilderness Act of 1964, which is perhaps the most famous and widely applied wilderness law in the world? The short answer is that these were pragmatic compromises necessary to achieve passage of the legislation (see Chapter 14). The people who agreed to these compromises candidly stated that they were a case of not allowing the perfect to be the enemy of the good. Many American wilderness areas have no mining claims or water diversions within their boundaries at all. In those that do, proposals to engage in new mining activity are usually met with fierce and broad-based public opposition, notwithstanding the initial legislative compromise that would allow them.

Comparisons of Wilderness Laws

Wilderness definitions generally include some combination of the following variables: size, intactness, permissible uses in wilderness, permissible degree of human use and occupation, and capacity of the land to be maintained or restored to a wilderness state. Determinations for each variable vary from country to country.

Some countries, such as New Zealand (see Chapter 10) and the United States (see Chapter 14), place great emphasis on the social aspect of wilderness as a place for solitude, recreation, and spiritual renewal. As a result, the legislative definitions focus to a significant degree on recreation and the human experience in wilderness, and less on biological questions beyond the fundamentally important object of constraining human interference with natural processes. Russia places a much greater emphasis on the biological rationale for protecting large areas, and has only recently begun to allow any visitors in some of their *zapovedniks* (see Chapter 11). Finland emphasizes wilderness as a place to preserve wild nature, as well as to protect the country's indigenous Lapp culture (see Chapter 6).

In the United States (as discussed above), livestock are allowed to graze in wilderness areas, and the Wilderness Act allows mining claims in existence at the time the Act was passed to remain active up to a certain date. In Finland, roads in wilderness areas are generally banned, except where they clearly benefit "the common good or the indigenous livelihoods in the area." Exceptions allow for some logging, but only in approximately 3.5 percent of the 1 million hectares (2.47 million acres) of designated wilderness in Finland. The law also allows Lapp herders to use the areas for reindeer grazing. Finland therefore allows for a degree of resource extraction and infrastructure to facilitate indigenous Lapp livelihoods, and wilderness areas in fact have slightly less protection than some of Finland's other protected areas. The Finnish law, with all the activities it allows, pushes the wilderness concept to its outside edge.

Size is sometimes addressed in wilderness laws. The United States allows for wilderness areas of "at least [two thousand hectares or] five thousand acres" or of "sufficient size as to make practicable its preservation and use in an unimpaired condition." Finland did not establish size considerations in its law, but has focused on areas greater than 15,000 hectares (37,000 acres). Iceland states that a wilderness area is "an area of land at least 25 square kilometers [9.6 square miles] in size, or in which it is possible to enjoy the solitude and nature without disturbance from manmade structures or the traffic of motorized vehicles on the ground, which is at least five kilometers [three miles] away from man-made structures or other evidence of technology, such as power lines, power stations, reservoirs and main roads, where no direct indications of human activity are visible, and nature can develop without anthropogenic pressures" (see Chapter 7). New Zealand does not establish a statutory size threshold, though New Zealand's 1985 Wilderness Policy, published by the Department of Lands & Survey for the Wilderness Advisory Group, states that a wilderness area should be large enough to take at least two days' foot travel to traverse.

In some cases, a wilderness protected area might not easily meet a stricter biological definition for a large wilderness area— either because it is not sufficiently intact in terms of habitat or faunal assemblages, or because they may be too small to be viable in the longer term. However, decision makers might be inclined to include it in a wilderness protected area system for any number of other reasons: because the land over time can be restored to a wilderness state; because it could be integrated into a larger land-scape conservation approach that makes it viable; or because the area nonetheless affords an excellent opportunity for recreation in a wild area. Or, sometimes, because in a fragmented world it is the best that can be done.

The Future Importance
of Wilderness Laws in the World

While wilderness laws have been effective in many places and their use is expanding around the world, far more wilderness has been liquidated across the planet than has been protected since the first wilderness laws appeared. The pace of destruction of wilderness in the twentieth century was breathtaking. The Millennium Ecosystem Assessment of 2005 has documented that we are now exhausting nature's resources. Wilderness laws thus take on increased urgency, as they are needed to protect the basic ecological processes that sustain us in our current state of civilization.

Today we accept as given that wilderness is essential to the full range of life on earth. Wilderness has been and continues to be fundamental to the development of human culture. It is the source of the air we breathe, the rain that falls, and the water we drink. It is an important source of economic benefits.[28] It offers opportunities for profound and perspective-altering recreation and spiritual development. It offers hope to those who never visit it. It is home to wild species, especially the big predators that humans do not tolerate very well. Wilderness is that part of the world that we do not control but that we still depend on. It is a profound paradox that the very survival of wilderness is in the hands of a single species.

Wilderness laws and policies are an essential part of any institutional framework that humans could create to build a culturally and ecologically sane twenty-first century society out of the ashes of the last. This book is the first effort to describe in detail the full variety of legal and policy tools available across the world to legally protect wilderness values. If we have missed any, we will be very pleased to include them in future editions.

Ravine des Casoars Wilderness Protection Area,
Kangaroo Island, South Australia, Australia.
Photo by Bill Doyle.

CHAPTER 2

The Matrix
A Comparison of International Wilderness Laws

Peter Landres[1], Brad Barr[2], and Cyril F. Kormos[3]

Summary

The following matrix provides a comparison of wilderness laws around the world. This matrix is divided into four parts, each focusing on a key area of wilderness legislation: the definition of wilderness; the overall legislative purpose; uses allowed by the legislation; and administration and management requirements under law. A more thorough analysis of individual wilderness laws follows in the ensuing chapters. The purpose of this matrix is to provide a highly condensed overview of the subject matter and to facilitate quick comparisons of the different approaches used in different countries or states/provinces.

Another important point is that the matrix focuses only on what is made explicit in the wilderness laws themselves. Thus, where the statute itself is silent on one of the issues in the matrix, we use the caption "not identified."

The matrices are largely self-explanatory, though a few brief notes are in order. First, the laws used in this exercise are listed in the first section in the left hand column. The names of the laws are not repeated in the three subsequent sections. For Australia and Canada, two countries in which state and provincial law are central given that most land is not held by the federal government, we included the states of New South Wales and South Australia for Australia, and the provinces of Ontario and Newfoundland and Labrador for Canada. These are also discussed at greater length in the ensuing case studies. We did not include state wilderness laws in the United States, as most wilderness protection occurs at the federal level, and all laws subsequent to the Wilderness Act of 1964 specify that the newly designated wilderness areas will be managed according to the provisions of the 1964 Wilderness Act. We do include the Mission Mountains Wilderness Area, established by The Confederated Salish and Kootenai Tribes in Montana, U.S., on their reservation lands, in this matrix. We have also chosen to include Mexico's wilderness definition, even though, as the chapter on Mexico below indicates, the final modalities for Mexico's wilderness protection programs have not yet been finalized.

Finally, two of the columns listed in Matrix D might require additional clarification. The first is the "Minimum Necessary Management Tool" column, which refers to a requirement in the United States, and also used by the Confederated Salish and Kootenai Tribes, that the least intrusive management tools be used in wilderness area. For example, hand tools such as axes and saws are favored over mechanical tools.

Matrix A: Definitions

Country	Law	Legislated Definition of Wilderness
Australia	National Parks and Wildlife Conservation Act of 1975	Not identified
Australia–State of New South Wales	Wilderness Act of 1987	a. the area is, together with its plant and animal communities, in a state that has not been substantially modified by humans and their works or is capable of being restored to such a state; b. the area is of sufficient size to make its maintenance in such a state feasible; and c. the area is capable of providing opportunities for solitude and appropriate self-reliant recreation.
Australia–State of South Australia	Wilderness Protection Act of 1992	a. the land and its ecosystems must not have been affected, or must have been affected to only a minor extent, by modern technology; b. the land and its ecosystem must not have been seriously affected by exotic animals or plants or other exotic organisms. [Sec. 3(2)]
Canada	Canada National Parks Act of 2000 [Chapter 32, Section 14]	… any area of a park that exists in a natural state or that is capable of returning to a natural state [Section 14(1)].
Canada–Province of Ontario	Provincial Parks and Conservation Reserves Act, 2006	The objective of wilderness class parks is to protect large areas where the forces of nature can exist freely and visitors travel by non-mechanized means, except as may be permitted by regulation,

Matrix A: Definitions

Country	Law	Legislated Definition of Wilderness
Canada–Province of Ontario, *continued*		while engaging in low-impact recreation to experience solitude, challenge and integration with nature. 2006, c. 12, s. 8 (2).
Canada–Province of Newfoundland and Labrador	Wilderness and Ecological Reserves Act	The Lieutenant-Governor in Council may set aside, as wilderness reserves, areas of the province that are subject to no or little human activity, a. to provide for the continued existence of those areas as large wilderness areas to which people may come and in which they may hunt, fish, travel and otherwise experience and appreciate a natural environment; b. to allow within those areas undisturbed interactions of living things and their environment; c. to preserve those large areas that may be necessary for the continued survival of a particular species; or d. to protect those areas with primitive or extraordinary characteristics. [Section 4]
Confederated Salish and Kootenai Tribes	Mission Mountain Tribal Wilderness Ordinance 79A of 1982 and Resolution 82-173	A wilderness is hereby recognized as an area where the earth and its community of life are untrammeled by man, where man himself is a visitor who does not remain. An area of wilderness is further defined as an area of undeveloped tribal land, retaining its primeval character and influence, without permanent improvements or human habitation, which is protected and managed so as to preserve its natural conditions. [Section 2]

Matrix A: Definitions

Country	Law	Legislated Definition of Wilderness
Finland	Act on Wilderness Reserves of 1991	Wilderness areas comprise the areas listed in Section 3. [Section 1]
Iceland	Nature Conservation Act of 1999	An area of land at least 25km^2 in size, or in which it is possible to enjoy the solitude and nature without disturbance from manmade structures or the traffic of motorized vehicles on the ground, which is at least 5 km away from manmade structures or other evidence of technology, such as power lines, power stations, reservoirs, and main roads, where no direct indications of human activity are visible and nature can develop without anthropogenic pressures. [Article 3(4)]
Japan	Nature Conservation Law of 1972	Area that preserves its original characteristics without any influence of human activities.
Mexico		Areas where habitats, biotic communities, and natural processes remain predominantly intact; where the footprint of industrial civilization and its infrastructure is not present; where human activities are developed without leaving evidence of their presence; and, are sufficiently ample to provide opportunities for the reconciliation of man as a species with nature.
New Zealand	Wilderness Policy of 1985	They will be large enough take at least 2 days' foot travel to traverse; They should have clearly defined topographic boundaries and be adequately buffered so as to be unaffected, except in minor

Matrix A: Definitions

Country	Law	Legislated Definition of Wilderness
New Zealand *continued*		ways, by human influences; They will not have developments such as huts, tracks, bridges, signs, nor mechanized access.
Russia	Federal Law on Specially Protected Natural Areas of 1995	On the territory of strict state nature preserves (zapovedniki), the following is completely withdrawn from economic utilization: specially protected natural areas, complexes, and objects (land, water, mineral resources, the plant and animal worlds) which have protected status; areas with scientific or environmental/ecological educational significance as models of natural environment; typical or rare landscapes; and areas for the preservation of genetic funds of plants and animals. [Article 6(1)]
South Africa	National Environmental Management: Protected Areas Act of 2003 and Protected Areas Amendment Act of 2004	… an area designated in terms of section 22 or 26 (to protect and maintain the natural character of the environment, biodiversity, associated natural and cultural resources and the provision of environmental goods and services; to provide outstanding opportunities for solitude; to control access which, if allowed, may only be by non-mechanized means.)
Sri Lanka	National Wilderness Heritage Areas Act of 1988	Not identified, but see Matrix B
United States	Wilderness Act of 1964	A wilderness, in contrast with those areas where man and his works dominate the landscape, is hereby recognized as an area where the earth and its community of life are untrammeled by man, where

Matrix A: Definitions

Country	Law	Legislated Definition of Wilderness
United States *continued*		man himself is a visitor who does not remain. An area of wilderness is further defined to mean in this Act an area of undeveloped Federal land retaining its primeval character and influence, without permanent improvements or human habitation, which is protected and managed so as to preserve its natural conditions and which (1) generally appears to have been affected primarily by the forces of nature, with the imprint of man's work substantially unnoticeable; (2) has outstanding opportunities for solitude or a primitive and unconfined type of recreation; (3) has at least [two thousand hectares or] five thousand acres of land or is of sufficient size as to make practicable its preservation and use in an unimpaired condition; and (4) may also contain ecological, geological, or other features of scientific, educational, scenic, or historical value. [Sec.2(c)]

Matrix B: Legislative Purpose

Country	Goal(s) of Wilderness Legislation
Australia	A wilderness zone shall be maintained in its natural state and shall be used only for scientific research authorized by the Director and such recreational and other purposes, other than the recovery of minerals, as are specified in the plan of management relating to the wilderness zone [Section 10(5)].
Australia–State of New South Wales	a. to provide for the permanent protection of wilderness areas, b. to provide for the proper management of wilderness areas, c. to promote the education of the public in the appreciation, protection and management of wilderness [Section 3]
Australia–State of South Australia	An Act to provide for the protection of wilderness and the restoration of land to its condition before European colonization; and for other purposes.
Canada	Not identified
Canada–Province of Ontario	See definition under Ontario in Matrix A above. The objectives of Provincial Parks generally, including Wilderness Class Parks, are: 1. To permanently protect representative ecosystems, biodiversity and provincially significant elements of Ontario's natural and cultural heritage and to manage these areas to ensure that ecological integrity is maintained. 2. To provide opportunities for ecologically sustainable outdoor recreation and encourage associated economic benefits. 3. To provide opportunities for residents of Ontario and visitors to increase their knowledge and appreciation of Ontario's natural and cultural heritage. 4. To facilitate scientific research and to provide points of reference to support monitoring of ecological change on the broader landscape. [Section 2]

Matrix B: Legislative Purpose	Page 2
Country	**Goal(s) of Wilderness Legislation**
Canada–Province of Ontario, *continued*	And: Ontario's provincial parks and conservation reserves are dedicated to the people of Ontario and visitors for their inspiration, education, health, recreational enjoyment and other benefits with the intention that these areas shall be managed to maintain their ecological integrity and to leave them unimpaired for future generations. [Section 6]
Canada–Province of Newfoundland and Labrador	See definition under Newfoundland and Labrador in Matrix A above.
Confederated Salish and Kootenai Tribes	It is the principle objective of this Ordinance to protect and preserve an area of land in its natural conditions in perpetuity. This Wilderness shall be devoted to the purposes of recreational, scenic, scientific, educational, conservation, cultural, religious and historical use only insofar as these uses are consistent with the spirit and provisions of this Ordinance. Human use of the Area must not interfere with the preservation of the Area as Wilderness. [Ordinance 79A]
Finland	1) Preserve wild areas, 2) Safeguard Lapp culture and indigenous livelihoods, 3) Develop the potential for diversified use of nature.
Iceland	The purpose of this Act is to direct the interaction of man with his environment so that it harms neither the biosphere nor the geosphere, nor pollutes the air, sea, or water. The Act is intended to ensure, to the extent possible, that Icelandic nature can develop according to its own laws and ensure conservation of its exceptional or historical aspects. The Act shall facilitate the nation's access to and knowledge of Icelandic nature and cultural heritage and encourage the conservation and utilization of resources based on sustainable development. [Article 1]

	Matrix B: Legislative Purpose Page 3
Country	**Goal(s) of Wilderness Legislation**
Japan	Not identified
New Zealand	Wilderness areas are wild lands designated for their protection and managed to perpetuate their natural condition and which appear to have been affected only by the forces of nature, with any imprint of human interference substantially unnoticeable ... Wilderness designation preserves resources and thus options for future use of the land.
Russia	The following goals are assigned to strict state nature preserves (zapovedniks): a) realization of the protection of natural areas with the dual goals of preservation of biological diversity, and the maintenance of protected natural complexes and objects in a natural condition; b) organization and performance of scientific research including maintenance of Letopis Prirody (Chronicles of Nature); c) realization of ecological monitoring within the framework of the general state system of the natural environment monitoring; d) environmental education; e) participation in State Ecological Expertiza (environmental impact assessment) of projects and schemes, i.e. schemes of placement of economic (industrial) and other types of objects; f) assistance in training the scientific community and specialists in the sphere of protection of the natural environment." [Article 7]
South Africa	... designated ... for the purpose of retaining an intrinsically wild appearance and character or capable of being restored to such and which is undeveloped and roadless, without permanent improvements or human habitation. [Sec. 1(1)].
Sri Lanka	For the purpose of preserving in their natural state, unique eco-systems, genetic resources; or physical and biological formations and precisely delineated areas which constitute the habitat of threatened species of animals and plants of outstanding universal values from the point of view of science or conservation; for enhancing the natural beauty of the wilderness of Sri Lanka and for promoting the scientific study and enjoyment thereof by the public. [Sec. 2(1)]

Matrix B: Legislative Purpose	Page 4
Country	Goal(s) of Wilderness Legislation
United States	In order to assure that an increasing population, accompanied by expanding settlement and growing mechanization, does not occupy and modify all areas within the United States and its possessions, leaving no lands designated for preservation and protection in their natural condition, it is hereby declared to be the policy of the Congress to secure for the American people of present and future generations the benefits of an enduring resource of wilderness. For this purpose there is hereby established a National Wilderness Preservation System to be composed of federally owned areas designated by Congress as "wilderness areas," and these shall be administered for the use and enjoyment of the American people in such manner as will leave them unimpaired for future use as wilderness, and so as to provide for the protection of these areas, the preservation of their wilderness character, and for the gathering and dissemination of information regarding their use and enjoyment as wilderness. [Section 2(a)]

Matrix C: Allowed Uses of Wilderness

Legislated Public Uses (Yes = allowed/permitted; No = not allowed/prohibited/restricted)

Country	Scientific	Subsistence or Traditional	Commercial	Extractive Activities	Motorized	Preexisting Rights	Roads, Buildings, Structures	Other Uses
Australia	Yes [Section 10(5)]	Not identified	Not identified	No [Section 10(5)]	No [Section 10(5)]	Not identified	No [Section 10(5)]	No timber felled, excavation [Section 10(5)]
Australia–State of New South Wales	Yes [Section 5(e)]	Not identified	Not identified	No–Section 2(1) prohibits development, which includes vegetation clearing. However, mining or other extractive activities might be allowed if a preexisting "interest" under Section 8(5).	Not identified	Yes–Protects any preexisting "interests" including any authority, authorization, permit, lease, license, or occupancy, whether or not arising under the act. [Section 8(5)]	No–Section 2(1) prohibits "development," which includes: buildings, work, subdivision, clearing of vegetation, **unless** by the approval of the Minister if the Minister is of the opinion the development will have no adverse effects.	Not identified
Australia–State of South Australia	Yes [Section 12(k)]	Yes [Section 12(n,o)]	Yes [Section 8(4)]	Not in wilderness protection areas, but permitted in wilderness protection zones, by proclamation of	Yes [Section 41(2)(q)]	Yes (mining, subsistence) [Sec. 25(3)-(5)].	No [Section 26(1)(b)]	Grazing of stock and all other forms of primary production are

Matrix C: Allowed Uses of Wilderness

Page 2

Legislated Public Uses (Yes = allowed/permitted; No = not allowed/prohibited/restricted)

Country	Scientific	Subsistence or Traditional	Commercial	Extractive Activities	Motorized	Preexisting Rights	Roads, Buildings, Structures	Other Uses
Australia–State of South Australia *continued*				the Governor Section 25(3), and subject to restrictions in Section 25(5)—the proclamation must be simultaneous to the wilderness declaration, and to enable exercise of preexisting mining rights.				prohibited. [Section 26(1)(a)]
Canada	Not identified	Yes [Section 17 by reference to [Section 14(3)(d)]	Not identified	Traditional resource harvesting in specified parks [Section17].	Yes [Section 14(3)]	Yes	Basic user facilities including trails, rudimentary camp-sites may be permitted. [Section 14 (3)(c)]	Air access permitted to remote parts of wilderness areas [Section 14(3)(e)].
Canada–Province of Ontario	Yes [Section 2(4)]	Yes [Section 4] reaffirms existing aboriginal	Yes [Section 14]	No commercial timber harvest, generation of electricity, mining activity, extracting aggregate, topsoil	Yes—to address certain needs, such as	Yes—exceptions made for preexisting oil and and gas wells, aggregate pits,	Yes—Subject to approval, roads to mining claims or to access minerals or timber outside a Provincial Park allowed.	No Hunting not allowed, unless permitted by regulation

	Matrix C: Allowed Uses of Wilderness							Page 3
	Legislated Public Uses (Yes = allowed/permitted; No = not allowed/prohibited/restricted)							
Country	Scientific	Subsistence or Traditional	Commercial	Extractive Activities	Motorized	Preexisting Rights	Roads, Buildings, Structures	Other Uses
Canada– Province of Ontario *continued*		and treaty rights of the aboriginal peoples of Canada under Constitution Act 1982.		or peat, or other industrial uses. [Section16]. Building a facility for electricity generation for Provincial Park purposes also allowed if no reasonable alternative. (Also see Preexisting column.)	non-conforming pre-existing uses, for use by First Nations, to access in-holdings, for permitted air access to remote parts of the park. [Section 54(3)]	electricity generation, and timber operations in Algonquin Provincial Park. Electricity generation allowed only if no reasonable alternatives or for communities not connected to the main electrical grid.	Utility corridors for electrical transmission also allowed. Roads must be closed if not used for 5 years.	under the Fish and Wildlife Conservation Act of 1997 and in certain townships incorporated into Algonquin Provincial Park [Section 15(1)(2)]
Canada– Province of Newfound-land and Labrador	Yes [Section 20]	Yes [Section 3.1]	Not identified	No. No cutting or logging of trees, agriculture, mining, prospecting, or claims staking. [Section 24]	No [Section 24]	Yes [Section 25], but activities must not be increased.	No [Section 24], includes prohibition on landing aircraft.	No altering water flows into or within a wilderness reserve [Section 24]; no spraying

Matrix C: Allowed Uses of Wilderness

Page 4

Legislated Public Uses (Yes = allowed/permitted; No = not allowed/prohibited/restricted)

Country	Scientific	Subsistence or Traditional	Commercial	Extractive Activities	Motorized	Preexisting Rights	Roads, Buildings, Structures	Other Uses
Canada Province of Newfoundland and Labrador *continued*								against insect infestations without approval by the Minister [Section 24]. Note: General exemption from prohibited activities in Section 24 if deemed necessary for management of the reserve.
Confederated Salish and Kootenai Tribes	Yes [Section 5(e)]	Yes [Section 1]	No [Section 5(d)]	Not identified	No [Section 4(d)]	Yes, for livestock grazing [Section 5(a)]	No [Section 4(d)]	Non-tribal members are subject to management restrictions for entry, group

Matrix C: Allowed Uses of Wilderness

Legislated Public Uses (Yes = allowed/permitted; No = not allowed/prohibited/restricted)

Country	Scientific	Subsistence or Traditional	Commercial	Extractive Activities	Motorized	Preexisting Rights	Roads, Buildings, Structures	Other Uses
Confederated Salish *continued*								size, length of stay, use of firearms [wilderness.net]
Finland	Not identified	Yes [Section 4]	Not identified	Restricted logging [Section 7], but has only been permitted in one area to date. No mining unless permitted for a compelling social purpose [Section 4]	No [Section 5]	Yes [Section 12]	No, unless permitted for a compelling social purpose [Section 6]	Not identified
Iceland	Not identified	Yes [Article 12]	Not identified	Not identified	No [Section 3(4)]	Not identified	No [Section 3(4)]	Not identified
Japan	Not identified	Not identified	Not identified	Not identified	Not identified	Not identified	Not identified	Activities negatively impacting the ecosystem are strictly prohibited.

Matrix C: Allowed Uses of Wilderness

Legislated Public Uses (Yes = allowed/permitted; No = not allowed/prohibited/restricted)

Country	Scientific	Subsistence or Traditional	Commercial	Extractive Activities	Motorized	Preexisting Rights	Roads, Buildings, Structures	Other Uses
New Zealand	Not identified	Not identified	No, unless permitted.	No	No	Not identified	No	Horses may be allowed where strong historical links exist, and where legislation permits.
Russia	Yes	Not identified	Not identified	Yes [Article 6(2)]	Not identified	Not identified	Not identified	Not identified
Sri Lanka	Yes, if permitted [Section 3(2)]	No	No selling of forest products, wildlife [Section 4]. Ecotourism or non-extractive activities are not identified.	No	Not identified, presumably no.	Not identified	No [Section 4]	No cultivation [Section 4]

Matrix C: Allowed Uses of Wilderness

Page 7

Legislated Public Uses (Yes = allowed/permitted; No = not allowed/prohibited/restricted)

Country	Scientific	Subsistence or Traditional	Commercial	Extractive Activities	Motorized	Preexisting Rights	Roads, Buildings, Structures	Other Uses
South Africa	Not identified	Not identified	Not identified	No [Section 22(2)(c) and Section 26(2)(c)]	No [Section 22(2)(c) and Section 26(2)(c)]	Not identified	Not identified	Not identified
United States	Yes, if permitted [Section 4(b)]	No, unless allowed by legislation (e.g. Alaska)	No, unless permitted [Section 4(d)(6)]	No, unless permitted [Section 4(d)(3)]	No [Section 4(c)]	No, except aircraft or motorboats [Section 4(d)1] and livestock grazing [Section 4(d)4]	No [Section 4(c)]	Not identified

Matrix D: Administration and Management

Page 1

Legislated Administration and Management of Wilderness

Country	Management Goal(s)	Buffer Zones Outside Wilderness	Use of "Minimum Necessary Management Tool" Concept	Treatment of In-holdings	Reporting and Accountability
Australia	Not identified	Not identified	Not identified	Not identified	Annual Report on operations by Director of National Parks and Wildlife (Section 52)
Australia—State of New South Wales	a. to restore (if applicable) and to protect the unmodified state of the area and its plant and animal communities, b. to preserve the capacity of the area to evolve in the absence of significant human interference, c. to permit opportunities for solitude and appropriate self-reliant recreation.	Not identified	Not identified	Not identified	Not identified
Australia—State of South Australia	The wilderness code of management will address: a. preservation of wildlife and ecosystems; b. restoration of land and its eco-systems to their condition before European colonization and the	Yes [Section 22(5)]	Not identified	Not identified	Yes—Annual Report by the Minister containing the names and locations of wilderness protection areas and zones, and the extent to which wilderness criteria are met

Matrix D: Administration and Management

Legislated Administration and Management of Wilderness

Country	Management Goal(s)	Buffer Zones Outside Wilderness	Use of "Minimum Necessary Management Tool" Concept	Treatment of In-holdings	Reporting and Accountability
Australia— State of South Australia *continued*	protection of land and its ecosystems from the effects of modern technology and exotic animals and plants and other exotic organisms; c. preservation of Aboriginal sites and Aboriginal objects; d. preservation of historic sites and objects and structures of historic or scientific interest; e. preservation of features of geographical, natural or scenic interest; f. destruction of dangerous weeds and the eradication or control of noxious weeds and exotic plants; g. control of vermin and exotic animals and other exotic organisms; h. control and eradication of disease of animals and vegetation; i. prevention and suppression of				by each; identification of former reserves or parts of reserves that are now wilderness protection areas or zones; extent of mining operations; restoration activities; list of management plans; portions of wilderness protection areas or zones that the Minister has declared as prohibited areas and reasons for the declaration; an account of money received and expended on management; an account of royalties.

		Matrix D: Administration and Management			Page 3
		Legislated Administration and Management of Wilderness			
Country	Management Goal(s)	Buffer Zones Outside Wilderness	Use of "Minimum Necessary Management Tool" Concept	Treatment of In-holdings	Reporting and Accountability
Australia—State of South Australia *continued*	bush fires and other hazards; j. conduct of firefighting and other emergency operations; k. conduct of scientific research l. education of the public as to the significance of wilderness protection areas and zones; m. use of wilderness protection areas and zones by members of the public; n. hunting in wilderness protection areas by Aboriginal people; o. the entry in and use of wilderness protection areas and zones by Aboriginal people to observe Aboriginal tradition. [Section12(2)]				
	"Not authorize any activity to be carried on in a wilderness area that is likely to impair the wilderness character of the area." [Section 14(2)]				

Matrix D: Administration and Management

Page 4

Legislated Administration and Management of Wilderness

Country	Management Goal(s)	Buffer Zones Outside Wilderness	Use of "Minimum Necessary Management Tool" Concept	Treatment of In-holdings	Reporting and Accountability
Canada– Province of Ontario	Not identified, but see definition and legislated purposes above.	Not identified	Not identified	No, [Section 13] though the minister may extend an existing lease or may grant new leases for private noncommercial purposes if the lease is consistent with the Act and its regulations.	Yes—Report required every 5 years on state of the parks. Report includes degree of ecological representation, ecological and socioeconomic benefits, number and area of parks, and threats to ecological integrity. [Section 11(1-4)] Also: Annual report on finances [Section 27(4)].
Canada– Province of Newfoundland and Labrador	The minister may carry out measures or programs in a reserve, a. for the preservation and protection of the reserve; b. for biological or physical research; or c. for anything necessary for the purpose of this act.	Not identified	Not identified	Yes [Section 23]	Yes—Advisory Council to report to the minister on the expenses and operations of the Advisory Council [Section 15].

Matrix D: Administration and Management

Page 5

Legislated Administration and Management of Wilderness

Country	Management Goal(s)	Buffer Zones Outside Wilderness	Use of "Minimum Necessary Management Tool" Concept	Treatment of In-holdings	Reporting and Accountability
Confederated Salish and Kootenai Tribes	Protect and preserve natural conditions in perpetuity [Section 4].	Yes (see case study on www.wilderness.net).	Yes (see case study on www.wilderness.net).	Not identified	Not identified
Finland	Preserve forests in their natural state or tended using natural forestry practices [Section 7].	Not identified	Not identified	Easements, usufructs, in the area may be redeemed [Section 8].	Not identified
Iceland	Not identified	Not identified	Not identified	Not identified	Report required on the condition, construction, and other aspects of concern for the management of these areas [Article 6].
Japan	Not identified	Not identified	Not identified	Not identified	Not identified
New Zealand	Not identified	Not identified	Not identified	Not identified	Not identified
Russia	Not identified	Not identified	Not identified	Not identified	Not identified

Matrix D: Administration and Management

Page 6

Legislated Administration and Management of Wilderness

Country	Management Goal(s)	Buffer Zones Outside Wilderness	Use of "Minimum Necessary Management Tool" Concept	Treatment of In-holdings	Reporting and Accountability
Sri Lanka	Not identified	Not identified	Not identified	Private property within the wilderness is deemed to be required for a public purpose and may be acquired [Section 2(4)].	Not identified
South Africa	Not identified	Not identified	Yes	Not identified	Not identified
United States	1) Preserve wilderness character. 2) Administer the area for the other purposes for which was established while preserving its wilderness character [Section 4(b)].	Not explicitly identified in Wilderness Act, but in at least 22 wilderness laws, buffers are not allowed.	"...except as necessary to meet minimum requirements for the administration of the area for the purpose of this Act" [Section 4(c)].	"Adequate access" is assured to state or private land within wilderness [Section 5(a)].	Annual report required on status of the wilderness system [Section 7].

Part II

Statutory Wilderness

Great Egret, Everglades National Park, Florida. Photo by
Rodney Cammauf, courtesy of the National Park Service.

Editor's Note

Part II includes eleven chapters covering ten countries and one Native American tribe in the United States, all of which have laws establishing wilderness as a special form of protected area, and many of which also require an act of the legislature to establish wilderness areas. These countries correspond to Class I and Class II under WILD's classification as described in Chapter 1. Turkey is in the process of developing new biodiversity protection legislation that would include a wilderness classification, though the law has not yet been passed.

Budawang Wilderness Area, Morton National Park, New South Wales,
Australia. Photo by John Reid, School of Art,
© Australian National University.

CHAPTER 3

Australia

James Prest[1]

Introduction

Protecting wilderness areas remains an important component of nature conservation strategies throughout Australia, particularly given the current shift away from species-specific biodiversity conservation approaches in favor of more comprehensive ecosystem conservation approaches.[2] Indeed, recent scientific analysis has bolstered the case that wilderness areas are key to nature conservation strategies, particularly in the face of human-induced climate change.[3] As Mackey, et al. state:

> Wilderness areas and areas of high wilderness quality, all other
> things being equal, will provide for larger reserves, support
> larger or better connected meta-populations, reduce extinction
> risk, be less fragmented, and possess greater resilience.[4]

At the same time, it would be fair to say that wilderness is not always a popular cause within government in Australia, and has even been criticized in some conservation circles.[5] One criticism has been that that wilderness conservation is insensitive to indigenous cultures, though in fact conservation organizations in Australia are working very actively with indigenous groups to develop and implement a common vision on wilderness conservation.

Despite criticism, wilderness has endured. There are still a substantial number of areas in Australia with good wilderness qualities, the objective of wilderness conservation is at the least passively acknowledged by most governments, and wilderness provisions have not been removed from the statute books despite occasional agitation from anti-environmental forces. For example, although a large number of proposed amendments to federal environmental law were presented to Parliament by government in October 2006, those provisions did not propose substantial changes to the federal protected areas regime, of which wilderness forms an important part.[6] Environmentalists also successfully persuaded the Queensland legislature to enact the Wild Rivers Act 2005[7], emulating earlier statutes in Victoria and New South Wales. Six wild rivers were declared by the Queensland government in 2006, with concessions for limited low-impact mineral exploration activity.[8]

Australia: Background

Australia has a federal system of government, which includes a central commonwealth government operating in conjunction with six states and two self-governing territories (the "provincial governments"). Because there is no direct reference to the environment or environmental protection in the Commonwealth Constitution, land management is largely left to the states.

New South Wales (NSW) and South Australia (SA) are the only states with specific purpose wilderness legislation: the Wilderness Act of 1987 in NSW and the Wilderness Protection Act of 1992 in SA. Most of Australia's other states and territories have wilderness provisions within their general nature conservation legislation, or within their parks and reserves legislation. These include Queensland, Victoria, Western Australia, Australian Capital Territory, and Northern Territory. The Commonwealth has provisions contained within the omnibus Environment Protection and Biodiversity Conservation Act 1999. Finally, in Tasmania and at the national level in the Nature Conservation Act 2002 and the National Parks and

Reserves Management Act 2002, wilderness is not a separate category of protected area, but simply a management objective for particular zones in national parks.

There are three different models of wilderness legislation in Australia: comprehensive legislation, minimalist legislation, and nonexistent (Whitehouse, 1993).[9] The comprehensive legislation model involves explicit wilderness legislation. These Wilderness Acts do not depend on categories derived from protected areas legislation. Instead, they stand alone, presenting comprehensive management principles for wilderness areas and providing for public input into the identification and declaration of wilderness areas. "Minimalist" wilderness legislation in Australia applies the concept of wilderness, but usually as a subset of protected areas management legislation. The so-called "nonexistent" legislative model provides protection to wilderness by the designation of wilderness zones within protected areas.

This chapter focuses in particular on New South Wales and South Australia, the two jurisdictions with a comprehensive legislation model for wilderness, but mentions other states and territories where relevant to highlight contrasting approaches.

Definitions of Wilderness

There are a variety of definitions of wilderness in Australia, each emphasizing different factors—for example the intactness of a particular area, its remoteness, the absence of exotic species, its size, its suitability for self-reliant recreation, etc. This section reviews several of these definitions.

New South Wales

In NSW, land can be declared as a wilderness area under the Wilderness Act of 1987, whether it is reserved as a protected area under the National Parks and Wildlife Act, is privately held land, or is held in another Crown land tenure.

The director of the NPWS makes a determination based on the following criteria:

a. The area is, together with its plant and animal communities, in a state that has not been substantially modified by humans and their works or is capable of being restored to such a state;

b. The area is of a sufficient size to make its maintenance in such a state feasible; and

c. The area is capable of providing opportunities for solitude and appropriate self-reliant recreation.

NSW legislation avoids the approach taken in jurisdictions such as Victoria and Queensland, which emphasizes remoteness criteria and which may inadvertently place too much weight on perceived barriers to declaring wilderness rather than focusing on the benefits. Instead, the emphasis in NSW is on naturalness of the environment. The legislation also makes allowance for future restoration of disturbed areas. Thus, the presence of some unsealed roads does not preclude the identification of an area as wilderness.[10]

Memory Cove Wilderness Protection Area, Port Lincoln National Park, South Australia. Photo by Bill Doyle.

The Act provides that the director may consider:

a. The period of time within which the area of land could reasonably be restored to a substantially unmodified state;

b. Whether, despite development which would otherwise render it unsuitable, the area of land is needed for the management of an existing or proposed wilderness area; and

c. Any written representations received by the director from any person (including a statutory authority) as to whether the area of land should be identified as wilderness.

South Australia

In South Australia, land can be proclaimed as a wilderness area or zone under the Wilderness Protection Act of 1992 if it meets the following criteria:

a. The land and its ecosystems must not have been affected, or must have been affected to only a minor extent, by modern technology; and

b. The land and its ecosystems must not have been seriously affected by exotic animals or plants or other exotic organisms.

The SA wilderness criteria therefore focus on integrity and lack of disturbance rather than questions of remoteness.

Commonwealth

The Commonwealth's Environment Protection and Biodiversity Conservation Act 1999 provides that Australia's executive government must assign any new reserve in the Commonwealth to one of the seven listed IUCN protected area categories, including IUCN Category Ib Wilderness. The Commonwealth Act largely adopts the IUCN definition of wilderness, stating that a commonwealth wilderness reserve or zone consists of a large area of land, sea or both that:

1. is unmodified, or only slightly modified, by modern or colonial society; and

2. retains its natural character; and

3. does not contain permanent or significant habitation.

Queensland

In Queensland, wilderness is defined under the Nature Conservation Act of 1992 as an area that is, or can be restored to be:

a. of sufficient size to enable the long-term protection of its natural systems and biological diversity; and

b. substantially undisturbed by modern society; and

c. remote at its core from points of mechanized access and other evidence of society.

Tasmania

Natural areas in Tasmania are protected via the National Parks and Reserves Management Act 2002 and the Nature Conservation Act 2002. However, Tasmania does not have a wilderness act, and its protected areas legislation does not specifically provide for the declaration of wilderness areas. Rather, Tasmanian national parks have statutory management objectives that include the preservation of the natural, primitive, and remote character of wilderness areas.

Wilderness areas in Tasmania are therefore only protected by a secondary layer of control, through management plans and associated statutory provisions.[11] Wilderness zones are one of four zonings set out in the Tasmanian Wilderness World Heritage Area Plan of Management: wilderness zones, self-reliant recreation zones, recreation zones, and visitor service zones. A wilderness zone of 1 million hectares (2.47 million acres) was established within the Tasmanian Wilderness World Heritage area under the 1992 management plan.

The fact that wilderness areas are not protected by legislation creates a danger of ad hoc development approvals and inconsistent management plan activities and amendments. Governments are also free to excise certain lands from wilderness areas, and the legislation makes allowances for development interests. On the other hand, proposed changes are subject to public review, and changes must be circulated to the National Parks and Wildlife Advisory Council as well as the Resource Planning and Development Commission.

Tasmanian legislation also enables a national park management plan to provide for grants of authorities for uses and development of the land not in accordance with the reserve's management legislation. For example, an authority other than the Parks Service may construct dams and other infrastructure. Such grants of authority, however, must be approved by both houses of Parliament.

Declaration and Revocation of Wilderness Areas

The process for the identification, assessment and declaration of wilderness areas—and conversely, the process of revoking wilderness status—are key elements of any wilderness protection system. The following sections review the different approaches to establishing and declassifying wilderness areas in Australia.

Declaration of Wilderness Areas

New South Wales

NSW legislation provides for a two-stage process for declaring wilderness areas. Lands meeting the statutory criteria in the Wilderness Act[12] are first officially identified, and then declared as wilderness by the director-general of the NPWS. One of the statutory objects of the Wilderness Act is "the *permanent* protection of wilderness areas" (emphasis added).

A key aspect of NSW law is the fact that any person or organization may propose that an area be identified and declared as a wilderness area.[13] The director-general must assess the proposal and advise the minister for the environment within two years of receiving it.[14] In the 1990s, the issue of significant delays arose between the identification of wilderness areas in NSW and their actual declaration.

There are three routes by which an area of land may be declared to be wilderness in NSW. These are primarily distinguished by the tenure of the land, and all depend on the land being officially identified as meeting statutory wilderness standards.

Existing Park

Where the land is already reserved or dedicated under the National Parks and Wildlife Act 1974, it can be declared a wilderness area under provisions of the Wilderness Act once it has been identified as a wilderness area.

Conservation Agreement

Where land is either leased or privately owned, is within an identified wilderness area, and the holder of that interest chooses to enter into a conservation agreement with the relevant minister under the National Parks and Wildlife Act, the minister is obliged by law to declare the land to be a wilderness area. At the time of this writing, there was only one such parcel of private land subject to such a declaration, in the Budawang wilderness adjoining the Budawang National Park in the South Eastern Highlands bioregion. [15]

Wilderness Protection Agreements

A wilderness protection agreement under the Wilderness Act is between the environment minister and either a statutory authority or the minister administering Crown land. This involves the land-holder—either the Crown or a statutory authority (such as those responsible for rail or road infrastructure, but not a government department)—that owns or controls land within an identified wilderness area to establish a wilderness area. The minister is again obliged to declare the land a wilderness area when a Wilderness Protection Agreement is signed.

To date, in all but one instance, wilderness areas in NSW have been declared over existing national parks. As a result, Wilderness Areas in NSW typically have not increased the total area of protected landscapes.

South Australia

South Australia's legislation requires an expert body, the Wilderness Advisory Committee (WAC), to identify and consider wilderness proposals. The committee performs the following functions:

- Assesses land to identify places that meet the statutory wilderness criteria;
- Assesses partly degraded lands to examine whether they warrant restoration to a condition that justifies protection as wilderness;
- Makes reports to the minister regarding wilderness assessments;
- Makes recommendations to the minister regarding the management of wilderness areas and zones;
- Commissions research into the effect of extractive industries, grazing, and other primary industries on wilderness; and
- Educates the public regarding the significance of wilderness.[16]

Following recommendation by the committee, wilderness areas and wilderness zones are created by proclamation of the governor.

Public Participation Provisions in NSW and SA

Community participation is a central aspect of wilderness protection legislation in NSW and SA. Both laws provide for public participation in wilderness identification and management planning. For example, the NSW act specifically provides that any person or organization may make a wilderness proposal to the director of National Parks and Wildlife.[17] At least some level of community input has preceded the majority of NSW wilderness declarations. In South Australia, eight terrestrial wilderness areas have been protected, all following nominations by the Wilderness Society (Australia). Eight additional marine wilderness areas have been proposed by the Society.

The wilderness legislation in these two jurisdictions also contain third-party enforcement provisions enabling any person to bring a civil action to enforce their provisions.[18] These provisions have facilitated access to the courts by NGOs seeking to protect wilderness.

For example, the Stealth Bomber case involved a successful legal challenge by environmentalists to the approval of commercial filming in a wilderness area of the Blue Mountains near Sydney. The court held that the grant of licenses by the National Parks and Wildlife Service for the production of a commercial feature film within a declared wilderness area in a World Heritage-listed national park was inconsistent with purpose and objects of the Wilderness Act and the management principles for national parks set out in the National Parks and Wildlife Act (Land and Environment Court NSW: Blue Mountains Conservation Society Inc. v Director-General of National Parks and Wildlife & Ors (29 April 2004).

Provisions to Revoke Wilderness Status

A related issue is the security of a wilderness declaration: once wilderness status is conferred, how easily can it be revoked? Australian legislation falls into two classes—those acts that permit the designation of wilderness to be revoked "at the stroke of a pen" by the executive, and acts that protect wilderness designations by requiring a resolution of both houses of Parliament.

NSW requires an act of Parliament to revoke a declared wilderness area, though areas can be modified by notification by the minister for environment published in the Gazette. In SA, a wilderness area or zone can be altered or revoked only upon resolution of both houses of Parliament. In Victoria and the Northern Territory, revoking wilderness status requires action by the legislative assembly. In the Australian Capital Territory, a change in wilderness status requires only public review and consultation with the conservator of flora and fauna, though the requested change may be disallowed by the legislative assembly.

Wilderness proclamations are the least secure in Western Australia (WA), Queensland, and Tasmania. In WA and Queensland, proclamation by the governor is sufficient to revoke wilderness status. Tasmania requires only a change in the protected area's management plan.

It is important to note that the removal of wilderness designation usually will not mean that the area is no longer protected. Wilderness designation is often an additional layer of protection applied to already protected areas such as national parks or nature reserves.

Wilderness Management Principles

Several Australian laws provide management principles for wilderness areas, referring to IUCN's definition of wilderness under Category 1b for guidance.

Commonwealth Management and Administrative Principles for Wilderness Areas

Regulations made under Australia's Federal Environment Protection and Biodiversity Conservation Act 1999 (Cth) set out administrative and management principles for wilderness areas.[19] Some of the key principles are listed below:

Administrative Principles

1. Community participation

Management arrangements should, to the extent practicable, provide for broad and meaningful participation by the community, public organizations, and private interests in designing and carrying out the functions of the reserve or zone [...]

4. Minimum impact

The integrity of a reserve or zone is best conserved by protecting it from disturbance and threatening processes. Potential adverse impacts on the natural, cultural, and social environment and surrounding communities should be minimized as far as practicable [...]

7. Joint management

If the reserve or zone is wholly or partly owned by Aboriginal people, continuing traditional use of the reserve or zone by resident indigenous people, including the protection and maintenance of cultural heritage, should be recognized.

Management Principles

2.01　The reserve or zone should be protected and managed to preserve its unmodified condition based on the following principles:

2.02　Future generations should have the opportunity to experience, understand, and enjoy reserves or zones that have been largely undisturbed by human action over a long period of time.

2.03　The essential attributes and qualities of the environment should be maintained over the long term.

2.04　Public access should be provided at levels and of a type that will best serve the physical and spiritual well-being of visitors and maintain the wilderness qualities of the reserve or zone for present and future generations.

2.05　Indigenous human communities living at low density and in balance with the available resources should be able to maintain their lifestyle.

States and Territories

New South Wales

The NSW Wilderness Act provides the following statutory management principles for wilderness areas:

"A wilderness area shall be managed so as to:

a. Restore (if applicable) and protect the unmodified state of the area and its plant and animal communities,

b. Preserve the capacity of the area to evolve in the absence of significant human interference, and

c. Permit opportunities for solitude and appropriate self-reliant recreation."

Queensland

The Queensland Nature Conservation Act 1992 states that "A wilderness area is to be managed to protect or restore the wilderness values, and the cultural and natural resources, of the area to the greatest possible extent ..." [20]

This provision shows important recognition of cultural resources of a wilderness area, suggesting recognition of indigenous interests in wilderness. Queensland's legislation also largely replicates subparagraphs (b) and (c) of the NSW legislation above.

Victoria

Victorian legislation, the National Parks Act 1975, states in section17A that:

> 2. The secretary must ensure that each wilderness park is controlled and managed in accordance with the objects of this Act in a manner that will protect and enhance the park as a wilderness including, insofar as is practicable and appropriate, the taking of measures:
>
> a. to preserve and protect
>
> > i. the natural environment including indigenous flora and fauna and features of ecological, geological or scenic significance; and
> >
> > ii. features of archaeological or historic significance; and
> >
> > iii. features of scientific significance; and
>
> b. for the eradication or control of non-indigenous flora and non-indigenous fauna; and
>
> c. for the control of indigenous fauna to the extent necessary for the reservation and protection of any species; and
>
> d. subject to paragraph (a), for the removal of evidence of developments of non-aboriginal origin.
>
> 3. Subject to subsection (2), the secretary:
>
> a. must ensure that opportunities are provided for solitude and appropriate self-reliant recreation in a wilderness park; and
>
> b. must promote the understanding and appreciation of the purpose and significance of wilderness and the proper use of wilderness by the public.

Australian Capital Territory

ACT Land (Planning and Environment) Act 1991, section 195 sets out the following management principles for wilderness areas:

1. to conserve the natural environment in a way ensuring that disturbance to that environment is minimal;
2. to provide for the use of the area (other than by vehicles or other mechanised equipment) for recreation by limited numbers of people, to ensure that opportunities for solitude are provided.

Northern Territory

In NT, the Territory Parks and Wildlife Conservation Act provides (section17) that "a wilderness zone shall be maintained in its natural state and shall be used only for purposes specified in the plan of management relating to the wilderness zone." Construction, logging, and the use of vehicles and vessels are prohibited except where carried out by the Conservation Commission in accordance with the management plan, "for purposes essential to the management of the park or reserve."[21]

Regulating Extractive Industries

There are two sources of Australian legislation regulating extractive industries in wilderness areas: specific restrictions arising from wilderness legislation, and general restrictions from protected areas legislation. An example of restrictions arising from wilderness legislation can be found in the management principles prescribed by the Wilderness Act in NSW. These state that "a wilderness area shall be managed so as to ... protect the unmodified state of the area and its plant and animal communities, [and] to preserve the capacity of the area to evolve in the absence of significant human interference."[22] That provision is expressed to prevail over other acts and instruments.

An example of the latter are the Commonwealth regulations made under the Environment Protection and Biodiversity Conservation Act 1999, which create offenses of excavating, building, and works within all types of protected areas, damaging and defacing features. The act also regulates other activities including commercial fishing.[23]

Activities must generally be consistent with plans of management for protected areas. For example, under the National Parks and Wildlife Act 1974 (NSW), no operations shall be undertaken in relation to the reserved lands subject to a management plan unless they are in accordance with that plan.[24]

Mining

New South Wales

Once an area has been formally declared to be wilderness in NSW, certain restrictions on mining come into force. Although the Wilderness Act itself does not explicitly prohibit mining, protection is derived from other sources. The first is the exclusion of the application of mining legislation—including the Mining Act 1992, the Offshore Minerals Act 1999, the Petroleum (Onshore) Act 1991 and the Petroleum (Submerged Lands) Act 1982—in protected areas classified under the national parks legislation, including national parks, historic sites, regional parks, nature reserves, and Aboriginal areas.[25]

Nevertheless, the Wilderness Act protects preexisting legal interests that may be associated with mining activity, including licenses, and interests that may be associated with mining such as mineral exploration licenses or mining leases.[26]

The second control is a general restriction on "development" in wilderness areas set out in the Wilderness Act, a restriction that appears sufficiently broad to constrain mining activity.[27] *Development*, in relation to wilderness areas, is defined to include:

a. the erection of a building in the area;
b. the carrying out of a work in, on, over or under the area;
c. the use of the area or of a building or work in the area;
d. the subdivision of the area; and
e. the clearing of vegetation in the area.

NSW planning law also makes a general prohibition on development of land that is, or is part of, a wilderness area.[28] Mining operations usually require planning approval, and larger mining operations are classified as designated development (coal mines; extractive industries involving excavating, dredging, tunneling or quarrying; limestone mines; other mines are likely to affect water bodies; or mines over a surface area impact threshold of 4 hectares [10 acres]). However, if consent has been granted under the Wilderness Act, that prohibition does not apply. Such consent may be granted to statutory authorities

The Wilderness Act restricts the capacity of statutory authorities to carry out development in wilderness areas that are subject to a wilderness protection agreement (where the land is owned and controlled by the Crown or a public authority, or is leased Crown land) or a conservation agreement (that is, where the land is privately owned or leased from the Crown).[29] Such development requires the consent of the environment minister and that consent can only be given if the minister believes that the proposed development will not adversely affect the wilderness area.[30] Where development by a pubic authority is proposed in a wilderness area, that development must be subject to environmental impact assessment which must involve consideration of the effect of that development on any wilderness areas.[31]

Preexisting mining interests are not rendered invalid by the declaration of a national park or other protected area in NSW.[32] Further, prospecting for minerals on behalf of the government is permissible in all categories of protected areas with ministerial approval, subject to a process of disallowance by both houses of Parliament.[33] The Wilderness Act does not expressly prevail over provisions of the National Parks and Wildlife Act 1974 (NPWA) concerning land within a wilderness area.[34] As a result, permissions for mining under the NPWA may prevail over the controls on development in the Wilderness Act.

South Australia

In South Australia, rights of entry, prospecting, exploration, or mining cannot be acquired or exercised in declared wilderness areas or zones proclaimed under the Wilderness Protection Act 1992 (SA).[35] However, mining may be permitted in wilderness protection *zones*, subject to conditions, by means of proclamation of the governor. Such a proclamation must be made either simultaneously with the proclamation that creates the wilderness protection zone, or, if later, by resolution of both houses of Parliament. If a mining tenement preexists the establishment of a wilderness protection zone, rights of entry, prospecting, exploration, or mining under the tenement may only be exercised if a proclamation is made simultaneously with the proclamation that creates the wilderness protection zone. If a person has no lawful authority to do so, it is an offense to intentionally cause damage to any part of a wilderness protection area or zone, a provision that can be enforced by any person under SA law.

Other Jurisdictions

Victorian legislation contains some specific protections for wilderness areas. For example, the Petroleum Act 1998 prohibits petroleum operations (exploration or production) on wilderness land and states that no authorities can be granted for such activity.[36] Further, land in a wilderness park or national park cannot generally be made the subject of a license for mineral exploration, mining, or searching.[37] However, this restriction does not affect an exploration or mining license granted before the declaration of the national park or wilderness park. Further, such licenses may be renewed after a park declaration. Where an area of a park has been declared as a "remote and natural area" under the National Parks Act, road construction, building and structures, facilities, earthworks, and vegetation removal are prohibited.[38]

Some legislation, such as in Queensland, protects wilderness by means of a general protection of protected areas from the grant of mining interests under the Mineral Resources Act 1989.[39] However, a multiple-use philosophy has permeated a significant proportion of Australian protected-areas legislation. For example, in Queensland, mining is permissible in "resource reserves."[40] In the Northern Territory, under the Territory Parks and Conservation Act, mining activity may be carried out in parks and reserves and wilderness zones, provided that it is in accordance with the management plan for that park.[41] Exploration licenses and exploration retention licenses can be granted within wilderness zones of protected areas in the NT by the minister for mines, subject to conditions imposed by the minister administering the Parks and Conservation Act.[42]

Forestry

In NSW, forestry is restricted where wilderness areas have either been declared or identified within part of a national park or other protected area. This protection derives from the status of the wilderness area as national park, rather than from its status as wilderness.[43]

Between 1987 and 1998, where an identified (but not yet declared) wilderness area was within state forests under the Forestry Act there was little protection, due to the fact that mere identification did not invoke the protections afforded by wilderness declaration. As a result of the Forestry and National Parks Estate Act 1998 (NSW), there is now an additional difficulty in protecting forested wilderness. This special purpose forestry legislation excludes the operation of wilderness legislation from areas of public forest subject to a logging approval—an Integrated Forestry Operations Approval (IFOA)—preventing any further wilderness areas from being either identified or declared. IFOAs have been issued for forestry within the Eden, Southern Region, Lower North East, and Upper North East regions.[44] At this stage, no IFOA has been completed for Western NSW.

Forestry within indigenous or nonindustrial native forests is not a significant land use in South Australia. In other jurisdictions, restrictions on forestry in wilderness areas derive from general restrictions in protected areas legislation.

Provisions Restricting or
Prohibiting Grazing and Pastoralism

NSW legislation provides that land subject to a wilderness protection agreement may contain terms restricting the use of the area.[45] South Australian legislation prohibits "the grazing of stock and all other forms of primary production" in wilderness areas or zones.[46]

Victorian legislation provides that within a wilderness zone there is to be "no use of any non-indigenous animal,"[47] and further, the secretary is obliged to ensure that "no commercial activity or development is carried out" in such zones.[48] However the statute permits continued cattle grazing in five wilderness zones within the Alpine National Park.[49]

Special Projects Legislation
Overriding Wilderness Legislation

To present a full picture of environmental legislation in Australia, one must take into account the effect of special projects legislation enacted specifically to facilitate development and to override provisions of environmental legislation that would normally restrict that development.

Special projects legislation has been used to vary the boundaries of wilderness areas to allow pipeline developments in NSW: Eastern Gas Pipeline (Special Provisions) Act 1996 (NSW) (s.6, Schedule 3). To this list must be added the Forestry and National Parks Estate Act 1998 (NSW), which was discussed above and which seeks to prevent further wilderness identifications or declarations in respect of state forest lands.

The Filming Approval Act seeks to facilitate commercial filming (via a specific approvals regime) in wilderness areas, contrary to prohibitions in wilderness and protected areas legislation. That act was the political reaction to the successful legal challenge by environmentalists to commercial filming in the Blue Mountains. It sought to reverse the broader implications of the decision of the Land and Environment Court in Blue Mountains Conservation Society Inc. v Director-General of National Parks and Wildlife & Ors (29 April 2004). The Filming Approval Act 2004 provides in section 6(1)(b) that filming approvals under that act authorize activities that would otherwise be prohibited by the Wilderness Act 1987 (or the National Parks and Wildlife Act 1974).

The Snowy Mountains Cloud Seeding Trial Act 2004 (NSW) has also recently been enacted. The act approves an artificial cloud seeding exercise over the Snowy Mountains, which fall within the Kosciuszko National Park in NSW, part of an interconnecting network of alpine national parks in three jurisdictions. The act excludes the operation of planning and environmental impact approvals legislation, and modifies the operation of national parks legislation, pollution control law, threatened species conservation law, fisheries law, and local government law.[50] Section 4 provides some limited protection for a declared wilderness area within that national park. It states that cloud-seeding agents are not to be discharged in land-based operations from within the Jagungal wilderness area.

Hunting and Fishing

Australian protected areas legislation generally prohibits hunting within national parks and other reserves, subject to limited exemptions for traditional indigenous hunting. Victorian legislation permits continued deer hunting in two wilderness zones within the Alpine National Park.[51]

Transport Access

Some wilderness protection legislation restricts transport access. The question of access is separate to that of access for resource utilization—for example for mining, pipelines, forestry, grazing, and so forth—which is covered by other provisions.

Four separate issues of transport access are identified in the legislation:

- Roads, tracks, and vehicles;
- Aircraft and motor boats;
- Animal transport;
- Access for recreation.

Much of the Australian legislation takes its lead from prohibitions provided by the United States Wilderness Act 1964, which, broadly speaking, ban roads and motorized access, though with a range of exceptions as noted in Chapter 3 above.

Roads, Tracks, and Vehicles

The full breadth of the questions raised in relation to this topic are subject to extensive review by Scott (1994) and are not repeated here.[52] Included below is a brief survey of the range of restrictions within Australian legislation.

South Australian legislation prohibits the use of "vehicles" within wilderness areas. However the prohibition does not apply to driving on tracks which have been designated as fit for vehicle use by the director of parks.[53]

The Victorian National Parks Act 1975 obliges the secretary to ensure that in a wilderness park, there is no use of "any form of motorized or mechanical transport."

The creation of vehicle tracks is prohibited in wilderness areas in Victoria is also prohibited. This prohibition does not apply to any road or use of motorized transport which the secretary considers to be "essential for the responsible management of the park."[54]

In Victoria, additional roads provisions apply in relation to "remote and natural areas" declared under the National Parks Act 1975. These include an obligation of the secretary to ensure that in a remote and natural area:

a. no new roads or tracks for vehicles are constructed; and
b. existing roads or tracks for vehicles are not widened or upgraded in any way so that they can carry increased traffic or heavier vehicles; and
c. no new structures are constructed; and
d. no new facilities are installed; and
e. no new works are carried out that will adversely affect the natural condition or appearance of the area.[55]

In NSW, management principles in the Wilderness Act do not provide clear guidance on acceptable uses. However, as most wilderness areas are contiguous with national parks, activities within wilderness areas are managed via management plans for national parks and by regulations under the National Parks and Wildlife Act. No operations may be undertaken on the specified area unless in accordance with the management plan.[56]

Further, the legislation provides the following statutory management principles for wilderness areas:

A wilderness area shall be managed so as:

    a. to restore (if applicable) and to protect the unmodified state of the area and its plant and animal communities;

    b. to preserve the capacity of the area to evolve in the absence of significant human interference; and

    c. to permit opportunities for solitude and appropriate self-reliant recreation. [57]

The NSW National Parks and Wildlife Regulation 2002 specifically prohibits a number of additional activities within national parks without permission. For example, Regulation 6 states that a person "must not drive a vehicle into a park otherwise than on a road leading into or traversing the park."[58] These protections apply to wilderness areas within national parks.

Additional restriction of access in NSW is achieved via wilderness protection agreements, which may contain terms binding on a statutory authority and possibly the Crown, but not the public, "prohibiting, except where necessary for health or safety or essential management reasons or in emergencies, access to the area by motor vehicles, motor boats or other forms of transport."[59]

Legislation in the Australian Capital Territory (of which approximately 70 percent is in nature reserves), creates offenses of establishing roads or tracks in a wilderness area. Further, it provides that it is an offense to use motor vehicles in wilderness zones, except on tracks that were in existence at the time of the declaration of the wilderness area, and that were "formed for the use of vehicles having four or more wheels."[60]

Western Australia's Control of Vehicles (Off-Road Areas) Act 1978 allows public and private lands to be gazetted either as prohibited or permitted areas for the use of off-road vehicles. Private lands may be gazetted as prohibited areas against the wishes of the owner if it is considered in the public interest because of:

    a. the need to provide for the protection of livestock or the preservation of any wildlife or flora;
    b. the environmentally sensitive nature of the land or things growing on the land;
    c. the proximity of any land used for residential purposes, or for purposes likely to be incompatible with the use of vehicles in the vicinity; or
    d. the provisions of any town planning scheme.[61]

Aircraft and Motor Boats

The Victorian National Parks Act 1975 obliges the secretary to ensure that in a wilderness park there is no use of "any form of motorized or mechanical transport."[62]

South Australian legislation is more specific, providing that the recreational use of aircraft over wilderness areas or zones is prohibited at altitudes below 1,500 meters (4,900 feet) above ground level.[63] This prohibition extends to landing of aircraft used for recreational purposes. Non-recreational uses of aircraft are not prohibited. Landing other forms of aircraft are permitted with the permission of the director.

With respect to boats, South Australian legislation appears to go furthest. The use of boats within wilderness areas or zones is prohibited in SA.[64] Boats are defined extremely broadly, as virtually any vessel—including boats, jet-skis, sailboards, rafts, pontoons or any other man-made objects capable of floating on water, including hovercrafts.[65]

Animal Transport

Access on horseback is another important issue in terms of wilderness protection and control of access. The Victorian National Parks Act 1975 obliges the secretary to ensure that in a wilderness park there is no use of any non-indigenous animal.[66] In WA it is prohibited to enter wilderness areas by means of an animal.[67]

In NSW, control of access issues to wilderness areas is achieved via general provisions in the National Parks and Wildlife Act 1974. Thus, where a wilderness area overlaps with a national park, the provisions of regulations made under the NPWA prohibiting the use of motor vehicles[68] (and other activities) in national parks can be used to control activities in wilderness areas. The Wilderness Act contains provisions that provide for the continued operation of the provisions of the National Parks and Wildlife Act 1974 (NPWA) in relation to land within a wilderness area.[69] By implication, this provision applies to regulations made under the NPWA.

Access for Recreation and Commercial Tourism

Certain wilderness legislation provides for a general ban on commercial activities within wilderness areas, but with an exemption for certain tourism activities. For example, the Victorian National Parks Act 1975 provides that "any commercial tours or activities not involving motorized or mechanical transport or the use of animals which the secretary considers appropriate for the appreciation and understanding of wilderness" may be permitted in a wilderness park.[70]

South Australian law enables the making of regulations which may restrict or entirely prohibit access to wilderness protection areas or zones or parts of them.[71]

Other Prohibited Activities
in Wilderness Areas

There are three approaches to regulating uses in Australia wilderness areas: a general approach, which sets out broad management principles for wilderness areas; a specific approach, enumerating those uses of wilderness that are not appropriate; and a default approach, which relies on the prohibitions of activities generally applied by protected areas legislation.

NSW legislation takes the general approach, setting out statutory objects and management principles, as well as providing for third-party rights to challenge administrative decisions (and actions taken in reliance upon them) that are inconsistent with the legislation.[72] It also relies upon protected-areas legislation to achieve specific prohibitions.[73]

NSW law also restricts pro-development clauses in planning legislation that would normally act to fast-track development approvals, where the land in question is a wilderness area. For example, neither the concept of exempt development nor complying development in NSW planning law can be applied to land that is part of a wilderness area.[74] Similarly, the exemptions from environmental laws found in plantation legislation in NSW do not apply to wilderness areas.[75]

The South Australian approach is far more prescriptive. The regulations provide for the prohibition on the following activities in wilderness areas:

- camping, except in designated areas;
- the lighting of fires;
- the use of chainsaws;
- the use of generators or alternators;
- the use of metal detectors;
- the possession and use of firearms (with exceptions for Aborigines);
- the possession and use of explosives or fireworks;
- swimming or diving, except in designated areas or with permission;
- entrance to a cave without permission of the director (or a number of other specified acts inside caves)
- rock climbing, rappelling without permission, except in designated areas;
- flying of model planes or gliders.[76]

Exceptions to this prohibition can be made by proclamation under South Australian legislation so that "rights of entry, prospecting, exploration, or mining may be acquired and exercised in respect of land constituting a wilderness protection zone" if a proclamation is made to that effect.[77]

Restriction on the Grant of Leases and
Licenses over Wilderness Areas
In New South Wales, the National Parks and Wildlife Act 1974 provides that leases, licenses, franchises, easements, and rights of way cannot be granted over areas of land that are declared as wilderness areas.[78] This helps to restrict private dealings with land and private commercial activities within wilderness areas. Similarly, nature conservation legislation in the Australian Capital Territory, which largely relies upon the operation of a leasehold system, provides explicitly that leases cannot be granted over areas of public land designated as wilderness areas.[79]

Education Provisions
under Wilderness Legislation
The NSW Wilderness Act includes as one of its objectives "to promote the education of the public in the appreciation, protection, and management of wilderness," and the director-general of NPWS is directed "to promote such educational activities as the director considers necessary in respect of wilderness or wilderness areas."[80]

Under the SA Act, the statutory Wilderness Advisory Committee is required to prepare, in consultation with the director, a draft management code of wilderness protection areas and wilderness protection zones for submission to the minister. The act specifies that the management code must set out policies to be implemented in relation to the management of wilderness areas including "education of the public as to the significance of wilderness protection areas and zones." [81]

Under the Victorian Act, the goals of the National Parks Act include to make provision for the use of parks by the public for the purposes of enjoyment, recreation, or education and for the encouragement and control of that use.[82]

The act also contains broad provisions stating that national parks are to be managed in order to "preserve and protect the park in its natural condition for the use, enjoyment, and education of the public." [83]

Queensland has similar general provisions relating to education of the public within its Nature Conservation Act 1992, which provides that the object of the act is to be achieved as follows:

> The conservation of nature is to be achieved by an integrated and comprehensive conservation strategy for the whole of Queensland that involves, among other things, the following:
>
> (a) Gathering of information and community education etc.
> - gathering, researching, analyzing, monitoring and disseminating information on nature;
> - identifying critical habitats and areas of major interest;
> - encouraging the conservation of nature by the education and cooperative involvement of the community, particularly land-holders ... [84]

Conclusion

Although there are many approaches to wilderness legislation in Australia, it is possible to identify a number of essential ingredients for Australian wilderness legislation. One review of wilderness protection provisions of Australian State and Territory legislation[85] generated the following list of key elements:

- Adequate provision for systematic identification of wilderness areas;
- Detailed frameworks for management of wilderness areas;
- Provision for consultation with indigenous communities; and
- Provision for public participation in identification, assessment and management of wilderness areas.[86]

A number of additional features of comprehensive wilderness legislation were identified by Whitehouse (1994):[87]

- A definition of wilderness that emphasizes ecological protection rather than recreational qualities.
- A process for expert identification of wilderness areas.
- A process for expert evaluation of proposed wilderness areas.
- Identification of wilderness not limited to the public conservation estate but considering freehold and leasehold land.
- Inconsistent uses and development restricted during the assessment process.
- Inconsistent uses and development restricted upon designation as wilderness.
- Management of wilderness by an expert public agency with statutory backing.
- Wilderness management principles are specified in legislation. These principles constrain the use and management of wilderness areas.
- Statutory constraints to the removal or revocation of wilderness designation.
- Controls over edge effects and boundary developments.
- Legislative provision for adequate funding of the wilderness assessment and management process, with adequate funding for acquisition of wilderness areas on private and leasehold land.
- Provision for civil enforcement of wilderness legislation by government land management agency and by third parties.
- Regular public reporting on administration of legislation.

The need for systematic processes for identifying wilderness areas, clear guidelines for wilderness management, and public participation, which has been a key factor in developing wilderness legislation and enforcing wilderness provisions, are all worth emphasizing. Indeed, a crucial aspect of wilderness protection legislation in NSW and South Australia are provisions for community participation:

providing for public participation in wilderness identification and management-planning processes, as well as third-party enforcement provisions enabling any person to bring a civil action to enforce its provisions.[88]

The issue of wilderness law and policy remains particularly important in Northern Australia, Western Australia, the Northern Territory, and Queensland, all of which have large areas of wilderness, but where wilderness legislation is neither as sophisticated, nor as keenly utilized as in the southern states. For example, in Queensland there have been no formal wilderness designations under the Nature Conservation Act 1992. Instead, wilderness has only been protected within national parks and through the management-planning process. In the Northern Territory, there are no formally protected wilderness areas, with the exception of a wilderness zone within Australia's largest national park, the federally managed Kakadu National Park. In that park, wilderness zonings are under threat, as the draft plan of management released in February 2006 proposed to delete the existing wilderness zone (along with all other land-use zonings in the park).

Broadly speaking, the future of wilderness conservation in Australia must be seen in the context of three key issues concerning the protected areas system: first, the role of wilderness within protected-areas policy; second, difficulties with the implementation of wilderness and protected-areas legislation; and third, the involvement of indigenous Australians in the management of wilderness and other protected areas.

The first issue concerns the future of the protected-areas system, particularly the contribution of parks to biodiversity conservation objectives. It has become increasingly recognized by scientists that an "across the landscape" approach, which goes beyond a protected-areas strategy, is essential for biodiversity conservation. This point has been recognized by the Wilderness Society (Australia) in its Wild Country project, which is seeking to assemble a mosaic of protected and quasi-protected areas to better meet ecosystem conservation objectives. The network of areas envisaged will include indigenous protected areas as well as zones on privately held land, to complement the operation of traditional protected areas.[89] The Wilderness Society-Australia stated in a submission to the 2006 Senate Inquiry into Australia's national parks that "the Protected Area estate will fail to meet even its most basic biodiversity conservation objectives if it is treated as islands in an ocean of unsustainable land and sea management."[90]

The second key issue arising in the Australian experience with wilderness legislation involves implementation—in particular, lack of resources for wilderness management and delays in declaration of wilderness areas—to such an extent that these issues are of equal if not greater importance than questions of the adequacy of legislation. To a significant degree, the implementation of environmental laws cannot be isolated from questions of politics and political will.[91] It remains difficult to minimize political and ministerial discretion by means of legislative drafting techniques.

Mount Owen, Budawang Wilderness, Morton National Park,
New South Wales, Australia. Photo by John Reid, School of Art,
© Australian National University.

The third ongoing issue in the future of wilderness conservation and legislation in Australia concerns the participation of indigenous peoples in protected-areas management. Legislation in many jurisdictions (e.g., Qld, NSW, NT, Cth) provides for the comanagement of protected areas with indigenous people.[92] For example, in NSW, nine protected areas are comanaged by the National Parks Service with indigenous people. The federal government operates an indigenous protected areas program under which thirteen indigenous protected areas have been declared over Aboriginal land following the signing of a voluntary agreement by traditional owners, covering more than 3.1 million hectares, and significantly expanding the National Reserve System.[93] The federal government has recognized a principle of joint management of its protected areas in Regulations. Its regulatory reserve management principles provide:

> If the reserve or zone is wholly or partly owned by Aboriginal
> people, continuing traditional use of the reserve or zone by
> resident indigenous people, including the protection and
> maintenance of cultural heritage, should be recognised.[94]

In this context, the wilderness concept has been criticized as inappropriate in Australia because of its Eurocentric origins and assumptions and on the grounds that it suggests a misguided hands-off approach to environmental management of protected areas.[95] This critique has been met head-on by wilderness advocates in recent years. For example, the Wilderness Society in its Wild Country program has proposed that:

> Australia's first people, and their own vision for their future,
> will also be a core part of the Wild Country vision and out-
> comes, including returning country to traditional owners, and
> using indigenous knowledge and skills in nature management.

However, a history of conservative politicians making cynical use of national park proclamations in order to defeat Aboriginal land-rights claims in states such as Queensland, combined with the history of dispossession of Australia's indigenous peoples, have left a legacy of mistrust and suspicion around the creation of protected areas.[96] For these historical and other reasons, indigenous people have sometimes shown limited amount of interest in wilderness designations.

Nonetheless, alliances between conservationists and Australia's indigenous peoples have played an important role in recent campaigns against destructive development proposals throughout Northern Australia in the past decade. A combined Aboriginal and environmentalist campaign between 1996 and 2001 did much to lead to the closure of the Jabiluka uranium mine within the Kakadu World Heritage area in March 2001. More recently, a coalition between NT environmentalists and indigenous communities has campaigned against the grant of approval for the expansion of the McArthur River lead-zinc mine.[97]

Both the Wilderness Society and other prominent wilderness advocates have acknowledged that, particularly in relation to areas of Northern Australia, there is a need for active land management within protected areas. According to Keith Muir, "you cannot separate people from wilderness because wilderness needs management."[98] The Wilderness Society in its submission to the Senate Inquiry into Australia's Protected Areas (2006) stated:

> There is mounting evidence, particularly in Northern Australia, that changes to traditional land management practices across all land tenures is linked to extensive biodiversity declines in otherwise 'intact' ecosystems. Halting these declines may require a significant investment in supporting indigenous Australians to maintain or restore traditional practices and/or to help deal with new problems such as invasive species and inappropriate use of traditional homelands over the past two hundred years. Across Northern Australia, real partnerships between indigenous communities and businesses and non-indigenous communities and businesses need to be encouraged and supported by all levels of Government to help achieve improved environmental outcomes.

For these and other reasons, the Wilderness Society and other conservation organizations such as the ACF have sought to actively involve indigenous people in their campaigns, such as the Starcke campaign on Cape York, the Cape York Heads of Agreement, and the campaign for protection of Shoalwater Bay. Nevertheless, some areas of contention occasionally arise, including questions of hunting within wilderness areas, permanent settlements, and the off-road use of four-wheel-drive vehicles within wilderness areas.

As argued at the outset of this chapter, there is a strong scientific foundation for the view that the protection of wilderness can make substantial contributions to biodiversity conservation. The challenge will be to ensure the protection of areas that have not yet been subjected to significant disturbance by industrialized society through the process of devising and revising management plans for protected areas, and by involving traditional owners and indigenous communities in the management process.

Tallek Arm of Nachvak Fiord, Torngat Mountains National Park Reserve, Labrador, Canada. Photo by Ian MacNeil, Parks Canada.

CHAPTER 4

Canada

Kevin McNamee[1]

Introduction

For more than a century, starting with the creation of Banff National Park in 1885, Canada has taken actions to protect its wilderness areas. Over time, these efforts were adjusted to changing circumstances and priorities. However, in the end, they were always about conserving land and wildlife in some form of protected area status. This chapter outlines the evolution of efforts to protect wilderness in Canada, with a focus on specific pieces of wilderness legislation, as well as the use of national parks to protect wilderness areas. While other forms of protected areas contribute significantly to protecting wilderness in Canada, such as British Columbia's Class A provincial parks, such protected areas without an explicit wilderness mandate are not addressed in this chapter.

The first national and provincial parks established by Canadian governments were not about protecting wilderness values per se. Objectives ranged from protecting spectacular mountain scenery; promoting tourism; conserving wildlife and wildlife habitat, forests, and watersheds for their utilitarian and recreational value; promoting regional economic development through nature-based tourism; and the construction of facilities such as in national parks. These objectives only started to embrace wilderness as an explicit goal in the 1970s.

However, even though many of Canada's protected areas do not have an explicit goal of conserving wilderness values, they make an important contribution to preserving natural areas in a wilderness state.

This century of action has been characterized by a range of legislative and policy initiatives, campaigns to protect to specific wilderness areas, an ongoing debate over the types of uses that should be prohibited, and most important, an increase in the number of natural areas protected from industrial development. However, no single approach has emerged as *the* model, given that the conservation of natural areas is the responsibility of fourteen separate governments— the federal, provincial, and territorial governments—and is also influenced by agreements with Aboriginal people.

This chapter suggests that there are four basic themes when reviewing wilderness conservation activities in Canada. These themes may not necessarily apply to other countries, but they do provide some sense of how the wilderness concept has evolved and been applied in Canada, and more to the point, how it will succeed in the future. The basic themes are:

- Fashion a basic definition of the wilderness concept that prohibits industrial development, and develop mechanisms that ensure that actions are taken to develop, review, and designate wilderness areas, be they land-use planning, conservation initiatives, or specific protected area initiatives.

- Ensure that the wilderness concept adopted provides for the rights and aspirations of Aboriginal people, and, where necessary, traditional harvesting activities by non-aboriginal people that are not harmful to natural ecosystems.

- Use scientific concepts including representation and ecological integrity to drive the design of protected-area systems and the location of specific sites. These concepts are a means to engage stakeholders who are unsympathetic to the philosophical underpinnings of the wilderness concept. To a certain extent, they focus discussion away from the never ending wilderness versus development debate.

- In Canada, the concept of ecological integrity has become central to the management of protected areas, more so than wilderness. It is therefore important that institutions developing wilderness policies make explicit efforts to link the wilderness concept to such scientific concepts.

Above all, it is important to ensure that there is ongoing public and political support for designating and maintaining wilderness areas.

A Wilderness Called Canada

Casting his eye north to Canada in 1966, Aldo Leopold noted in his classic book *A Sand Country Almanac* that in Canada "there are still large expanses of virgin country" and wondered "to what extent Canada … will be able to see and grasp their opportunity is anybody's guess."[2] Forty years later, it is possible to state that Canadian governments, responding to public support for the protection of wilderness areas, have grasped opportunities to protect wilderness areas. Almost 10 percent of the nation is set aside in some form of protected-area status.

Almost 1 billion hectares (2.5 billion hectares) in size, Canada is the second largest country in the world. But it only ranks thirty-seventh in terms of population. These two factors, plus the fact that more than 90 percent of Canada's population is located within 160 kilometers (62 miles) of its southern border, suggests that there is a tremendous amount of wild, open country and wildlife. According to a 1992 survey, outside of Antarctica, Canada has 20 percent of the planet's remaining wilderness. Thus, Canada bears an enormous responsibility and opportunity for action in conserving a large percentage of the planet's remaining wilderness for future generations.

The superlatives don't stop at the amount of wilderness found in Canada, or the fact that it possesses large intact boreal, arctic, temperate, and marine ecosystems, or that it has the world's longest coastline. Canada has within its borders:

- 20 percent of the world's fresh water;
- 25 percent of the world's temperate rainforest;
- 30 percent of the world's boreal forest;
- half of the world's population of barren ground caribou; and
- one-third of the world's wolf population.

However, Canada is also a country that perpetuates the myth that its footprint is confined to a thin populated strip along the United States border. In 1992, it was estimated that over 65 percent of the country has been developed or is allocated to development, including logging, mining, agriculture, oil and gas extraction, and urbanization, and that one square kilometer of wilderness was lost to development every hour. For example, more than 400,000 hectares (1 million acres) of boreal forest are logged in Canada every year.[3]

Perhaps in response to earlier indicators that Canada was starting to lose its wild lands, according to Dr. Robert Page, by 1970 wilderness had become more than a biological concept to Canadians: "it had become part of their cultural and intellectual identity. In the literature of the early 1970s … a cult of the wilderness began. It was a literature of protest against the development ethic implicit in the evolution of Canada."[4] Even the sitting prime minister at the time, the Right Honorable Pierre Elliot Trudeau, observed: "If part of our heritage is our wilderness, and if the measure of Canada is the quality of life available to Canadians, then we must act should there be any threat to either."[5]

Efforts to protect the Canadian wilderness have been marked by several milestones. In the early 1970s, proposals by the Ontario government to possibly permit logging in some of the province's iconic provincial parks—Quetico and Algonquin—sparked a strong public movement to protect these areas. Similarly, an international campaign to stop the logging of the old growth temperate rainforest of the South Moresby archipelago in British Columbia's Queen Charlotte Islands not only brought national attention to the plight of Canada's wilderness lands, it also sparked the launch of a ten-year campaign spearheaded by World Wildlife Fund Canada to encourage governments to complete their respective protected-area networks.

While the bottom line is that there are no laws that require governments to continually create new national parks and protected-areas, nor to increase the amount of protected wilderness, action has been taken by politicians, civil servants, Aboriginal people, and conservation groups. While estimates vary, as of April 2003, approximately 8 percent of Canada is legally protected from development, most of it in a wilderness state.[6] Collectively, the efforts that led to this level of wilderness protection speak to the need for broad public support and political leadership to designate new areas.

Canadian Realities
and the U.S. Wilderness Act of 1964

One cannot examine wilderness concepts and processes to protect wilderness areas without making reference to the U.S. Wilderness Act of 1964. While Canada has not passed its own federal wilderness legislation, the constant shadow of the American legislation has inspired similar actions. There have been some attempts to duplicate the American act, but no national wilderness vision or program has ever been adopted by government agencies; work has focused more on the protection of wilderness areas in national parks and protected areas. But that's not to say there have not been attempts to duplicate the American experience.

On March 27, 1990, federal member of Parliament Mr. Bob Wenman tabled a private member's bill (C-292) in the House of Commons entitled the Wilderness Protection Act.[7] Using much the same wording as the U.S. Wilderness Act in its purpose and definition statement, Mr. Wenman proposed amending the existing National Parks Act to set out criteria and provide a mechanism for the establishment of wilderness areas. As with most private members' bills that are tabled by individual members of Parliament and are not supported by the political party in power, it died on the order paper.

In 1991, buoyed by Mr. Wenman's attempt, the Canadian Environmental Advisory Council recommended in its report *A Protected Areas Vision for Canada* that the "federal Parliament should pass a Canada Wilderness Act to promote the heritage values of wilderness to Canadians, to require the protection of wilderness in federal land-management policies and programs, and to promote cooperative action across Canada to protect and properly manage nationally significant wilderness landscapes."[8] No action was taken on the council's suggestion.

Perhaps one reason Mr. Wenman's bill did not garner much debate or support was that it did not acknowledge the constitutional rights of Aboriginal people in the use of natural resources. Indeed, today this is a key factor in the designation of wilderness areas in Canada, particularly in the case of proposed national parks. But not until the last few decades have protected area legislative and management frameworks evolved to encompass the views and aspirations of Aboriginal people. For example, the evolution of the national park concept in Canada has moved from one in which Aboriginal people were removed from areas designated as national parks, to being central to the management of these areas.

In discussing Aboriginal interests in the creation and management of national parks and protected areas, Morrison points out:

> North American parks and protected areas have generally
> been created in the name of the "public interest." Most
> conservationists fully support this concept, insisting that it is
> a governmental responsibility to protect significant regions of
> the country for the benefit of future generations. Aboriginal
> people, however, dispute the inclusiveness of the term
> "public." In their view it automatically places the interests of
> the general society above those of minorities.
>
> It is fair to say, therefore, that indigenous people have
> borne the costs of protecting natural areas, through the loss of

access for hunting, trapping and other harvesting activities. As
[former Grand Chief of the Assembly of First Nations
George] Erasmus puts it, the doctrine of public interest made
"an ancient way of life subject to the apparent modern-day
whims of an alien culture, all in the name of conservation.[9]

Over the last few decades, the national park concept has
evolved most in the area of dealing with Aboriginal peoples in a
number of ways:

- While the protection of wilderness areas is still a primary out-
  come in the national park establishment process, the focus
  and the terms used in consultations with Aboriginal people
  focus more on protecting representative areas, maintaining
  the ecological integrity or health of the landscape, conserving
  wildlife populations and habitats, and protecting watersheds.
  These terms provide a more common basis for discussion.
  And, if achieved, the protection of these elements invariably
  leads to wilderness protection.
- The management of national parks is done on a much more
  cooperative basis with Aboriginal people. Land claim agreements, particularly in northern Canada, set out the terms and
  conditions of relationships between Parks Canada and
  Aboriginal people. This relationship is maintained through
  the establishment of cooperative management boards, and in
  the case of the Inuit, negotiation of formal impact and benefit agreements.
- Land claim agreements, which take precedence over the
  Canada National Parks Act, ensure that Aboriginal people can
  continue traditional ways of life within national parks,
  including legally designated wilderness areas. These agreements increasingly include a chapter specifically on the
  establishment and management of national parks, detailing
  the principles and processes that will guide establishment and
  management. For example, the 1993 Nunavut Land Claim

Agreement states that national parks in Nunavut, subject to the terms of an impact and benefit agreement, shall contain a "predominant proportion" of special preservation and wilderness zones.

The success of the federal government in the last few decades in working with Aboriginal people is seen in the fact that over half the land designated as national park land has been protected as the result of arrangements negotiated with Aboriginal people. In addition, in eighteen of Canada's forty-two national parks, Aboriginal people continue their traditional practices and ways of life.

One site that exemplifies this situation is the proposed national park for the East Arm of Great Slave Lake in the Northwest Territories. In 1970, the federal government withdrew 770,000 hectares (1.9 million acres) of wilderness from development for national park purposes. That same year, officials from Parks Canada explained to a local Aboriginal community that while the park would bring economic benefits to them, they could not exercise their traditional use of the land;

Nakvak Brook, Torngat Mountains National Park Reserve.
Photo by Ian MacNeil, Parks Canada.

hunting and trapping would be prohibited. Local people refused to support the park proposal, and so it sat for over three decades.

However, thirty-six years later, as national parks legislation and policy evolved to respect these activities, that same community signed and celebrated in October 2006 an agreement with the federal minister in charge of national parks that has launched a joint feasibility study to determine the feasibility of establishing a national park within a 3.3 million-hectare (7.4 million-acre) study area.

Thus, in Canada, it is imperative that government officials and conservation groups advocating the protection of specific wilderness areas in national parks and other forms of protected areas have a clear understanding of the specific agreements that govern the relationship between governments and Aboriginal people in those places.

A National Campaign to Protect the Canadian Wilderness

Perhaps among the single most important events in the Canadian history of wilderness protection was the ten-year Endangered Spaces Campaign. Launched by World Wildlife Fund Canada in 1989, this campaign was a sustained, well-funded, and focused national campaign to get governments to complete their representative-protected area networks by 2000. A large range of national and regional conservation groups participated in the campaign. The campaign was a success in that it pressed governments to establish one thousand new protected areas, increasing the amount of protected wilderness and natural areas from 2.95 percent in 1989 to 6.84 percent in 2000. In addition, the number of natural regions represented by protected areas was doubled from 66 to 132; in total, jurisdictions have divided Canada into 486 natural regions.[10]

The campaign was a success in part because it adopted a set of very simple criteria. To contribute to the goal of protecting Canadian wilderness, a protected area had to be legally protected, and could not allow logging, mining, oil and gas extraction, or hydroelectric

development. The focus was clearly on prohibiting industrial activities, which ensured that the campaign did not become embroiled over
such divisive issues as sport hunting, recreation, and the extraction of
renewable resources.

How the Endangered Spaces Campaign resulted in the doubling
of protected wilderness and natural areas over a ten-year period is a
subject that should be further researched. However, given that the
author participated in the campaign from start to finish, it is possible
to identify several key elements in the campaign:

- Strong public support was secured for the campaign goal with
  over 600,000 Canadians signing the Canadian Wilderness
  Charter, a document produced very much in the style of the
  Canadian Charter of Rights that called for action to protect the
  nation's wilderness. This support was tracked during the campaign by a series of public opinion polls. Editorial support
  from major national and regional newspapers was secured, as
  well as significant funding from corporate and foundation.

- The campaign worked to secure political commitments to
  complete their protected-area networks by the year 2000
  from government leaders and as many political parties as
  possible. Each year, a national report card grading each jurisdiction on its annual progress was released across Canada. In
  1992, the federal, provincial, and territorial ministers in
  charge of environment, parks, and wildlife released their own
  statement of commitment, pledging to complete their protected area networks by the year 2000.

- During the life of the campaign, a range of likely and unlikely
  alliances was developed. For example, as part of an accord
  that was signed by the mining industry, governments,
  Aboriginal organizations, environmental groups, and labor,
  all five groups agreed that governments should complete
  their protected-area networks, in part, to provide the mining
  industry with a high degree of certainty as to which lands are
  open and which are closed to development.

- Rather then simply focus on the concept of wilderness, which is subjected to so many different and sometimes conflicting definitions, the Endangered Spaces campaign focused on science, and on encouraging governments to complete their own system plans. The campaign was science-based, but it also worked hard to appeal to the emotional value of protecting natural areas and wilderness.

In the end, one can observe that it took Canada a century to protect almost three percent of its landscapes from industrial development. Then, in ten short years, it more then doubled its amount of protected wilderness with a focused, science-based national campaign backed by strong public support and linked to the priorities of Aboriginal people to protect their traditional territory, industry to gain some certainty over land use, and Canadians generally to ensure the protection of life-sustaining natural ecosystems.

Evolution of the Wilderness Concept in Canada

Jurisdiction over the designation and management of protected wilderness areas rests with a number of Canadian governments. Of prime importance is the role of the ten Canadian provinces, who have jurisdiction over 60 percent of the country, including the most biologically diverse and productive regions. Various provincial governments have adopted different means to protect wilderness. In the following sections, a select number of jurisdictions and their approaches are reviewed.

Province of Ontario

Ontario was the first jurisdiction in Canada to pass legislation that gave government explicit powers to protect wilderness areas. In 1959, the Ontario legislature passed the Wilderness Areas Act, five years before the U.S. Wilderness Act was signed into law by President

Lyndon Johnson. The Ontario Act stated that the provincial cabinet could "set apart any public lands as a wilderness area for the preservation of the area as nearly as may be in its natural state in which research and educational activities may be carried on, for the protection of the flora and fauna, for the improvement of the area, having regard to its historical, aesthetic, scientific or recreational value, or for such other purposes as may be prescribed."[11]

The act came into being for several reasons. First, organizations such as the Federation of Ontario Naturalists had long advocated government action to set aside nature reserves as sanctuaries for representative and unique features, for endangered plants and animals, and as research areas. While the language used in the act clearly suggests nature reserves, the government called them wilderness areas. Second, government drafters of this bill were also aware of the efforts being made in the United States to develop federal wilderness legislation, and may have adopted the term.

However, despite the promise of the wording, the Ontario government responded to the concerns of the mining industry by limiting the protective powers of the Wilderness Areas Act. The act stated that a wilderness area could be no larger then 259 hectares (640 acres). Initially, conservation groups did not criticize the government for this decision, in part, because it was a positive response to their campaign to establish nature reserves, and because it did prompt some action. But the act never became a powerful conservation tool and was seldom used.

By 1961, thirty-five separate areas had been designated wilderness areas, with all but one of these areas being small in size and within the 259-hectare (640-acre) limit. There was one exception: one of the designated wilderness areas was 580,000 hectares (1,432,600 acres) and protected important habitat for polar bears, snow geese, tundra wolves, and caribou. The area would be later enlarged and designated as Polar Bear Provincial Park, now 1.8 million hectares (4.4 million acres). Years later, however, many of these areas would become larger provincial parks.[12]

In 1964, the government designated another wilderness area that, due to its lack of mineral and timber potential, exceeded the 259-hectare (640 acre) limit. Located on the north shore of Lake Superior, this area would eventually be transferred to the federal government to be established and managed as Pukawska National Park of Canada. So, while often ignored or criticized for its very limited application, the Wilderness Areas Act was an important conservation tool that resulted in the protection of a number of significant wilderness areas.

Over the years, however, Ontario has relied more on a policy approach to the protection of wilderness areas. Starting in 1978, the Ontario government recognized wilderness parks as one of six official categories of provincial parks. A *wilderness park* was defined as an area "where the forces of nature are permitted to function freely and where visitors travel by non-mechanized means and experience expansive solitude, challenge and personal integration with nature."[13] Other pieces of provincial legislation were used to ensure that the areas were, in fact, placed off limits to logging and mining.

This policy approach had its drawbacks. The lack of rigid guidelines allowed governments to change their perspective on what type of activities should be prohibited in wilderness. In 1983, the provincial Conservative government established 155 new provincial parks, including 6 new wilderness parks. But in its decision, it allowed logging, mining, hunting, and trapping in many of these new parks, undermining its own parks policy that prohibited such activities. Eight years later, a new Liberal government changed this policy, eliminating these nonconforming uses. This episode underscored the fact that, lacking a legal framework and a legislative requirement to consult the public on policy changes, governments can unilaterally permit activities that can harm wilderness values.

It was not until June 2006 that the Ontario legislature passed legislation to ensure permanent legal protection of the province's provincial parks, including those designated as wilderness areas. In passing its Provincial Parks and Conservation Reserves Act, the Ontario legislature repealed the Wilderness Areas Act and legally enshrined wilderness parks as an official category in the province's protected areas system. However, the definition used is essentially the one used in the province's 1978 policy document, with a strong focus on the recreational and spiritual value of wilderness areas. The legislation states:

> The objective of wilderness class parks is to protect large areas
> where the forces of nature can exist freely and visitors travel
> by non-mechanized means, except as may be permitted by
> regulation, while engaging in low-impact recreation to
> experience solitude, challenge and integration with nature.[14]

But the legislation also makes it clear that wilderness parks are to be managed "to maintain their ecological integrity and to leave them unimpaired for future generations."

The process to establish wilderness parks is guided by Ontario's provincial park planning and management policies, which call for a wilderness park to be established in each of Ontario's thirteen site regions for the purpose of representing the biophysical diversity of each region. However, the policy also notes that, given the extent of development in the province's two most southernmost regions, wilderness parks cannot be established in these regions given that wilderness parks cannot be smaller than 50,000 hectares (123,500 acres).

The establishment of new wilderness parks has been guided by provincial land-use planning processes—one that was launched in the early 1980s, culminating in the designation of the six wilderness parks, and a second process that culminated in 2000 in the designation of a large number of new protected areas.

Province of Newfoundland and Labrador

The passage of legislation protecting wilderness areas in Ontario is no surprise. But the actions of the tiny province of Newfoundland and Labrador on the eastern shores of Canada to adopt wilderness legislation were unexpected. May describes 1980 as "a watershed in the province's conservation history" because one of the things the provincial House of Assembly passed was the Wilderness and Ecological

Reserves Act.[15] Provincial civil servants, concerned over the growing loss of wilderness habitat, secured the support of government officials and politicians to develop and present to the House legislation to protect wilderness area, which was easily passed.

The 1980 act states that:

- Cabinet may set aside, as wilderness reserves, areas that are subject to no or little human activity to:
  - protect wilderness areas in which people may hunt, fish, travel and experience and appreciate a natural environment;
  - allow within those areas undisturbed interactions of living things and their environment;
  - preserve those large areas that may be necessary for the continued survival of a particular species; and
  - protect those areas with primitive or extraordinary characteristics.[16]

The Newfoundland legislation is distinctive in that it clearly permits Newfoundlanders and Labradoreans to continue to hunt, trap, and fish in wilderness areas, as long as these activities do not threaten viability of populations or habitat. This is important in a

The carnivorous pitcher plant, Hudson Bay/James Bay lowlands, Canada. Photo by Evan Ferrari.

province that continues a strong tradition of local people using the land and maintaining a traditional way of life.

An important element of the Newfoundland wilderness legislation is the detailed attention paid to outlining the process to bring about the protection of wilderness areas. Three important elements of the legislation are: (1) the establishment of the independent Wilderness and Ecological Reserves Advisory Council to advise the minister responsible for wilderness areas; (2) the establishment of provisional reserves over candidate sites to ensure that the natural values of an area under consideration are not lost during the review process; and (3) the provision that any boundary changes must be subjected to public hearings. May outlines the basic steps:

- The Advisory Council hears proposals, including those advanced by public organizations; conducts interdepartmental reviews; resolves conflicts where necessary; and reports to Cabinet if a proposal has merit.
- If Cabinet agrees, an interim reserve is established and the council drafts a preliminary management plan that is subject to public hearings.
- The council then makes a second report to Cabinet, and the provincial cabinet that makes a final decision on whether to proceed.
- Once established, a range of activities are prohibited including logging, mining, agricultural development, hydroelectric development, and road and facility construction.[17]

Despite having been in place for almost three decades, the Government of Newfoundland and Labrador has only established two wilderness reserves totaling almost 400,000 hectares (988,400 acres)—the Bay du Nord Wilderness Reserve (289,500 hectares/ 715,000 acres) protects one of the last major natural areas on the island of Newfoundland, and the Avalon Wilderness Reserve (107,000 hectares/264,000 acres) conserves the habitat for the most southerly caribou herd in Canada. In 2006, the provincial government also announced that it would consider protecting a third wilderness area in the Lac Joseph-Atikonak area of southwestern Labrador.

Overall, the province's wilderness legislation is a promising model that, aside from its lack of "triggers," is worth consideration by other jurisdictions.

Government of Nova Scotia

The Government of Nova Scotia passed its Wilderness Areas Protection Act in 1998 at a time when the rationale for protecting natural areas was much more rooted in the global effort to protect biological diversity. The legislation was also passed at the end of a decade-long government effort to identify and consult on a list of thirty-one candidate-protected areas. The act formalized the rationale as well as protection of almost 5 percent of the province's total land base, a very important conservation achievement.

Under its Wilderness Areas Protection Act, the Government of Nova Scotia stated that it can:

Establish, manage, protect and use wilderness areas, in perpetuity, for present and future generations, to:

- maintain and restore the integrity of natural process and biodiversity;
- protect representative examples of natural landscapes and ecosystems;
- protect outstanding, unique, rare and vulnerable natural features;
- provide reference points for determining the effects of human activity on the natural environment; and
- protect and provide opportunities for scientific research, environmental education and wilderness recreation.[18]

This legislation provides a more expansive rationale for the protection of wilderness areas than the examples of Ontario or

Newfoundland and Labrador, giving prominence to the conservation of biodiversity and providing benchmarks to study the impacts of human activity on the natural world, while maintaining a focus on providing opportunities for research, education, and recreation. This is due to the fact that it was advanced at a time that protection of bio-diversity was in the ascendancy in public policy debates. Unlike Ontario or Newfoundland and Labrador, which passed their wilder-ness legislation and then identified and protected areas, Nova Scotia used the legislation to formalize the protection of thirty-one wilder-ness areas, totaling 285,000 hectares (704,000 acres). Most significantly, this meant that almost 20 percent of the province's Crown land was set aside from logging and road development, hydro-electric development, transmission or pipe lines, and mining except for preexisting commitments.

While the act does not compel the government to establish new wilderness areas, it does call on the responsible minister to establish policies and programs as necessary to guide, among other things, the establishment of wilderness areas. To date, there are no initiatives sim-ilar to the landmark program of the 1990s. The legislation also calls on the minister to promote the voluntary establishment of privately owned lands as new wilderness areas or as additions to designated wilderness areas. This is an important undertaking in a province where the land base is 70 percent privately owned.

National Parks of Canada

A major conservation tool in the protection of Canadian wilderness areas is the national park system established by the Government of Canada under the Canada National Parks Act. Over 31 percent of the land designated as protected in Canada is managed by the Parks Canada Agency as national parks. This section focuses on the evolu-tion of the national parks as a tool to protect wilderness areas.

To date, there are forty-two national parks and reserves. They protect more than 27 million hectares (roughly 68 million acres) or almost 3 percent of the Canadian landscape from industrial development and sport hunting. The national parks differ in size, with the largest being Wood Buffalo National Park at 4,479,200 hectares (roughly 11 million acres—larger then the country of Switzerland) and the smallest being Point Pelee National Park at 1,500 hectares (3,700 acres). Together, they represent the physical and biological features of twenty-eight of the thirty-nine natural regions that make up the national parks system. There are plans to add seven more national parks over the next several years, which could add an additional 9 million hectares (22 million acres) of protected wilderness to Canada's national park system.

Canada is the third country in the world, after the United States and Australia, to establish a national park, starting with Banff National Park in the Canadian Rocky Mountains in 1885. Over the decades, the key concepts behind the establishment and management of national parks have changed as governments have amended the legislation and policy governing national parks. To date, the key principles behind the management of national parks are as follows:

- National parks are designed to be representative of their natural regions, of which there are thirty-nine defined by Parks Canada that make up the national park system;
- national parks are dedicated to the people of Canada for their benefit, education, and enjoyment;
- national parks are to be maintained and made use of so as to leave them unimpaired for the enjoyment of future generations;
- the first priority in the management of the parks is maintenance or restoration of ecological integrity through the protection of natural resources and processes;
- when a park management plan identifies an area for declaration as a wilderness, the minister shall recommend to Cabinet its designation within one year;
- legislation prohibits logging, mining, oil and gas extraction, and hydroelectric development; and

• legislation is required to either reduce or eliminate a
national park.

Together, these principles and processes go a long way to
ensuring that Canada's national parks contribute to the protection of
wilderness areas.

Canadian National Parks and the Wilderness Concept

Passage of the U.S. Wilderness Act in 1964 has helped to shape the
establishment and management of Canada's national parks, and
helped to set in motion actions that have resulted in the legal designation and protection of specified wilderness areas within those
parks. While the Canadian Parliament and Parks Canada did not
specifically adopt the definition of the American legislation, they were
reminded of its existence by Justice Thomas Berger, when he delivered
his landmark report on his inquiry into a proposed pipeline along the
Mackenzie Valley in the Northwest Territories in 1977.

In his report, Justice Berger recommended a ten-year morato-
rium on the development of such a pipeline, calling for a range of
actions including the designation of a wilderness park and the settlement of native land claims. Justice Berger explicitly identified the
protection of northern wilderness as a priority action in advance of
development, citing passage of the U.S. Wilderness Act as the culmination of the idea of preserving wilderness. Berger observed: "We have
not yet in Canada developed a legislative framework for the protection of wilderness, but a model exists in the United States."[19] To
Berger, that model was the U.S. Wilderness Act. He suggested that
"wilderness constitutes an important—perhaps an invaluable—part
of modern-day life; its preservation is a contribution to, not a repudi-
ation of, the civilization upon which we depend."[20]

Berger rejected the idea of building a gas pipeline across the
northern Yukon, instead recommending that the calving grounds of
the Porcupine caribou herd be protected under the national park
system as a wilderness park. But he also introduced what was then a

new idea—that Native people should continue to practice their traditional ways of life within this new wilderness park.

> The park that I propose for the Northern Yukon should be
> set up under the National Parks system, but it would be a
> new kind of park—a wilderness park. It would afford
> absolute protection to wilderness and the environment by
> excluding all industrial activity within it. Of course there
> would have to be guarantees permitting the native people to
> continue to live and to carry on their traditional activities
> within the park without interference.[21]

Berger's recommendations indirectly led to actions by the Canadian federal government to create five new national parks, and to amend the National Parks Act to explicitly protect wilderness areas within national parks.

In 1978, Parks Canada announced plans to consult Canadians on the creation of five new national parks to protect large wilderness areas in northern Canada, one of which was proposed for the northern Yukon.[22] It took twenty-five years for Parks Canada to realize the initiative's completion. The first national park to be established under this initiative was Ivvavik National Park, and it protected the calving grounds of the Porcupine caribou herd as recommended by Berger. Ivvavik also set a precedent in that it was the first national park established as part of a broader land claim agreement between the Government of Canada and Native people; in this case, the Inuvialuit. The fifth and final park established under this initiative was Ukkusiksalik National Park in 2003. All told, the five national parks (Ivvavik, Quttinirpaaq, Aulavik, Tuktut Nogait, Ukkusiksalik) were established, protecting over 10 million hectares (24.7 million acres) of northern wilderness from industrial development.

That same year, also in reaction to Berger's report, Parks Canada released a policy document outlining the concept for a new category of national parks called national wilderness parks. However, environmental groups such as National and Provincial Parks

Association of Canada (now the Canadian Parks and Wilderness Society), the Canadian Nature Federation (now Nature Canada), and the Sierra Club did not support this new concept. They were concerned that this wilderness-class park could result in the southern national parks being devalued. There was evidence to support this fear; in 1978, the Tourism Industry Association of Canada supported the proposed National Wilderness Park designation and argued that as a result, national parks such as Banff should be termed National Recreation Areas.[23]

The end result of the discussion over the National Wilderness Park concept was twofold. First, Parks Canada adopted a new policy in 1979 that did not mention the concept. Instead, the policy identified a five-tier zoning system, including a wilderness zone, whose purpose it is to ensure that the majority of national park lands and associated natural resources are protected in a wilderness state with a minimum of facilities. Second, starting in 1983, the Canadian Parks and Wilderness Society turned its attention to seeking amendments to the National Parks Act that would permit the legal protection of wilderness zones within the national parks.

Legal Protection of Wilderness Areas in National Parks

In 1988, the Canadian Parliament approved a series of amendments to the National Parks Act. Two of those amendments are particularly relevant for this review. First, the concept of ecological integrity was enshrined into the legislation, stating that "maintenance of ecological integrity through the protection of natural resources shall be the first priority when considering Park zoning and visitor use in a management plan." Second, the idea of legally protecting wilderness areas within national parks was also put into legislation in that the federal Cabinet was given the power to declare any part of a national park to be a wilderness area, and the government was not to authorize activities within those areas that could impair their wilderness character.

However, the clear focus of subsequent work by Parks Canada in implementing these amendments was on the ecological integrity concept. Policy papers, workshops, ecosystem stress questionnaires, staffing, and other activities all reflected the "first priority" principle behind the concept of ecological integrity. In fact, not one wilderness area was designated in the years following this amendment.

In 2000, the government-appointed Panel on the Ecological Integrity of Canada's National Parks issued an important report and recommendations on how best to ensure that ecological integrity is maintained across the Canadian national park system. With respect to wilderness areas, the panel made an important observation: "Parks Canada currently has at its disposal an excellent way to maintain ecological integrity within national parks: formal designation of sensitive or undeveloped areas as 'wilderness.'"[24] Observing that since 1988, no wilderness areas had been legally designated, the panel recommended the National Parks Act be amended by including a trigger that would compel the government to legally designate all existing wilderness areas within one year of the legislation coming into effect.

That same year, Parliament overhauled the national parks legislation and passed a new Canada National Parks Act. Under this act, "Cabinet may declare any area of a park that exists in a natural state or that is capable of returning to a natural state to be a wilderness area." Furthermore, the minister "may not authorize any activity to be carried on in a wilderness area that is likely to impair its wilderness character." The act further states that the minister:

may authorize activities in a wilderness area for:

- park administration and public safety;
- provision of basic user facilities i.e. trails, rudimentary campsites;
- carrying on of traditional renewable resource harvesting; [or]
- access by air to remote parts of the wilderness area.[25]

Finally, in responding to the panel's recommendation, Parliament added a provision that is essentially a trigger to compel action to designate wilderness areas within an existing national park (but not new national parks). Section 14(4) of the Act now states: "Where a new or amended management plan sets out an area for declaration as a wilderness area, the Minister shall recommend such declaration ... within one year after the plan or amendment is tabled [in Parliament]."

The key here is that a management plan, which is subject to public consultation, must identify a wilderness area for declaration. As Parks Canada's *Action Plan for the Declaration of Wilderness Areas in National Parks* points out:

> In some parks, it may not be appropriate to declare areas as wilderness. The park or candidate areas may be so small or of such configuration as to mitigate against the protection of wilderness values. In other parks, conditions of park establishment may make the declaration of wilderness areas inappropriate. For example, some northern parks have their wilderness character defined through land claims/establishment agreements. In these cases, declaration of wilderness areas may be redundant or not acceptable to Aboriginal partners.[26]

Kesagami Provincial Park, Wilderness Class Park, Ontario.
Photo by Evan Ferrari.

In October of 2000, the federal government finally designated the first legally protected wilderness areas under the Canada National Parks Act in the four national parks that comprise the core of the Canadian Rocky Mountains World Heritage Site—Banff, Jasper, Kootenay, and Yoho. In one sense, this action was the culmination of an idea that Justice Berger initiated in his Mackenzie Valley report in 1977. It was his report that first raised the idea of a national wilderness park, which eventually evolved into the idea of designating wilderness areas within national parks in 1988, and then to the first designation of such sites in 2000.

Conclusion

Canadian governments and conservation groups have been involved in promoting, establishing, and managing national parks and protected areas for well over a century. The concept of wilderness has been, and continues to be, a defining concept. Images of wilderness areas continue to inspire the Canadian population, promoting alarm over the diminishing state of wilderness lands, and inspiring politicians and the public to seize the opportunity that Canada still possesses to act.

From this experience emerge some lessons. While the following is clearly not an exhaustive list, it could help others to consider how to proceed in protecting wilderness areas:

1. In defining wilderness, keep it simple and inclusive. Try to adopt a definition that speaks to a broad range of values, and avoid the strong focus some definitions place on recreational aspects of wilderness. The Canada National Parks Act and Nova Scotia legislation offer examples.

2. Identify a short list of prohibitions, including the need to eliminate industrial activities such as logging, mining, oil and gas extraction, hydroelectric development, and associated road development. Provincial legislation such as that adopted by Ontario in 2006 or Nova Scotia in 1998 provide examples.

3. Ensure that definitions and prohibitions do not run counter to constitutional or treaty obligations to Aboriginal people, and find means to accommodate the continuation of traditional renewable resource harvesting activities when they are central to the social fabric of a region. Canadian national parks created since 1984 offer some interesting examples.

4. In developing wilderness or associated forms of legislation, make sure the legislation requires public notification and hearings, as well as legislation, to reduce or revoke legal protection from wilderness areas. Investigate the potential application of triggers to compel action to designate wilderness areas. The Canada National Parks Act provides some examples.

5. Critical to the process of establishing new protected wilderness areas is the idea of applying interim protection measures to candidate sites to ensure that the very values that gave rise to their consideration as potential protected areas are not lost during the time they are reviewed. The Newfoundland and Labrador legislation provides an interesting example.

Despite the issues inherent in defining and applying the concept in Canada, wilderness is still a concept that garners public attention and support. However, it is clear that as a defining concept behind the management of national parks, it has taken a backseat to more scientific frameworks such as ecological integrity. But as Justice Berger noted in 1977 and the Panel on the Ecological Integrity of Canada's National Parks noted in 2000, the protection of landscapes in a wilderness condition clearly contributes to maintaining the ecological health of some of our most sensitive and enduring landscapes.

Wilderness is a powerful term, one that has been used to promote action to protect natural areas for almost a century in Canada. But with an increasingly urbanized population, and with growing numbers of citizens who come from different countries from around the globe, wilderness may be a concept that has less meaning over time. We must therefore place a priority on using our national parks and protected areas to reinforce wilderness values through direct visitor experience and educational programs, lest we lose what so many other places have lost—their wilderness heritage.

*McDonald Peak, Mission Mountains Wilderness,
Montana, U.S.A. Photo courtesy of
Confederated Salish and Kootenai Tribes.*

CHAPTER 5

The Mission Mountains Tribal Wilderness Area
Confederated Salish and Kootenai Tribes

The area known today as the Mission Mountains Tribal Wilderness was a small part of a vast landscape that our people have taken care of from time immemorial. We were not only connected spiritually and physically to this place, but we enjoyed an intimate relationship with all of the lands in our aboriginal territory. We were tied to this land by our ancestors' and elders' stories that related our oral history and told us of Coyote's travels and activities. John Stanislaw, tribal elder, told me that every drainage, every lake, and every mountain, valley, and prairie had a significant story.

Today we still depend on this land for our game, our fish, and our plants. The elders have told us how important it is to protect it. We not only have to protect the Mission Mountains Wilderness, but we have to watch over all of the places in our aboriginal territory. Our ancestors kept our rights to continue our relationship with our homelands in the 1855 Treaty of Hellgate. We honor our ancestors through our stewardship of the land and by maintaining and exercising the rights we kept in our treaty. This is our generational responsibility that we grow up with as Indian people.

—Terry Tanner, CS&KT Wildland Recreation Program

History: The First Tribal Wilderness

The striking peaks found in the Mission Mountains of the Flathead Nation of western Montana crown a wilderness range unique in the United States both in majesty and management. Standing more than a mile above the farmlands and towns of the Mission Valley, the western front of the range provides one of the most spectacular valley landscapes in the Rocky Mountain region. But the range is more than a natural wonder. It is the first place where an Indian nation has

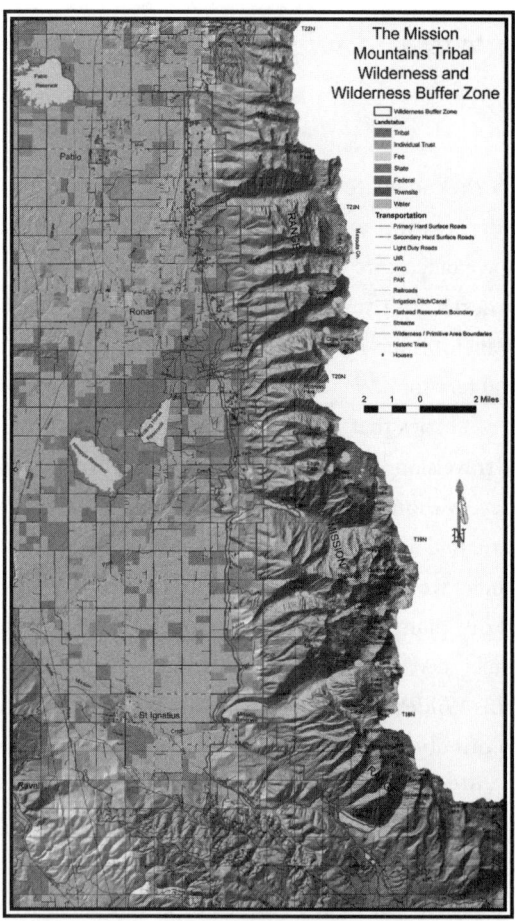

Map courtesy of the
Confederated Salish and Kootenai Tribes.

matched, and possibly exceeded, the U.S. Federal Government in dedicating lands to be managed as wilderness.

The Confederated Salish and Kootenai Tribes are comprised of descendants of Salish (Flathead), Pend d'Oreille, and Kootenai Indians, tribes that traditionally occupied an 8 million-hectare (20 million-acre) area stretching from central Montana to eastern Washington in the United States, and north into Canada. The signing of the Hellgate Treaty of 1855 ceded the vast majority of those ancestral lands to the United States government in return for the approximately 0.5 million hectares (1.2 million acres) now known as the Flathead Indian Reservation.

In the words of Isaac Stevens, then-governor of the Washington Territory, the treaty gave access to "much valuable land and an inexhaustible supply of timber" and enabled settlers "to secure titles to land and thus the growth of towns and villages." The loss of this vast wilderness meant the potential loss of traditional Indian society. Every aspect of Indian culture, from hunting and food gathering to religious practices, depended on a wilderness setting.

To the Salish, Pend d'Oreille, and Kootenai Indians, the Mission Mountains were one part of this wilderness homeland, distinct in its incredible ruggedness and extreme weather but no more wild or primeval than anywhere else. Like other features of the landscape, the Mission Mountains influenced the culture and economy of the tribes. The area could be crossed only through certain passes on a network of trails that had been used for thousands of years by the Salish, Pend d'Oreille, Kootenai, and other tribes. They enjoyed the striking natural beauty; fished the lakes; hunted elk, deer, goats, and sheep; and harvested plants from the forests and ridge tops. They also practiced spiritual traditions throughout the area.

The first attempt by the tribes to officially protect the Mission Range occurred in 1936, during a period of extensive trail construction in the mountainous areas of the reservation by the Indian Civilian Conservation Corps. That year, the newly established Tribal Council voted to set aside about 40,500 hectares (100,000 acres) of the western slope of the Mission Mountains as an Indian-maintained national park. The tribes sought to retain ownership of the lands but planned to parallel the National Park Service in its administration of the area. With support of the local Bureau of Indian Affairs (BIA) superintendent, the council wanted to encourage tribal member use of the park. They envisioned an area of traditional encampments and opportunities for Indian guides to bring visitors into the park. In a 1936 press release, the BIA superintendent of the Flathead Agency wrote:

> It is planned to maintain the park in its present natural state. Roads will not be built … . A complete system of trails will be, and some trails are already constructed. … These trails will, for the most part, follow old Indian trails. At natural camp places, shelters will be erected for the convenience of the traveler and explorer, with corrals in connection where necessary. Indian guides will be available to conduct parties through the park.

Ironically, just one year later, then-commissioner of Indian affairs, John Collier, signed an order drafted by then-chief forester for the same office of Indian affairs, Bob Marshall, which classified the Mission Range as a roadless area. The order established twelve such roadless areas and four wild areas on twelve reservations across the country. Its stated purpose:

> If on reservations, where the Indians desire privacy, sizeable areas are un-invaded by roads, then it will be possible for the Indians of these tribes to maintain a retreat where they may escape from constant contact with white men.
>
> Establishment of Roadless and Wild Areas on Indian Reservations, 3 Fed. Reg. 1408,1409 (1938).

A second goal was to preserve some untouched land for future generations. But because the federal government established the areas without consent of the tribes, the affected nations petitioned to have them declassified. The Confederated Salish and Kootenai formally protested the Marshall Order in 1939, and in 1958 they officially requested that the part of the order applying to the Flathead Reservation be withdrawn. The Mission Mountains Roadless Area was declassified in the Federal Register in 1959.

During the early 1970s, the BIA's Flathead Agency proposed to log portions of the remaining roadless area on the western front of the Mission Range on behalf of the tribes. The proposal, as well as other development activities (clearcuts, roads, poor logging practices, pipelines, dams, and so forth) fueled a renewed interest in preserving the Mission Mountains in a natural state and in protecting other reservation areas.

It was about this time that Thurman Trosper (a tribal member, retired U.S. Forest Service employee, and past president of the Wilderness Society) returned home to the Flathead Reservation. He proposed the idea of establishing a tribal wilderness area to the council. Also at about this time, three greatly respected grand-mothers (*YaYas*)—Annie Pierre, Christine Woodcock, and Louise McDonald—protested the timber sales proposed for the Missions and led the way for other community leaders to organize the Save the Mission Mountains Committee, a group led by tribal businessman Doug Allard. Its purpose was to stop the timber sales proposed for the Missions. The committee circulated a petition in 1975 asking the council to designate the range a tribal primitive area in which logging would be banned. Soon after this, the council seriously began to con-sider some type of wilderness protection.

Several proposals were advanced, all of which lacked overall management considerations other than a prohibition on logging. A proposal containing the least acreage included only those lands unfea-sible for timber harvesting. Advocates of this proposal were concerned about loss of income from reductions in commercial timber lands.

Allard's Save the Mission Mountains Committee proposed a boundary that came to the base of the mountain range and included private and roaded lands, which made it politically unfea-sible. Their interest centered on protecting aesthetic values and preserving the wilderness character of the area, thereby helping to retain some of the cultural and spiritual values important to most tribal members.

In 1976, at the recommendation of Thurman Trosper, the Tribal Council contracted with the Wilderness Institute of the University of Montana to develop a draft boundary and management proposal for a Mission Mountains Tribal Wilderness Area. Two years later, the institute presented the drafts—which were a compromise of previous proposals—to the council for review. The council took no immediate action, but a year later they approved the draft boundary and decided to create a new tribal program to oversee the interim management of the area. Called the Wildland Recreation Program, it was also charged with developing a wilderness management plan to meet the specific needs and values of the tribes.

The program completed the plan in spring 1982, and on June 15 the council voted overwhelmingly to approve Ordinance 79A, the Tribal Wilderness Ordinance, and adopted the Mission Mountains Tribal Wilderness Management Plan.

The Mission Divide makes up the eastern boundary of the Flathead Reservation, and the east side of the Mission Range is managed by the U.S. Forest Service. In 1931, a portion of this range was classified as a primitive area. Named the Mission Mountains Primitive Area, it encompassed 27,000 hectares (67,000 acres). An additional 3,400 hectares (8,500 acres) were added in 1939. Officially classified as wilderness in 1975, the 30,000-hectare (73,877-acre) area is now managed in accordance with the federal Wilderness Act. A high level of cooperation exists between managers of the tribal and federal areas.

Three *YaYas*

In 1974, as the Tribal Council was considering a proposal to log Ashley Creek, in the heart of the Mission Range, three *YaYas*, "grandmothers," accompanied by Germaine White, went to visit the council. The chairman greeted them, and the *YaYas* requested a moment of the council's time to talk about Ashley Creek. The council agreed and each of the elders spoke. They said that people are only on earth for a short time, and that it is important to take care of what's here and to pass it on to the children in good condition. They said that this task is our responsibility, and they told the Tribal Council that the Mission Mountains were a treasure and that it was important we not destroy them in the short time we are here.

The Tribal Council listened and when the last of the *YaYas* had spoken, the chairman thanked the grandmothers and waited for them to sit down. But the *YaYas* continued to stand. So the chairman asked if there was anything else they wanted to say. One of the *YaYas* replied, "Well, we'll just wait here until you vote."

According to Germaine, it soon became clear the women were not leaving. The councilmen looked back and forth at each other until finally the chairman called for a vote. That was the end of the Ashley Logging Unit, and the Ashley Creek sale was the last proposed timber sale for what would become the Mission Mountains Tribal Wilderness.

Protection of the Mission Mountains:
Tribal Ordinance 79A

Wilderness ... is the essence of traditional Indian religion and has served the Indian people of these Tribes as a place to hunt, as a place to gather medicinal herbs and roots, as a vision seeking ground, as a sanctuary, and in countless other ways for thousands of years.

—Tribal Ordinance 79A

The Mission Mountains Tribal Wilderness is established by a tribal ordinance, Ordinance 79A. Article II of the Constitution and Bylaws of the Confederated Salish and Kootenai Tribes provides that "all final decisions of the Tribal Council on matters of general and permanent interest to the members of the Confederated Tribes shall be embodied in ordinances."

Ordinances are not permanent enactments; they can be revised or rescinded by a simple majority vote of the Tribal Council. However, popular support for the wilderness would make it difficult for the council to rescind the ordinance or weaken its provisions. The only stronger protection than the current ordinance would be an ordinance passed by the council and approved by a referendum vote of the tribal membership, an option a future Tribal Council may consider.

The Tribal Council's action in 1982 to approve Ordinance 79A was historic: it was the first time that an Indian tribe had decided on its own accord to protect a sizable portion of its lands as wilderness, and to provide policy and personnel to fulfill its purpose.

The Tribal Wilderness Ordinance states:

Wilderness has played a paramount role in shaping the character of the people and the culture of the Salish and Kootenai Tribes; it is the essence of traditional Indian religion and has served the Indian people of these Tribes as a place to hunt, as a place to gather medicinal herbs and roots, as a vision seeking ground, as a sanctuary, and in countless other ways for thousands of years. Because maintaining an enduring resource of wilderness is vitally important to the people of the Confederated Salish and Kootenai Tribes and the perpetuation of their culture, there is hereby established a Mission Mountains Tribal Wilderness Area and this area, described herein, shall be administered to protect and preserve wilderness values.

Because of the precedent-setting nature of the designation, no legal definition of wilderness existed at the time other than that found in the federal Wilderness Act. As a result, much of the language in the tribal ordinance, particularly the definition of wilderness, matches that found in the federal act:

> A wilderness is hereby recognized as an area where the earth and its community of life are untrammeled by man, where man himself is a visitor who does not remain. An area of wilderness is further defined as an area of undeveloped tribal land, retaining its primeval character and influence, without permanent improvements or human habitation, which is protected and managed so as to preserve its natural conditions.
>
> It is the principal objective of this Ordinance to protect and preserve an area of land in its natural conditions in perpetuity. This Wilderness shall be devoted to the purposes of recreational, scenic, scientific, educational, conservation, cultural, religious and historical use only insofar as these uses are consistent with the spirit and provisions of this Ordinance. Human use of this area must not interfere with the preservation of the area as wilderness.

A significant difference between the tribal ordinance and the federal Wilderness Act, however, is that Ordinance 79A states unambiguously that a primary purpose of the Mission Mountains Tribal Wilderness is the preservation of tribal culture, and it acknowledges the importance of wilderness to the perpetuation of traditional Indian religion.

In writing the ordinance, the authors reflected upon and borrowed from the federal wilderness language, but they also consulted cultural and spiritual leaders in the tribal community. Although there was a strong belief that traditional Indian culture was and is part of the natural world, the consensus among these leaders was that the value of the Mission Mountains for future tribal cultural and religious purposes would be substantially diminished if human use was allowed to degrade the area's exceptional natural qualities. They were especially concerned about the impacts of non-Indian use and the potentially damaging impacts of twentieth-century technologies. In the end, they decided preservation of the area as wilderness had to take precedence over human use.

In that spirit, the ordinance prohibits permanent the building of roads in the wilderness, stating:

> Except as necessary to meet the minimum requirements for
> administration of the Area for the purpose of this Ordinance
> (including measures required in emergencies involving the
> health and safety of persons within the area), there shall be no
> temporary road, no use of motor vehicles, motorized equipment
> or motorboats, no landing of aircraft or other form of mechan-
> ical transport, and no structure or installation within the area.
>
> —Ordinance 79A.

Management
Description of the Mission Mountains Wilderness Area

The Mission Mountains Tribal Wilderness is located on the western slopes of the Mission Range, and covers 37,000 hectares (91,778 acres). It ranges in elevation from 1,200 meters (4,000 feet) to over 3,050 meters (10,000 feet) at the mountain peaks and is approximately fifty-five kilometers (thirty-four miles) long and an average of eight kilometers (five miles) wide.

On the eastern slopes of the Mission Range, the U.S. Forest Service manages the federally protected Mission Mountains Wilderness, established in 1975. That area covers approximately 30,400 hectares (75,000 acres). Both wilderness areas combine with the Bob Marshall Wilderness to the east to form one large ecosystem. Geographic features include forested slopes and high mountain valleys, rocky cliffs, rugged rocky peaks, subalpine and alpine lakes, creeks, and some small glaciers.

On the tribal side, the forest cover is dominated by Douglas fir and subalpine fir trees mixed with cedar, larch, spruce, and stands of ponderosa pine and lodgepole pine. The Douglas fir communities on the lower slopes are proceeding toward climax stage, with some stands becoming quite dense. This density has resulted in increasing outbreaks of insects and disease, which has caused high mortality in some stands and resulted in blow down and a build-up of fire fuels.

Nine major streams issue from the Mission Mountains Tribal Wilderness area. In addition, approximately 113 lakes greater than 0.4 hectares (1 acre) can be found in the cirque basins created by the glaciers that formed the landscape. In the past, campsites along these lakes were used when Indians hunted and fished in the Missions, or as rest stops during journeys across the mountains to other traditional hunting grounds. For hikers, these high mountain lakes provide some of the most breathtaking and memorable sights on the reservation. Unfortunately, some have been degraded by excessive or inappropriate use, which has caused soil compaction and erosion, litter, multiple fire rings, and horse and human fecal contamination of surface waters.

Most trailheads are located at the wilderness boundary—some with campground facilities, others marked only by a trailhead sign. Many of the trails were built by members of the Tribes long ago; others were built by the Civilian Conservation Corps (CCC) in the 1930s during the Great Depression. Trailheads and campground areas contain some facilities, whereas campsites usually consist only of fire rings.

The number of trails and trailheads has varied through the years. A CCC inventory in 1941 counted twenty-six trailheads and forty trails; a 1963 inventory, twenty trailheads and twenty trails; and a 1972 inventory, only six trailheads and eight trails. Today there are nine developed trailheads and twelve major trails that are maintained and that receive regular use. An additional eight trails receive limited use and only "impact" maintenance. The trails are mainly used in summer, from June to September, although higher trails and lakes are not ordinarily used until midsummer after the snowpack melts. The trails are all located in prime wildlife habitats. Grizzly bears, elk, deer, mountain lions, mountain goats, eagles, black bears, and other wildlife use the area along with humans, which creates special management needs. Most campgrounds and trailheads are located in the Wilderness Buffer Zone, and they fall under less strict management guidelines than those within the Tribal Wilderness.

Many roads access the wilderness along the foothills of the Mission Range. County roads, private roads, irrigation roads, power-line access roads, and old tribal logging roads crisscross the landscape at and near the base of the mountains. Many private and tribal (BIA logging) roads run within the buffer zone and in some cases into the wilderness. All roads within the wilderness have been ordered to be closed; however some remain open due to closure logistics. These open roads are sometimes used for illegal activities such as permit noncompliance, Christmas tree and fuel-wood harvest, hunting by nonmembers, and vehicle use.

Management Plan

The Wilderness is currently managed under the Mission Mountains Tribal Wilderness Management Plan, revised in 1997, for the "protection and preservation of the area's natural conditions in perpetuity." Management of the area enables the tribes to monitor human uses and their influences, define limits of acceptable change, and act to prevent degradation or restore impacted areas. The wilderness plan is an administrative guide for tribal staff and the framework for human use of the area.

The Tribal Wilderness Ordinance provides for various human uses as long as they are consistent with the area's primary purpose: the protection and preservation of natural conditions in perpetuity. The protection of the wilderness resource is the dominant motivation in all management decisions where a choice must be made between wilderness values and visitors or their activities.

Also inherent in the ordinance is the recognition that, in addition to the benefits derived from the direct use of the area as wilderness, there are substantial indirect benefits to many tribal members. That is, tribal members draw spiritual and physical refreshment from simply knowing the area and the plants and wild animals it supports are protected as wilderness.

Management is necessary to ensure an enduring wilderness in the Mission Mountains. The manager's job is to monitor human uses and their influences, to identify how they are affecting or changing natural processes, to define the limits of acceptable human-caused change, and then to act in a manner consistent with the purpose of the wilderness. The policies contained within the plan help to define the limits of acceptable human-caused change.

Wilderness, as defined by the ordinance, has many elements. In managing the area, all these elements are considered. Losing one or more elements of the wilderness could seriously degrade the quality of the overall wilderness resource. Management therefore seeks to treat the wilderness as a whole and not as a series of discrete parts.

Management strives to maintain or, in special cases, reestablish natural distributions and numbers of plants and animals. Except as specifically provided for in the ordinance, natural processes, both physical and biological, are allowed to continue without human influence.

Management also seeks to preserve spontaneity of use and as much freedom from regulation as possible, while preserving the naturalness of the wilderness area. It emphasizes solitude, physical and mental challenge, and freedom from the intrusion of unnatural sights and sounds. Indirect methods of distributing use are favored over direct regulation.

Management also seeks to provide visitors with a spectrum of wilderness opportunities, ranging from a good selection of well-maintained trails on one end of the spectrum to an area without trails on the other. Another objective is to prevent the further degradation of naturalness and solitude and to restore heavily impacted, substandard areas to minimum standards.

Management is carried out in the least obtrusive manner possible. Tools used in the administration of the area are the minimum necessary to safely and successfully do the work. The tool, equipment, or structure chosen is the one that least degrades wilderness values, whether temporarily or permanently.

The Mission Mountains Tribal Wilderness is managed as a tribal wilderness: the needs and values of tribal members take precedent over those of non-tribal members. A common thread through all management considerations is the tribes' cultural and spiritual ties to wilderness.

Although wilderness-use trends may vary, the simple existence of wilderness in a region has economic benefits. Population growth over the past fifteen years in counties located adjacent to wilderness areas has been two to three-and-a-half times higher than in other counties, according to a study of 277 U.S. counties. In Montana during the 1980s, nine of the top twelve counties in terms of population growth were located next to wilderness areas. These "wilderness counties" became highly attractive to businesses and new residents because of the high quality of the local environment including many protected wilderness areas.[1] These counties grew economically in spite of severe fluctuations in the economy because the natural landscape "drew people there, kept them there, and helped them permanently sustain the local communities and economies."[2]

Zoning

Continuous impacts on the limited wilderness resources by human and livestock use have made it necessary to restrict certain activities in certain parts of the wilderness. Several zones in the Mission Mountains Tribal Wilderness receive special management considerations:

1. *Special Grizzly Bear Management Zone*—Established in 1982 along with and within the Tribal Wilderness, it covers approximately 4,049 hectares (10,000 acres) surrounding McDonald Peak and Ashley Lakes drainage. It is where, during the summer months, a number of grizzly bears gather to feed on insects. Each year, the entire area is closed to human use from July 15 (earlier if the situation warrants it) to October 1 (later if the situation warrants it) both to minimize disturbance to bears and to provide for the safety of people.

2. *Ashley Lakes Day Use Area*—The Ashley Lakes area and trail, located within the Special Grizzly Bear Management Zone, is restricted to day use only when the area is open to recreational use (when the grizzly bear closure is in effect, this

area is closed). During spring and fall, this area may receive heavy grizzly bear use and there is a potential for human-bear conflicts. This restriction is designed to both minimize disturbance to bears and to provide for the safety of people.

3. *Trailless Area*—When the Tribal Wilderness was established, this area, with a few minor exceptions, had no trails. Not only was it not economically feasible to develop new trails in this rugged and rocky terrain, the country was open enough that in most cases trails were not needed. In addition, for recreationists, the trailless area provides a wider spectrum of opportunities in cross-country travel, a greater chance to experience solitude, and a generally more primitive and wild camping and hiking experience.

4. *Spring Stock-Use Closure*—Since 1989, the entire Tribal Wilderness area is closed to all livestock use (including all pack and riding stock) from March 1 through June 30. This closure came about due to the damage and erosion problems to the trails and campsites caused by livestock when the soils are most vulnerable.

5. *North Fork Post Creek Fishing Closure*—Enacted in 1989 to protect naturally reproducing trout populations in the Summit Basin area from fishing harvest, this regulation affords protection to spawning runs in the tributary streams of Moon, Long, Frog, and Summit Lakes.

The following areas and resources are given special consideration when decisions are made regarding management of wilderness resources:

1. *Grizzly Bear Management Zone* and grizzly bear habitats for a sustainable grizzly population.

2. *Other endangered species* and habitats for maintenance of biological diversity.

3. *Cultural site* protection.

4. *Maintenance of fragile alpine/tundra* ecosystem.

5. *Sensitivity of riparian zones* for water quality and wildlife

protection.

6. *Municipal watershed* protection.
7. *Trailless area* maintenance.
8. *Wilderness Buffer Zone.*
9. *Trails and campsites* (locations, environmental impacts, and history of visitor use).
10. *Fisheries* management is weighted to give special attention to waters containing native West Slope cutthroat trout and native bull trout.

The following provisions govern use principally by non-tribal members:

1. *Use of any tribal wilderness lands or waters by non-tribal members* requires the purchase of a tribal conservation license and the appropriate activity stamp (fish, bird hunt, or camp).
2. *A group size limit* of eight people and eight head of livestock is in place for wilderness lands.
3. *Use of a campsite* for longer than three consecutive days is prohibited.
4. It is illegal to carry or use a *firearm.*
5. *No commercial use* of the Tribal Wilderness is allowed (no outfitting or guides).

The following plans, policies, codes and resolutions affect the wilderness:

1. Ordinance 79A, Tribal Resolution 82-137, which approved the plan to protect wilderness as a valuable resource.
2. Mission Mountains Tribal Wilderness Management Plan.
3. Mission Mountains Tribal Wilderness Buffer Zone Management Plan.
4. Grizzly Bear Management Plan for the Flathead Reservation.
5. Mission Mountains Tribal Wilderness Fire Management Plan.
6. Fisheries Management Plan of the Flathead Indian Reservation.

7. Reservation Class I Airshed Designation (See Chapter 9, Air.).
8. Ronan municipal water supply lease (Middle Crow Creek).
9. Snow Survey Measurement Agreement (See Chapter 10, Water.)
10. Ordinance 44D subject to Joint Tribal/State Hunting & Fishing agreement.

In addition to the policies established by the tribes and the BIA, other agencies involved in the management of similar resources adjacent to the Tribal Wilderness and Buffer Zone make an effort to standardize management goals. For example, the U.S. Forest Service is attempting to adopt the Tribes' wilderness regulation that limits group sizes.

In 1992, the Confederated Salish and Kootenai Tribes and USDA Flathead National Forest developed a joint wilderness map for the Mission Mountains wilderness complex. The purpose of the development of this map was to increase visitor awareness of the tribal wilderness regulations and wildlife protection zones and to reduce visitor pressure at high-use areas.

The first Flathead Nation wilderness manager stated: "Wilderness is, to a segment of the tribal population, vitally important. It is one part of the Indian culture that remains as it was. Preservation then, expresses reverence for the land and its community of life, as well as respect for Indian culture."

The Buffer Zone

The management goals of wilderness currently differ dramatically from the management goals of non-wilderness. Management strategies change abruptly at the Tribal Wilderness boundary, and impacts from activities occurring outside the Tribal Wilderness encroach, at least to some degree, on the wilderness. Accordingly, the Tribal Council decided to establish a buffer zone to act as a cushion to the Tribal Wilderness to protect it from outside influences.

In January 1986, the Confederated Salish and Kootenai Tribal Council approved Resolution 86-47, which established the Wilderness Buffer Zone Committee and charged it with drawing up a buffer zone boundary and management plan. Following council direction, the committee developed the following overall goal for the buffer zone: "to protect and preserve the integrity of the Tribal Wilderness."

In 1987, the Tribal Council adopted the Mission Mountains Tribal Wilderness Buffer Zone Management Plan. In 1990, the Tribal Council approved Resolution 90-73 reestablishing the Buffer Zone Administrative Use Committee, which revised the 1987 Mission Mountains Tribal Wilderness Buffer Zone Management Plan. The council adopted the plan in 1993.

The buffer zone is designed to control, to the extent possible, those activities that may adversely impact the Tribal Wilderness and erode its primary purpose. The intent of the plan is to establish interim tribal management practices for natural resources. It is not intended to represent an ultimate tribal governmental position on any aspect of natural resource management. Rather, it was enacted to deal with immediate management concerns in the least confrontational method possible, and to encourage other jurisdictions and interested individuals to offer advice and suggestions on how to more fully address—on an ecosystems basis—holistic natural resource management.

The buffer zone encompasses 56,398 hectares (22,833 acres) in the Mission Mountains foothills. The lower foothills are used for a multitude of purposes including, but not limited to, cultural uses, livestock grazing, timber harvest, recreation, home sites, Christmas tree harvest, and post and pole harvest.

The objective of the Wilderness Buffer Zone Management Plan is the development of an administrative process to ensure that management of the buffer zone will be conducted using an interdisciplinary approach, and that planning and decision-making will consider all the resources within the area. Additionally, the management plan provides resource managers with clear guidelines to follow when considering activities within the buffer zone. It includes the following policies:

1. All tribal, BIA, and other federal government programs conducting activities within the buffer zone will be governed by the guidelines set forth in the Wilderness Buffer Zone Management Plan.
2. Private landowners and all non-tribal governmental entities conducting activities within the buffer zone are encouraged to follow the guidelines in the Wilderness Buffer Zone Management Plan.
3. The Administrative Use Oversight Committee (AUO) will be responsible for implementation and monitoring of the Wilderness Buffer Zone Management Plan. The AUO will use the interdisciplinary approach to decision-making, and will call upon experts in appropriate fields as needs arise.
4. The Wilderness Buffer Zone Management Plan will be updated and amended as needed.

Benefits: What Has Been Gained Through Wilderness Designation

Tony Incashola, a cultural leader of our tribes, has said that we protect these areas not for ourselves, but for our ancestors, our elders, and our children. So protecting the wilderness is a way of honoring our ancestors and elders. It is also a way of telling our children that we care about them and their future.

In our comprehensive resources plan, our tribes have identified the following fundamental values, which are based on long-held cultural attitudes toward the land and its historical use of resources by our ancestors:

- Respect and live in harmony with each other and with the land, the latter of which we are borrowing from our children.
- Act on a spiritual basis when dealing with the environment.
- Preserve the abundance of animals, plants, and fish.
- Maintain hunting and fishing based on need and traditional use.

By establishing and maintaining the Tribal Wilderness, we help to sustain these deep-seated values, which are key to preserving our culture.

Other related benefits include:

- The Tribal Wilderness serves as an important retreat from roads, motorized vehicles, media, and all the other technologies and noises of our modern society. In so doing, it provides us and our children with an appropriate place to connect with our ancestors and our traditional cultural and spiritual practices.

- For many tribal people, wilderness is a peaceful sanctuary that provides much-needed solitude and an opportunity for spiritual renewal. For others, who may never visit the area, it puts their mind at peace to know that one of the most beautiful places on the reservation is protected in its natural condition for this and future generations of tribal members, and for the plant and animal communities that live in the mountains.

- Our tribal communities depend on opportunities for subsistence hunting and fishing close to home. Our spiritual traditions depend on sensitive species like grizzly bear, elk, mountain goat, wolf, lynx, and native trout. Those species in turn require undisturbed habitat to survive and thrive. Maintaining the Tribal Wilderness helps to preserve the diverse plant and animal life needed to keep tribal communities healthy.

- The reservation's cleanest water begins in the Tribal Wilderness and primitive areas. Tribal communities depend on that clean water for drinking, fishing, spiritual and cultural traditions, agriculture, and a host of other uses.

- The Tribal Wilderness provides our youth with healthy alternatives for recreation. It is a place free of pressures such as drugs and alcohol, a place where our young people can have extraordinary, even life-changing experiences, while learning in a concrete way about their cultural and spiritual traditions.

- Designation of the Tribal Wilderness has made the Confederated Salish and Kootenai Tribes a national leader in the conservation movement and brought international respect and acclaim to the tribes. The recognition undoubtedly helped the tribes in their endeavor to assume management responsibility of the National Bison Range.
- The Tribal Wilderness brings thousands of visitors to the reservation, many of whom spend money at tribal businesses.

Issues and Threats, Solutions and Approaches

Only by staying true to our values, remembering in our hearts who we are as Indian people, and reflecting those values in the way we protect and treat this place we call the Tribal Wilderness, will we be successful in passing onto our children something of great importance that is unique to our culture.

After the Tribal Council designated the Mission Mountains Tribal Wilderness and adopted a management plan, managers realized that many of the greatest threats to the integrity of the wilderness were coming from activities occurring outside of the boundary on lands adjacent or contiguous to the wilderness. They identified the following issues for areas both within and outside of the Tribal Wilderness boundary:

1. Home site development on tribal and private lands.
2. Methods of fire control and fuel management (such as wildfire prevention and protection by landowners and associated fuels reduction timber harvesting activities).
3. Shifts in tree species composition and increasing forest density due to 100 years of fire exclusion.
4. Impacts of recreation and other uses on fisheries and riparian zones.
5. Livestock use and grazing practices including seasons of use, stocking rates, sensitive areas (riparian habitats and wetlands), competition with wildlife, and the placement and maintenance of fencing.

6. Commercial outfitting within the wilderness.
7. Forest pest, disease, and weed management.
8. Protection of sensitive grizzly bear habitats from overuse by recreationists.
9. Roads leading up to or entering the wilderness.
10. Regulation and enhancement of recreational use and opportunities for the development and management of facilities.
11. Protection of cultural, spiritual, and historical sites.
12. Water quality for valley watershed.

Working closely with the Tribal Council and the tribal membership, managers have taken several approaches to addressing these issues. The most significant of these approaches include:

1. Developing and supporting a strong wilderness management program that monitors use and restores impacted areas, and that coordinates the activities of all tribal programs and departments in the wilderness.
2. Establishing the Mission Mountains Wilderness Buffer Zone to address threats to the wilderness from adjacent and contiguous lands.
3. Coordinating with Lake County's land-use-planning efforts so that activities on private lands adjacent to the wilderness are compatible with the purposes of the wilderness.
4. Working closely with the U.S. Forest Service on how it manages use in the adjacent federally protected Mission Mountains Wilderness, so that tribal policies, regulations, and closures can be adequately respected and enforced.
5. Developing a wilderness fire management plan and a reservation fire management plan, both of which take into consideration the special management needs of the Tribal Wilderness.
6. Creating a 4,049-hectare (10,000-acre) Grizzly Bear Conservation Area in the heart of the Mission Mountains to protect feeding grizzly bears. This twenty-year-old conserva-

tion area, which is closed to all human use for much of the summer, was one of the first of its kind in the nation. At the time it was created, other agencies were closing areas for short periods of time to protect hikers. This area is closed for an extended period on an annual basis to protect bears.

7. Developing a strong education program focused on residents living near the wilderness and visitors to the wilderness.

8. Acquiring land adjacent to the wilderness as opportunities arise to protect sensitive species like grizzly bears.

9. Making additions to the wilderness through the forest planning process.

We acknowledge with gratitude the help of many people in preparing and/or publishing this case study, among them David Rockwell, Vance G. Martin and The WILD Foundation, and Ken Wilson and The Christensen Fund.

Photo courtesy of the Confederated Salish and Kootenai Tribes.

Käsivarsi Wilderness Area, Finland. Photo by Tapani Vartiainen.

CHAPTER 6

Finland

Liisa Kajala[1]

Introduction

The Finnish Wilderness Concept

The historical roots of the wilderness debate in Finland date back to the 1950s, when modern forestry gradually made its way to Inari, Finland's northern timberline region.[2] The formal process that led to establishing statutory wilderness areas in Finland started in 1987 through the work of the Finnish Wilderness Committee.[3] Finland's Wilderness Act (official translation: Act on Wilderness Reserves) was passed in 1991.

The twelve existing Finnish wilderness areas were established to protect large roadless areas close to their natural state. More specifically, they were established "to preserve the wilderness character of the areas, to protect the Sámi culture and the traditional subsistence use of the areas, and to enhance possibilities for multiple-use of nature."[4] Thus, Finnish wilderness areas are protected areas, but not protected by the Nature Conservation Act (1996). Also, unlike the borders of areas protected by the Nature Conservation Act, borders of wilderness areas are not marked. They are a transitional type of nature-protection area, lying somewhere between national parks, other strict nature-conservation areas, and commercial land. This allows the wildernesses to be large in size, but leaves the arena open for several controversies over resource use. For instance, small-scale logging operations are allowed in certain parts of some Finnish wilderness areas.

Thus, the Finnish concept of wilderness is quite different from the Anglo-American one, given that resource use is an essential part of the Finnish wilderness areas. This is one of the main reasons why all Finnish wildernesses belong to IUCN category VI: Managed Resource Protected Area, even though many of Finland's wilderness areas remain in a wild state.

Extent of Finland's Wilderness

The designated areas cover about 1.5 million hectares (3.7 million acres) in northern Finnish Lapland, which is about 15 percent of the area of Lapland, and about 5 percent of the total area of Finland. In the sparsely populated north, the areas officially designated as wilderness are not islands surrounded by development, but rather parts of

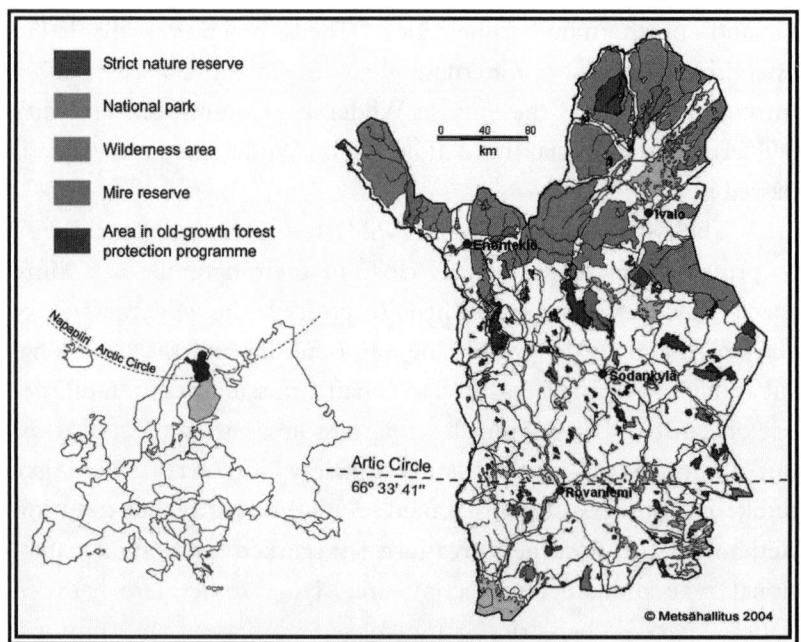

Map courtesy of Metsähallitus.

larger areas with a wilderness character. These large, wild areas are separated by relatively narrow zones with buildings, roads, and other man-made structures. The borders of the wilderness areas reflect the idea that it is important to protect both the natural environment and cultural values.

Some of the criteria applied when drawing the borders were that the areas need to be at least 15,000 hectares (37,000 acres), more than ten kilometers (6.2 miles) wide, and mostly roadless and uninhabited. Distance from the road was not strictly applied; more important was to create ecological entities with natural borders. The smallest Finnish wilderness area, Tsarmitunturi, is 15,000 hectares (37,000 acres), and the largest, Kaldoaivi Wilderness Area, is 294,000 hectares (726,000 acres).

The Finnish wilderness areas are managed by Metsähallitus (Finnish Forest and Park Service), and ten of them are in the Sámi homeland region. Metsähallitus is a state enterprise which also has community and official duties. These include taking care of protected areas and promoting nature conservation and outdoor recreation on state-owned lands and waters.

In addition to statutory wilderness areas, Finland has about 1 million hectares (2.47 million acres) protected by the Nature Conservation Act that are valuable for their wilderness character. These *de facto* wilderness areas are comparable to those established by the Finnish Wilderness Act and include national parks, strict nature reserves, peat land protection areas, and areas in the old-growth forest protection program. These areas are more strictly protected than wilderness areas. For example, in the Finnish national parks, motorized recreation and recreational hunting are forbidden. These *de facto* wilderness areas comprise about 1 million hectares (2.47 million acres), or nearly 3 percent of Finland's surface area. Together, statutory wilderness areas and *de facto* wilderness areas cover approximately 8 percent of Finland's area.

Within each national park there are several management zones. The most remote areas were previously called wilderness zones, though the name was recently changed to remote zone. However, the reason for establishing administrative wilderness zones is not to create strict protection areas. Rather, they are established where there is less recreational use and where more wilderness-like conditions prevail. Consequently, less regulation is needed in these zones, thereby providing visitors with a less regimented experience. This system is possible as long as only a few people are interested in going to these regions.

Finland's Wilderness Act was a one-time designation. Although more *de facto* wilderness may be protected in the future, there will be no new wilderness areas designated under Finnish wilderness legislation, simply because there are no more such areas that would fulfill the criteria set by law. Thus, contrary to other countries, designation of new wilderness areas under the law is not a concern in Finland. However, as described below, the delicate balancing act that Finland's wilderness legislation achieves makes drafting management plans for wilderness areas a significant challenge, which requires long and intensive public processes. Thus, Finland's wilderness protected areas are not by any means static.

Management of Finland's Wilderness

Ecological Dimensions

Finland's wilderness areas are situated in northern Lapland, in the timberline region. Their topography includes various types of peat lands, watersheds, and forests mainly of little or no commercial value. The country's most extensive upland areas are also within the designated wildernesses.

When Finland joined the European Union in 1995, Finland proposed that all the wilderness areas become part of the European Union's Natura 2000 network in 1998, some of them as a part of an even larger area. This means, among other things, that the importance of nature conservation issues and the role of Finland's Regional Environment Centers in wilderness protection have increased. For example, two sections (sections 65 and 66) of the Nature Conservation Act concerning evaluation of impacts now also apply to wilderness areas. On the other hand, because the protection of Natura 2000 habitats and species had already been implemented by the Wilderness Act, new legislation was not promulgated. The Wilderness Act protects these areas in a wild state, and therefore inclusion in Natura 2000 has not caused and is not likely to cause any changes in wilderness area management practices.

Social Dimensions

The Finnish wilderness concept has its roots in ancient hunting and fishing culture. In earlier days, Finns made long trips to *erämaa* (wilderness), a vast, uninhabited area abounding in game. For the nomadic and half-nomadic Sámi people, wilderness has traditionally been their home at least part of the year, so much so that their languages contain no word for it. The relationship between local people and nature is reciprocal; large wild areas have strongly affected the lives of the people of the north, and on the other hand people have for a long time had major impacts on the wilderness. Finnish wilderness is valued for livelihood, cultural tradition, and recreation. It provides income through reindeer husbandry, fishing, hunting, picking cloudberries, and nature tourism.

Even today, local people depend heavily on the wilderness areas for these traditional sources of livelihood. Therefore, one of the main reasons for establishing Finnish wilderness areas was to secure future possibilities for traditional sources of livelihood. There is also a goal to maintain a thriving Sámi culture, which is based on reindeer herding and other closely nature-dependent sources of livelihood. Thus, these areas are of substantial importance to the local people, not only economically, but also socially and culturally.

The Finnish Wilderness Act in itself was valuable to local people in that it provided protection for these areas against uncontrolled development. To the local people, however, there is no such thing as *wilderness* as defined by wilderness legislation. This is especially the case with the Sámi people, who in the past considered the whole wilderness as their home because they roamed these areas with reindeer herds. The local people traditionally simply go "to the mountains" or "to the forests," while wilderness is a more popular concept among non-local recreationists.[5]

Allowed Uses

The Wilderness Act brought a new perspective on the management and use of nature in northern Finland. It prohibited heavy development that would change wilderness significantly, yet at the same time it aimed at improving possibilities for traditional uses of nature. Wilderness legislation explicitly prohibits mining, building permanent roads, and giving or renting land for purposes other than reindeer herding, fishing, hunting, or picking berries and mushrooms. However, the Finnish government can make exceptions to the above restrictions, provided there are compelling social reasons. So far, there have been few such exceptions. The Ministry of the Environment has granted a permit to construct a short road for reindeer husbandry. On the other hand, it has forbidden a private project for tourism development. Currently, the Ministry of the Environment is dealing with an application for gold mining, requiring interpretation of both the Mining Act and the Wilderness Act.

The Wilderness Act allows for restricted forestry in small parts of five forested wildernesses (3.5 percent of the total wilderness areas). This reflects the fact that the Finnish Wilderness Act is in many ways a compromise. So far, logging has been implemented only in one wilderness area, Hammastunturi. Debate continues, but it seems unlikely that logging will be permitted in other wilderness areas. The process of developing management practices for wilderness forests has been significant in developing forest management of the northern timberline region. Wilderness forest management practices and silvicultural methods are now also applied in commercial forestry in the most northern forests managed by Metsähallitus. These methods imitate the natural succession of forests.

In addition to the Act on Wilderness Reserves, numerous other laws and statutes relating to hunting, fishing, reindeer herding, off-road traffic, and so forth regulate the management and use of wilderness areas. For example, motorized recreation (snowmobiles, transportation of tourists by aircrafts) is allowed, but can be regulated by permits (Off-Road Traffic Act, Act on Aviation).

Outdoor Recreation

Wilderness areas are popular recreation amenities. A few of the most popular areas have reservation and rental cabins, marked hiking trails, and snowmobile routes. However, in order to protect their wild character, most areas have not been provided with such facilities. The principle has been that outdoor recreation services are provided only at the most popular wilderness areas, and even there

Ice fishing in the Käsivarsi Wilderness Area, Finland.
Photo by Tapani Vartiainen.

at a very limited scale, in such a way that they enhance and guide the current use.

The Wilderness Act does not mention outdoor recreation or tourism directly. However, the third goal listed in the Wilderness Act, "enhancing possibilities for multiple use of nature," includes outdoor recreation. The justifications of the act explain that the goal of developing diversified use of nature means, among other things, providing for outdoor recreation.

The traditional public right of common access to lands and waters, no matter who owns or occupies them, has become a fundamental legal right in Finland. In practice, it means that everyone has a right to walk, ski, cycle, or ride freely in the countryside, without requiring any form of permission to do so, so as long as these activities cause no harm to property or nature. This largely unwritten code of practice is also valid in wilderness areas.

Related to the goal of "enhancing possibilities for multiple use of nature" are issues such as the acceptable amount of tourism and outdoor recreation facilities. However, due to traditional public right of common access, only indirect controls are available.

Lessons Learned in Finnish Wilderness Areas
Management Plans Are Essential

Management plans are essential to the protection of the wilderness values. The passage of the Wilderness Act in 1991 was a very significant step to conserve the last remaining extensive fell and forest areas and their natural and cultural values in Finland. The Wilderness Act states that a wilderness area is to be managed and used in accordance with a plan for management and use, drawn up by Metsähallitus and ratified by the Ministry of the Environment. Thus, management plans play an essential role in implementing the Wilderness Act. The importance of generating local agreement over the key principles of the management plans was already apparent when the law was being drafted. Therefore, the justifications of the act state that the Ministry of the Environment can either ratify or reject the entire plan or parts of it, but cannot change the plan.

Preparing management and land-use plans for wilderness areas has proven to be a complicated and demanding task that requires effective collaboration with various stakeholders. This is not least due to the fact that the main goals of the Wilderness Act conflict to some degree with one another. The primary challenge is to find a balance between land use and users, such as forestry, reindeer herding, hunting, fishing, off-road traffic, and tourism.

Preparing wilderness plans for the twelve wilderness areas was initially believed to be a project that would take a few years. Now, fourteen years after the passage of the Wilderness Act, only two plans have been confirmed: Hammastunturi and Kemihaara, though draft plans are available for five more areas (Kaldoaivi, Käsivarsi, Pöyrisjärvi, Tarvantovaara, and Vätsäri). It has become evident that wilderness planning is an ongoing development process and requires long-term commitment from Metsähallitus and its employees.

Wilderness management planning is integrative land use planning, aiming at reconciling numerous and often conflicting goals. One important aspect is zoning. Unlike management plans for nature conservation areas, Finnish wilderness management plans do not include regulations for users. Instead, they focus on administrative decisions, such as how Metsähallitus should act with regard to any particular wilderness area, what kinds of permits are available, and so forth.

Thorough Inventories of Wilderness Values Are Important
The planning process is influenced and complicated by the characteristics of the Finnish wilderness areas:

- The diverse, and sometimes conflicting, objectives of the Wilderness Act;
- Northern nature and timberline issues;
- The remoteness and vastness of the areas;

- The importance of traditional sources of livelihood (reindeer herding, hunting, fishing, berry picking) for both Sámi and other local people;
- Sámi culture;
- Land ownership claims;
- Nature tourism in some wilderness areas;
- Contradictory goals among interest groups, leading to intensive public participation in the planning process;
- The proximity of many wilderness areas to Finland's borders, requiring cooperation with neighboring countries (Norway, Russia, Sweden).

Consequently, thorough basic inventories of nature and culture—both past and present—are particularly important in the Finnish wilderness areas, as they are in the national parks and even more so than in many other nature protection areas in Finland.

Unanticipated Issues

There are many issues that were not anticipated when drafting the Wilderness Act and that cannot be solved through wilderness management, but this does not reduce the act's importance. For example, when establishing the wilderness areas, the focus was on forestry issues. The biggest challenge was to reconcile in the best possible way the requirements of forestry with wilderness, traditional use, and other uses including recreation. Currently, wilderness management and planning deal more and more with the planning of fell areas, where logging is not an issue, except for firewood.

After the passage of the Wilderness Act, the importance of preserving the Sámi culture and traditional subsistence uses has increased, especially in relation to other forms of land use in wilderness areas. Sámi legislation has developed significantly after the Wilderness Act was passed, including in particular the passage of The Act on Sámi Parliament in 1995. The interests of Sámi and the settlers of Finnish origin often conflict. As natural resources are limited, the central issue becomes: Who has the right to use wilderness and on what basis? Currently there are particular difficulties in reconciling the goals of preserving the Sámi culture, conducting different building projects for outdoor recreation, and allowing for off-road traffic. As the nature-based means of livelihood in large northern areas requires infrastructure, the building of this infrastructure on the basis of old utilization rights has caused most of the conflicts between these groups.

In addition to protecting Sámi culture, securing diversified use of wilderness—in the forms of nature-based means of livelihood and outdoor recreation—were also important when wilderness areas were designated.

Some new uses are already causing problems in the wildernesses. For example, sled-dog excursions are increasingly popular in northern Finland and current legislation regarding these new uses is ambiguous. Also, one of the most central issues, especially in fell wilderness, is the suitability of motorized recreation and tour operators. The increase in the popularity of these activities was not anticipated when the law was drafted.

Modern technology has also become a part of nature-based means of livelihood, making these livelihoods less traditional. The balance between these means of livelihoods and nature—if it ever existed—has now definitely been upset. The Committee for Constitutional Law stated in December 2004 that modern ways of practicing nature-based means of livelihood are part of the Sámi culture. As a result, modern technologies are allowed in wilderness areas when related to preserving Sámi culture, and Metsähallitus has little or no way of controlling this development.

In the case of the Pöyrisjärvi Wilderness Area, the Supreme Administrative Court overruled the Ministry of Environment's approval of the management plan and sent it back to Metsähallitus for redrafting because the Ministry had not negotiated sufficiently with the Sámi Parliament, though the Supreme Administrative Court did not rule on the particular issues that the Sámi Parliament and Metsähallitus disagreed about (for example, the building of cabins by local people and access to off-road traffic). It seems clear that in the future, the decisions of the Supreme Administrative Court, initiated by appeals made by some stakeholders, will lead to the final resolution of many conflicts. These decisions will also guide the implementation of the management of wilderness areas.

Compromise Is Better than No Wilderness Legislation

A Wilderness Act that makes necessary compromises is much better than no wilderness legislation at all. Though the passage of the Wilderness Act did not resolve the major land-use conflicts of northern Lapland as had been hoped, the passage of the Wilderness Act has played an important role in preserving the Sámi culture, and traditional subsistence use has increased, especially in relation to other forms of land use and land-use rights in wilderness areas.

The Wilderness Act is somewhat controversial. Land and resource rights remain unresolved—causing delays to the planning process required by the Sámi Parliament—and many plans remain to be finalized. That said, the Wilderness Act and the planning processes based on it have significantly contributed to preservation and sustainable use of the natural resources in the northern timber-line region.

First, the act has led to the development of area-specific information on the nature, culture, and use of wilderness areas. Second, the planning process is an important forum for local people and other stakeholders to discuss related issues about the area with Metsähallitus. Third, Metsähallitus as a land administrator of wilderness areas can implement many parts of the plans even if they are not yet ratified. This is a much better alternative than no plan at all, as Metsähallitus has to make everyday management decisions anyway, balancing requirements of different land uses including forestry, reindeer herding, hunting, fishing, off-road traffic, and tourism. For example, off-road traffic in fell areas is a significant issue. In the wilderness management planning process, the principles according to which Metsähallitus gives permits are discussed and agreed upon. Metsähallitus as a land administrator can implement these jointly set guidelines, even if the plan itself is not ratified. And finally, as an ongoing process, wilderness management planning gathers information on the nature, culture, and use of the areas. At its best, it is a mutual learning process.

*Herðubreið Mountain and Lindaá River in the Herðubreiðarlindir
Nature Reserve, one of the few oases in the desert-like Highland.
Photo by Trausti Baldursson.*

CHAPTER 7

Iceland

Trausti Baldursson[1]

Introduction

Background

Iceland covers an area of approximately 10.3 million hectares (25.5 million acres), about 2.5 million hectares (6.2 million acres) of which have a vegetation cover. The country is situated on the Mid-Atlantic Ridge and is traversed by an active volcanic zone. The landscape varies greatly, with many fjords and bays, mountains, glaciers, and lowlands. Woodlands cover only a small proportion of the country (about 1 percent) and these areas consist mostly of birch. Approximately 60 percent of the country is more than 400 meters (1,300 feet) above sea level, an area generally referred to as the Highland or the Central Highland. About 60 percent of the land is desert-like, including glaciers, of which Vatnajökull (*jökull* meaning "glacier") at 830,000 hectares (2 million acres) is the largest, both in Iceland and Europe. The highest mountain is Öræfajökull, which is 2,110 meters (6,923 feet) above sea level. The Icelandic coast is about 6,000 kilometers (3,728 miles) long.

Geologically speaking, Iceland is young: no more than about 15 million years old. Although a large part of the land is desert-like, Iceland receives a great deal of precipitation. However, evaporation is comparatively slight, and runoff is 1.73 metric tons per square kilometer (4.9 tons per square mile), among the highest in Europe. The rate of erosion is high and deposition of sediment is substantial. Both natural and man-made erosion have a great effect on the appearance of the landscape in Iceland. From the first period of settlement in Iceland between AD 870 and 930, the land has been used for grazing and hay-making. Most of the man-made erosion is due to a combination of overgrazing, volcanic activity, unfavorable climate (the "Little Ice Age"), and the easily eroded sandy volcanic soil. The flora and fauna in Iceland are relatively poor and resemble arctic flora and fauna. The only native land mammal in Iceland is the arctic fox.

There are about 300,000 inhabitants in Iceland, about two-thirds of whom live on the southwest coast around the capital city, Reykjavík. All major towns and villages in Iceland are situated along the coast and are less than 200 meters (656 feet) above sea level, as are most of the farming areas. There are no inhabitants above 350 meters (1,148 feet) above sea level in the Highland. However, these higher-altitude areas are not totally intact because they have been used for sheep grazing over the centuries.

Hlöðuvík bay (vík meaning "bay") in the Hornstrandir Nature Reserve in the Vestfjords of Iceland. Hornstrandir has not been inhabited for nearly eighty years, and the area has regained its wilderness character. A part of the area has always been wilderness. Photo by Trausti Baldursson.

A Brief History of Nature Protection and Conservation

Iceland's history of nature protection and conservation began with laws enacted to combat wind erosion and the destruction of vegetation to prevent loss of agricultural and grazing land. In 1907, an act concerning Planting of Woodland and Prevention of Wind Erosion was passed, followed in 1914 by a special act regarding Cultivation of Sandy Areas. Species protection was also of concern during this period: in 1913, a special act gave protection to eagles, and whales were protected from 1915 to 1935 following excessive hunting.

The start of the debate on nature conservation in the modern sense of the word is thought to have been a newspaper article written by Iceland's chief inspector of ancient monuments and historical buildings in 1907. He pointed out that other countries, inspired by the protection of national parks in the U.S., were making efforts to protect nature, and he encouraged Icelanders to follow suit. In 1913, the idea of protecting a specific area, Þingvellir, was taken up for the first time. It generated extensive debate, which culminated in 1928 when the *Althingi* (Iceland's parliament) approved protection for Þingvellir, which for centuries had been the central gathering place of Iceland's parliament—one of the oldest in Europe. Protection was approved mainly because of the area's historical importance and because of celebrations planned at Þingvellir in 1930 to commemorate the 1000-year anniversary of the founding of the Icelandic nation, though the area also has great natural beauty and a remarkable landscape. However, the law only conferred special protected status over Þingvellir (which today is a national park and World Heritage Site), and debate over whether it was necessary to have a special nature conservation act for other areas continued.

In 1940, the *Althingi* passed legislation protecting the island of Eldey, making this the first law to be adopted solely for the purpose of protecting nature. Sixteen years later, the *Althingi* passed more comprehensive legislation in the form of the Nature Protection Act of 1956. The 1956 act was revised in 1971, 1996, and then most recently in 1999. It was prior to the revision in 1999 that the wilderness concept was introduced as a possible part of the Nature Conservation Act.

Wilderness—(*ósnortin víðerni*)—under the Nature Conservation Act of 1999

Protected Areas and the Nature Conservation Strategy

Wilderness is not listed as a distinct protected area category under the Nature Conservation Act of 1999, No. 44 (articles 50–55), which only recognizes the following five categories of protection:

- *National parks*: The minister of the environment may declare an area of land a national park "because its landscape or biosphere is so unique, or because it has historical significance, which gives grounds for preserving it and its natural characteristics and allows public access to it in accordance with specific rules." The land of a national park is owned by the state unless there are special grounds for other arrangements.
- *Nature reserves* are areas that are important to preserve because of their landscape, geological formations, or biota. Land ownership in nature reserves varies.
- *Natural monuments* are natural formations such as waterfalls, volcanoes, caves, or rock outcrops, as well as locations of fossil beds, rare rocks, and minerals, which are important to preserve for their scientific value, beauty, or unique characteristics.
- *Organisms and their habitats and ecosystems* can also be protected.
- *Recreational areas* are established at the initiative of local authorities, who are also responsible for operating them. The objective is to ensure that the public have access to areas where outdoor recreation may be enjoyed.

Although wilderness is not a protected area category of its own, wilderness is an important criterion for establishing protected areas in Iceland. Articles 65–68 of the Nature Conservation Act are

Hornvík in the Hornstrandir Nature Reserve,
Vestfjords of Iceland. Photo by Trausti Baldursson.

the starting point for understanding the role of wilderness in Iceland's approach to nature protection. These articles call for the minister for the environment to draft a national nature conservation strategy ("the plan") to establish a registry of sites of natural interest, and to identify those sites on the registry that are deemed important to protect. An updated nature conservation strategy and registry must be submitted to the *Althingi* at intervals of no more than five years. Responsibility for compiling the data and information for the plan lies with the Environment Agency (which includes the Nature Conservation Division), which must do so in consultation with the Icelandic Institute of Natural History, nature research centers, and the relevant nature conservation committees.

The nature conservation strategy and registry must include the most relevant information possible on sites of natural interest for which protection is proposed, including the unique characteristics of these sites, their significance for the country's natural environment, the main habitat types and ecosystems, as well as geological formations. The plan also includes information on rare species; species in danger of extinction; sites unusually rich in number of species; sites sensitive to disturbance; sites necessary for maintenance of healthy stocks of important species; and sites with substantial scientific, social, economic, or cultural value, or that are important to the maintenance of natural evolutionary processes. Finally, in addition to the criteria above, article 66 states that the plan must also specifically consider four elements:

1. cultural and historic heritage;
2. the necessity of reclaiming habitat types;
3. anthropogenic utilization of nature; and
4. wilderness.

Thus, wilderness functions as an overarching element that must be considered when identifying sites of natural interest throughout the country, and the first nature conservation strategy, 2004–2008, included several wilderness areas. However, no area in Iceland has yet been protected, or proposed for protection, solely on the grounds that it is a wilderness area.

The Definition of Wilderness

Wilderness is defined in article 3 in Iceland's Nature Conservation Act (44/1999):

> Wilderness (*ósnortið víðerni*) is an area of land at least 25 km²
> (9.6 mi²) in size, or in which it is possible to enjoy solitude
> and nature without disturbance from man-made structures or
> the traffic of motorized vehicles on the ground, which is at
> least 5 km (3.1 mi) away from man-made structures or other
> evidence of technology, such as power lines, power stations,
> reservoirs and main roads, where no direct indications of
> human activity are visible and nature can develop without
> stress imposed by human activity.

The word *víðerni* in Icelandic translates most directly to "open space" or "open land with distant views," and does not necessarily describe land that is uninhabited, uncultivated, or free from all man-made impacts such as grazing. *Wilderness* has therefore been translated as *ósnortið víðerni* or open land that has not been affected by human activity (*ósnortið* meaning "untouched"). However, as mentioned before, almost all lands in Iceland have been or are still affected by sheep grazing. As a result, many people in Iceland feel that the two traditional words *óbyggði*, meaning "uninhabited land," and *öræfi*, meaning "wasteland," describe wilderness areas better, and many will rather use the term *óbyggð víðerni* for wilderness.

The Environmental Impact Assessment Act and the National Sustainable Development Strategy

The word *wilderness* occurs in one other law and one other national policy: the Environmental Impact Assessment Act and the National Strategy for Sustainable Development.

Annex 2 of the Environmental Impact Assessment Act contains a list of projects that may have substantial effects on the environment. These projects are assessed on a case-by-case basis, with regard to their nature, size, and location, to determine whether the project will be subjected to environmental impact assessment. Annex 3 of the act contains selection criteria for projects listed in annex 2. Among the issues to be

The open wasteland at Jökulsá á Fjöllum, a glacial river near Herðubreið Mountain. Photo by Trausti Baldursson.

investigated is the absorption capacity of the natural environment, paying particular attention to several objectives such as wetlands, geological formations, landscape, wilderness, and highland areas.

Iceland's National Sustainable Development Strategy, *Velferð til framtíðar, Sjálfbær þróun í íslensku samfélagi, Áherslur 2006–2009 samfélagi* (Welfare for the Future, Iceland's National Strategy for Sustainable Development in Icelandic Society, Main Objectives 2006–2009) also mentions wilderness. Wilderness is one of the main objectives in the nature conservation section of the strategy, and the strategy seeks to ensure that large and intact wilderness areas will continue to be found in uninhabited areas in Iceland, and that new major man-made structures are built outside of defined wilderness areas. Where this is not deemed possible, the strategy states that care should be taken to ensure that these structures will cause minimal damage to nature and have minimal visual effect on scenery and landscape.

Wilderness Designation and Monitoring in Iceland

The authority to create protected areas at the national level in Iceland lies with the minister of the environment, who does so after receiving the "proposals or opinion of the Environment Agency and the Icelandic Institute of Natural History," and on the basis of information in the nature conservation strategy and in the registry of sites of natural interest.

One important tool in establishing new protected areas is the official map of Iceland's wilderness areas, which is maintained by Iceland's Environment Agency (see Figure 1). This map includes both wilderness areas that are already protected—for example within national parks— and areas without statutory protection, but that correspond to the definition of wilderness in article 3 of the Nature Conservation Act listed above. The map is updated on an annual basis to include new projects in unprotected wilderness areas, allowing the government to monitor change over time. It provides a valuable instrument for decision makers in the administration of wilderness areas. The aim is to maintain information on two key indicators for wilderness in Iceland:

- Total area of wilderness areas and protected areas.
- Percentage of the total area of Iceland that is wilderness.

As mentioned, there are no areas in Iceland that have been protected solely on the basis of their wilderness qualities. However, as Figure 1 indicates, large areas of wilderness are protected in existing parks. The main wilderness areas are in the Central Highland or in large remote areas that include land that is higher than 300–400 meters (984–1,312 feet) above sea level. Wilderness areas in Iceland cover approximately 4 million hectares (9.9 million acres), of which 600,000 hectares (1.5 million acres) are inside protected areas. Some of the potential wilderness protected areas include existing huts or roads, though some of these areas could be restored as wilderness if the roads were closed, given that it is often the traffic more than the roads themselves that reduce the wilderness conservation value of the area.

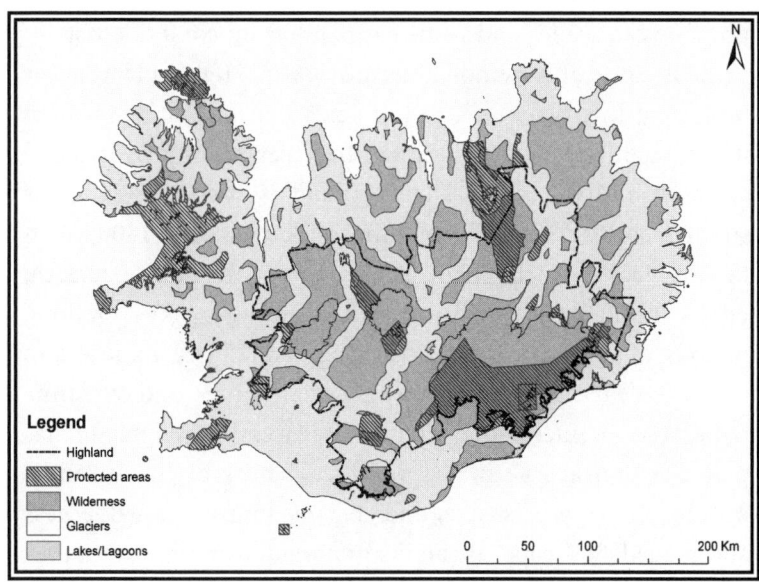

Figure 1—Wilderness areas in Iceland.
Map courtesy of Environment Agency of Iceland.

Iceland's Central Highland

Iceland's Central Highland is a dramatic landscape. An expansive plateau in the center of the country, the Central Highland is shaped by glaciers, active volcanoes, extensive geothermal activity, strong winds, waterfalls, and fast-flowing rivers. The colors in the Central Highland are as powerful as the landscape: black basalt sands and lava fields, brown tuff and yellowish pumice, white glaciers, bright greens from occasional vegetated oases, and red, yellows, and greens from rhyolite mountain areas. Although much of the plateau is covered by glacial deposits, there are some vegetated areas in the Highland with large wetlands that are important for bird species, including the pink-footed goose (*Anser brachyrrhynchus*). Arctic fox is the only native land mammal, though reindeer originally imported from Norway around 1750 are now found in the northeast and the southeast. Because there are no woodlands in the Central Highland, in good weather conditions and from the right location one can see Iceland's entire expanse from coast to coast.

Because of its remoteness, the Central Highland has never been used intensively. There has never been extensive farming in the Highland, though farming has been attempted in some areas around its edges. The Highland is used, however, for summer sheep grazing. From initial settlement until 1400, when the vegetation in the Central Highland was more extensive, people probably traveled across it more often. But for long periods of Iceland's history, the Highland was a remote and inaccessible place where outlaws had their refuge, and over time it became an increasingly mystical place. The Highland has played a central role in shaping the identity of the Icelandic people—its very existence, and the freedom of its wilderness and rugged landscape, are an inspiration and an important part of Iceland's heritage.

Until only forty or fifty years ago, the Central Highland was too remote for most people to reach, and it was considered an adventure to travel there. In recent years, however, the Highland has become much more accessible because of the construction of hydroelectric power plants, because four-wheel drive vehicles are now so widespread, and because roads are much improved. To this day, there are few paved roads. Nonetheless, it is now possible to reach almost any part of the Highland in just three to five days. What was once an endless magical land of unspoiled nature and adventure is shrinking rapidly.

However, measures to protect the Highland are underway. A new act for the protection of the Vatnajökull glacier and its surroundings, Vatnajökull National Park, was recently approved by the *Althingi*. The national park will be the largest in Europe, as well as the largest conserved wilderness area in Europe, and will include some of the greatest volcanic and geothermal areas in Iceland. The plan is to enlarge the park gradually so that it ultimately extends beyond the glacier's ice cap. Iceland has also approved a regional plan for the Central Highland, which will restrict projects and infrastructure to certain defined areas. A new mapping project of Iceland's roads has also begun, which will provide the basis for deciding which roads in the Highland should be maintained and which should be closed off, creating opportunities for enlarging or restoring wilderness areas.

Conclusion:
The Future of Wilderness in Iceland

Wilderness areas will likely grow more valuable in the future, both in an economic sense with respect to the tourist industry, and in a subjective sense, as access to untouched nature contributes to the quality of life in modern metropolitan society. It is therefore vital for us to protect wilderness areas and to take great care to minimize the visual impact of projects undertaken in such areas.

Compared to some countries in Europe, Iceland is a large area with very few inhabitants. And though our wilderness areas are not extensive compared to areas in Alaska, Canada, Australia, or Russia, Iceland does have some of the biggest wilderness areas in Western Europe. Tourism in Iceland has expanded in recent years, and more tourists now come to the country than there are inhabitants. Some tourist companies see this as an opportunity for better roads in the Highland, though this would have serious impacts on Iceland's wilderness areas. There is also increasing pressure for new roads across the Central Highland from the transport sector, which is interested in shortening travel times from the southwest coast to the north and east. All tourist surveys show that the main reason for visiting Iceland is the unspoiled nature, and the Icelandic Travel Industry Association has also stated that all further road building in the Highland should be considered very carefully so it won't spoil the wilderness character of the land. Nature conservation NGOs are also well aware of the threat to the Icelandic wilderness.

There has also been a great expansion in the production of aluminum in Iceland in recent years, and therefore in the use of electricity. This in turn calls for many more hydroelectric and geothermal power plants. All the major hydroelectric opportunities are in the Central Highland, and many of the geothermal hot spots are also in remote wilderness areas including areas that are already protected.

From 1998 and until recently, a plan for hydroelectric development in the northeast Highland caused the bitterest environmental debate Iceland has seen yet and divided the country into two opposing camps. A framework plan for hydroelectric and geothermal development was initiated in 1999 (and completed in 2003) in an attempt to evaluate potential sites or projects for energy development in Iceland and to classify and rank them according to four objectives: 1) environmental and cultural heritage, 2) impact on land use (tourism, grazing, fishing, hunting), 3) national, regional, and social consequences, and

4) to select and define the projects and describe their technical and economic aspects.

Four working groups were established. One of the groups had the task of evaluating the impact of different options in energy development on environmental and cultural heritage, including wilderness. The results clearly indicated that all energy development in the Central Highland, both hydroelectric and geothermal, will have lasting effects on wilderness areas in Iceland. It was also evident that there is a significant lack of knowledge in this field, and much work needs to be done to have a proper overview of wilderness areas in Iceland.

If Iceland's wilderness areas are to persist in the future, there must be better coordination of wilderness conservation and the continued utilization of the land and its natural resources. Iceland still has the opportunity to protect all its major wilderness areas. Whether this opportunity will be seized or whether other land uses will become higher priorities will be determined in the next few decades.

References

Nature Conservation Act no. 44/1999

Environmental Impact Assessment Act no. 106/2000

Velferð til framtíðar, Sjálfbær Þróun í íslensku samfélagi, Áherslur 2006–2009 *samfélagi (Welfare for the Future, Iceland's National Strategy for Sustainable Development in Icelandic Society. Main Objectives 2006–2009).* The Ministry for the Environment in Iceland 2007

Nordic Wetland Conservation: TemaNord Environment 2004:505

Nordic Scenery: Nord 2003:5

Framework plan for hydroelectric and geothermal development Niðurstöður 1. áfanga rammaáætlunar: Gefið út af verkefnisstjórn um gerð rammaááætlunar og iðnaðar- og viðskiptaráðuneytinu, Reykjavík, nóvember 2003. ISBN 9979-68-134-9.

www.lmi.is

www.landvernd.is

www.umhverfisraduneyti.is

www.ust.is

Shiretko World Heritage Site, Japan. Photo by Brian Caouette.

CHAPTER 8

Japan

Brian Caouette[1]

Introduction

As a highly industrialized and densely populated country in Northeast Asia, Japan is not generally recognized as a country of wilderness areas. The majority of Japanese live in crowded urban areas; approximately 90 percent of the population of 128 million people live on less than 10 percent of the land.[2] Nevertheless, much of the countryside remains relatively undeveloped, with numerous semi-wild areas offering promising opportunities for biodiversity conservation and landscape preservation.

Extending nearly 3,000 kilometers (1,900 miles) north to south, the rugged, mountainous islands forming the Japanese archipelago shelter a great diversity of species and ecosystems. From the humid subtropical Ryukyu Islands in the south to the boreal forests of the north island of Hokkaido, Japan is home to more than two thousand endemic species of plants and animals.[3] The country has a particularly high percentage of endemic mammals, including the Japanese macaque (*Macaca fuscata*) or snow monkey, the most northerly living nonhuman primate in the world. Japan is at the heart of the one of the world's great migratory flyways, the East Asian-Australasian Flyway, and supports important breeding and feeding grounds for myriad migratory birds such as the Steller's sea eagle (*Haliaeetus pelagicus*). Birdlife International has identified 167 Important Bird Areas in Japan (IBAs), of which 61 support globally threatened species.⁴

Japanese culture has a long history of nature reverence, particularly in the Buddhist and Shinto religious traditions. To this day,

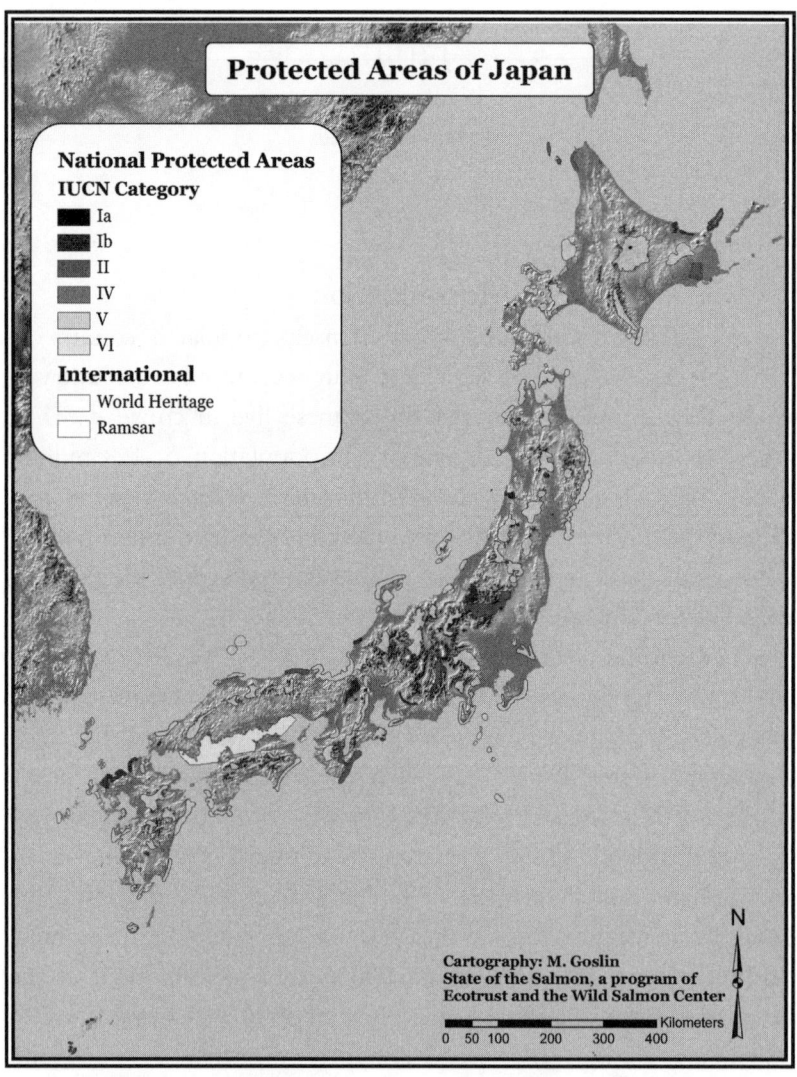

Protected areas of Japan. Map courtesy of the Wild Salmon Center.

Buddhist temple and Shinto shrine land often protect old growth forests and unique habitats from industrial development and other human intrusions.[5] Trees, rocks, and other natural objects are conserved and worshipped as sacred dwelling places for the gods. Scholars have noted, however, that nature in Japan has often been valued not as wilderness, but instead as humanized or cultivated nature.[6] A traditional Japanese garden represents nature in its ideal form: calm, cultured, and controlled.

Modern Japan's heady drive for economic growth has drastically altered the natural environment. As rapid industrial development enriched the country and bequeathed Japan one of the highest per capita GDPs in the world, it also imparted high environmental costs on the land including habitat fragmentation, species extinctions, degraded ecosystem services, and acute levels of industrial pollutants.[7] At least forty-seven recorded animal species are now extinct in Japan including the Japanese wolf (*Canis lupis hodophilax*), the Okinawa flying fox (*Pteropus loochoensis*) and Kokanee salmon (*Oncorhynchus kawamurae*). More than 2,600 animal and plant species are presently on the Japanese Red List of Threatened Species.[8]

Author Alex Kerr has labeled Japan a *dokken kokka* or "construction state"; public work projects including an assortment of dams, dikes, and roads are ubiquitous even in Japan's remotest corners.[9] In 2006, the Ministry of Land, Infrastructure and Transport's annual budget was 10 trillion yen or $84.1 billion,[10] exceeding the U.S. Department of Transportation's budget by nearly 20 percent, despite the land area of Japan being only one-twentieth the size of the U.S.[11] As a result of more than fifty years of *dokken kokka*, all but three of Japan's major rivers have been dammed.[12] Best estimates suggest that more than 2,700 large dams (greater than fifteen meters or fifty feet) and 55,000 smaller dams are sprinkled throughout the countryside.[13] In the north island of Hokkaido, more than 25 percent of aquatic habitat is now inaccessible from the sea due to dams and other obstructions.[14]

Protected Areas and Wilderness Policy

Four framework laws provide the authority for the creation of national-level protected areas.

The National Parks Law (1957)

This law provides the legal authority for the establishment of national parks in Japan. Its mission as stated in article 1 is "to protect the places of scenic beauty as well as promote its utilization as resources for the health, recreation, and culture of the people."[15]

- **National Parks** (IUCN protected area category II)—Designated and managed by the Ministry of Environment, national parks represent the largest share of protected land in Japan. There are currently twenty-eight national parks in Japan that protect more than 2 million hectares (4.9 million acres) of land (equivalent to 5.4 percent of the area of country). National parks in Japan often incorporate a zoning system that includes special protection zones, core areas "required to maintain scenic beauty." In this core, the construction of structures and man-made objects is strictly prohibited.

- **Quasi-National Parks** (IUCN protected area category V)—Designated by the Ministry of the Environment and managed by prefectural governments, there are currently fifty-five quasi-national parks in Japan covering approximately 1.3 million hectares (3.2 million acres) (equivalent to 3.5 percent of the area of the country). Due to lower budgets and few, if any staff, quasi-national parks are generally less protected than national parks.[16]

The Nature Conservation Law (1972)

The Nature Conservation Law makes provisions for the establishment of both wilderness areas and nature conservation areas. In consultation with relevant government agencies, the Ministry of Environment has authority to designate both types of protected areas.[17]

- **Wilderness Areas** (IUCN protected area category 1a)—
  Totaling five sites that protect 5,631 hectares (13,909 acres) of
  national forest land, wilderness areas in Japan are meant to
  preserve and maintain the original ecosystem and to be free
  from human influence. Wilderness areas often include no
  entry, or restricted zones that are only accessible for scientific
  research with required permits. Wilderness areas are generally
  "stand-alone" protected areas in Japan, not a component of
  larger protected areas as in some countries. However, there
  are a number of wilderness areas in Japan that are contiguous
  to national parks.
- **Nature Conservation Areas** (IUCN category IV)—Totaling
  ten sites that protect 21,593 hectares (53,335 acres), nature
  conservation areas are created to preserve and maintain
  ecosystems including alpine vegetation, natural forests,
  aquatic and marine habitats with valuable wildlife, and
  exemplary landforms and geological sites. Though less strict

Shiretko World Heritage Site, Japan. Photo by Brian Caouette.

than wilderness areas, nature conservation areas include restrictions on land development, hunting of wildlife, and plant gathering.

The Wildlife Protection and Hunting Law (1918)

This law empowers the Ministry of Environment and prefectural governors to establish both wildlife protection areas and special wildlife protection areas for up to twenty years.[18]

- **Wildlife Protection Areas** (IUCN category VI)—Fifty-nine national level areas limit hunting on 514,000 hectares (1,269,600 acres) of land. Hunting and disturbing wildlife are strictly prohibited.
- **Special Wildlife Protection Areas** (IUCN category VI)— Forty-six national level areas limit hunting on 117,000 hectares (289,000 acres). Special wildlife protection areas include restrictions on hunting and protections for natural habitat. Approval from the Ministry of Environment or prefectural governors must be obtained before land reclamation, timber harvest, or construction of any structures can be undertaken.

The Law for Conservation of Endangered Species of Wild Fauna and Flora (1992)

This law empowers the Ministry of Environment to create:

- **Natural Habitat Conservation Areas** (IUCN category IV), single species focused protected areas designed to conserve the habitat of threatened species on the Japanese National Red List. There are currently seven natural habitat conservation areas totaling a modest 863.38 hectares (2,132.55 acres).[19]

In terms of international conservation instruments, the Convention on Wetlands of International Importance Especially as Waterfowl Habitat (Ramsar Convention) has significant implications for wilderness protection in Japan. As of November 2005, Japan has designated thirty-three important wetland habitats as Ramsar sites, equaling more than 130,000 hectares (321,000 acres) of marshlands, lakes, tidal flats, mangrove forests, and other wetland types.[20] It is important to note that while Ramsar-site status can bring international recognition to the value of specific wetlands, the designation does not in itself translate into increased regulations. National or prefectural level protected areas designations are necessary for on-the-ground protections.

Protected Area Challenges in Japan

The original purpose of the National Parks Law in Japan was not to create a system for the protection of wildlife or ecosystem conservation, but rather to maintain scenic qualities for human recreation and enjoyment.[21] In many national parks and other protected areas, promoting recreational opportunities and related economic benefits have become the parks' *de facto* mission. Local governments and commercial enterprises often expect economic benefits from parks, sometimes leading to conflicts with park managers who try to limit access for restoration or conservation purposes.[22] In 2002, the National Parks Law was belatedly revised to include the conservation of ecosystems and biodiversity.

Another major issue of concern is the implementation of park regulations. Management plans are often inadequate and not fully staffed. As an example, Hokkaido's six national parks each employ, on average, three permanent staff. Overburdened staff spend most of their time managing visitors and processing paperwork and have virtually no time or training to manage wildlife.[23] (By comparison, the Yellowstone National Park in the U.S. has 460 permanent staff.[24]) Overlapping agency jurisdictions and lack of cross-agency communications have also plagued national park management. Among the twenty-two national parks in the main islands of Honshu, Shikoku, and Kyushu, private lands make up nearly half of protected areas, although there is no legal framework for enforcing park regulations on private land.[25] Other types of protected areas in Japan are either too few (wilderness areas), too small in size (natural conservation areas and natural habitat conservation areas), or are not intended for habitat conservation (wildlife protection areas) to significantly advance wilderness protection in Japan.

Few national-level protected areas have been created in Japan in the last twenty years; the newest national park was created in 1974, the newest wilderness area in 1980.[26] This may reflect a dearth of large, undeveloped tracts of land left in Japan. In contrast, a modest number of nature conservation areas and wildlife protection areas have been established in the last two decades.[27] Further, Japan has expanded its network of Ramsar sites considerably, although usually on land already under some form of protected area status.

Case Study:
Shiretoko World Heritage Site

Known as "Japan's Alaska," the Shiretoko Peninsula is a rugged, volcano-strewn peninsula separating the Pacific Ocean and Sea of Okhotsk coastline at the northeast edge of Japan. Shiretoko is arguably Japan's most authentic wilderness area. Translated in the native language of the Ainu as "end of Mother Earth," Shiretoko was added to the UNESCO World Heritage List in 2005. The Shiretoko World Heritage Site is comprised of the Shiretoko National Park, the Onnebetsu-Dake Wilderness Area and a newly created marine reserve. According to registration documents, "Shiretoko provides an outstanding example of the interaction of the marine and terrestrial ecosystems as well as extraordinary ecosystem productivity."[28] Shiretoko is Japan's third natural World Heritage Site after Shirikami Sanchi and Yakushima.

While the Shiretoko World Heritage Site incorporates many characteristics of a wilderness area including a relatively large size (71,000 hectares/175,000 acres), a largely inaccessible and protected core, and abundant wildlife (with one of the highest densities of brown bears (*Ursus arctos*) in the world),[29] there are numerous issues of environmental concern. Researchers estimate that approximately 331 dams have been built on the peninsula and at least 39 within the World Heritage Site itself.[30] As opposed to the outstanding example of the marine and terrestrial ecosystem interaction, dams and other public works such as dikes, roads, and coastal retaining walls all limit essential natural processes.[31] Salmon, a symbol of the connection between marine and terrestrial ecosystems, are unable to reach spawning grounds in many locations on the peninsula due to dams, overharvesting, and hatchery collection facilities.[32]

In response to calls from UNESCO and the IUCN, the Ministry of Environment launched the Shiretoko Liaison Committee in 2005 to coordinate interagency activities related to the Shiretoko WHS, including the development of a marine and terrestrial management plan.[33] The Committee has promised to generate a salmonid management plan and identify solutions to the limited fish passage on rivers in the world heritage site.[34] In a country known for *tatewari gyousei* or "vertically organized agencies," such an interagency body is a significant precedent for cooperative natural resource management in Japan. Shiretoko WHS may prove to be a springboard for improving management of remaining wilderness on the peninsula.

Conclusion:
Conservation and
Wilderness Protection in the 21st Century

Japan faces many challenges to effectively conserve its remaining wilderness and semi-wild nature areas in Japan. Nevertheless, there are signs of a growing commitment to conservation including the upgrade of the sub-cabinet level Environmental Agency to the cabinet level Ministry of Environment in 2001, and corresponding budgetary increase.[35] In the last decade, several new laws, as well as improvements of existing environmental laws, have come on the books including a new Invasive Species Law (enacted 2004), a revised Wildlife Protection and Hunting Law (enacted 1918, revised 2002), a revised River Law (enacted 1964, revised 1997), and a revised National Parks Law (enacted 1957, revised 2002).[36] In 2005, the number of Ramsar sites in Japan nearly tripled to thirty-three.[37] The development of an integrated management system on Shiretoko World Heritage Site also sets an important precedent.

In many ways, Japan is passing through the development bottleneck. Changing demographics and economic conditions in Japan are diminishing pressures on the land while providing new opportunities for restoration and conservation. Japan represents one of the few countries in East Asia where the rate of natural resource development is actually declining, particularly in rural areas. For example, the number of dam projects has decreased substantially in the last decade.[38] Further, domestic timber production declined by 40 percent between 1974 and 2004, allowing many forests in Japan to reestablish themselves.[39] The decline in anthropogenic pressures on the land can be partly attributed to a declining federal public works budget, labor shortage, and subsequent high labor costs in Japan. In 2006, the Japanese population began to shrink for the first time as the death rate surpassed the birth rate.[40] Depopulation in rural areas is even more pronounced as young people flock to cities. In Sarufutsu Town, Hokkaido, one of the most remote and least populated corners of Japan, the population has shrunk by 70 percent in the last forty years.[41] Farmland is lying fallow; forests are no longer being cut. It is in these regions where the greatest opportunities for protection of natural and wilderness areas could arise in the twenty-first century.

The El Carmen Complex, México. Photo by Patricio Robles Gil.

CHAPTER 9

México

Juan E. Bezaury Creel[1]

Introduction

As evidenced by the remains of pre-Hispanic cultures, which are found throughout México including the country's most remote corners, México's lands and waters have been used by humans for millennia. Given this long history of human use of natural resources, the wilderness concept has only recently begun to be discussed within governmental, academic, and conservation circles. This is largely as a result of the 8th World Wilderness Congress, held in Anchorage, Alaska, in 2005, where México's National Institute of Ecology (INE) sponsored a seminar[2] on wilderness. This chapter outlines the preliminary Mexican wilderness strategy that emerged from this seminar, and which attempts to define basic guidelines to implement the wilderness concept at a national level in México.

México's Protected Areas[3]

México's efforts to conserve biodiversity must be understood in the context of an overwhelming necessity to provide goods and services to its growing population. Thus, national conservation approaches deal primarily with practical issues rather than ethical concepts, recreation, solitude, or spiritual renewal. Strict reserves, especially biosphere reserve core zones, are established as natural benchmarks for long-term monitoring of environmental impacts to natural ecosystems resulting from their human use (as stated by UNESCO's Man and the Biosphere—MAB biosphere concept). They are not established with a wilderness concept in mind, even if on the ground they can become practically undistinguishable.

Protected areas constitute an important part of the Mexican strategy to protect its unique biodiversity. Currently, the majority of Mexican protected areas surface is conceptualized as multiple-use zones (83 percent, IUCN Category VI),[4] where activities are limited by the thresholds imposed by sustainable use of natural resources, and thus can not be considered as wilderness by any definition. This means that protected areas are not isolated from the national economy, but rather that they play an important role in enhancing and consolidating the well-being of México's rural population, though within the limits imposed by the vital need to conserve their "natural" condition.

A crucial characteristic of Mexican protected areas that can help demonstrate their social role is that land tenure within their boundaries is not altered by their establishment, but rather, land use is restricted through presidential decree in order to safeguard the land's environmental conditions on behalf of a greater public good. This apparent imposition (a "taking" in other legal systems) upon property rights has its legal basis in article 27 of the Mexican Constitution, which states that "originally all land belongs to the nation, who creates private and communal property but holds the right to impose modalities upon its use, in order to achieve a greater public good." Expropriation of lands to create protected areas has been used by some administrations, but is currently used only in exceptional cases when a specific strict no-use policy is required, and almost always with dire results. It is also important to clarify that private and communal property of land in México refers only to surface rights; subsoil rights—including mineral rights and all water rights—are national property by law.

México's Ecology Law[5] establishes the following objectives for Mexican protected areas:

- Preserve representative environments from all natural bio-geographic and ecological regions and their ecosystems;
- Safeguard the genetic diversity of wildlife upon which their evolutionary continuity depends and ensure preservation and sustainable use of biodiversity, especially of endangered, threatened, endemic, and rare species, and those subject to special protection;
- Assure sustainable use of ecosystems and their elements;
- Provide opportunities for scientific research and for the study of ecosystems and their balance;
- Generate, recover, and communicate traditional or new knowledge, practices, and technologies that will allow for preservation and sustainable use of biodiversity;
- Protect towns, communications and industrial infrastructure, agricultural lands, and the hydrological cycles of watersheds; and,
- Protect the natural surroundings of archaeological, artistic and historical zones, monuments and remains, tourism zones and other areas important for recreation, culture, and national and indigenous communities' identity.

Thus, even though the preservation of wilderness in itself has never been legally mandated by Mexican legislation, wilderness conservation would certainly be consistent with and help further some of the Ecology Law's objectives.

Wilderness Policy

There is currently no explicit policy or legislative definition of wilderness within México's law or protected areas classification system. However, México is developing several mechanisms to facilitate the implementation of wilderness protection. This derives from the unique opportunity created by a bilateral governmental and private sector commitment by the National Protected Area Commission (CONANP) and CEMEX S.A. de C.V. (one of the world's largest producers of cement), facilitated by The WILD Foundation and Agrupación Sierra Madre at the 8th World Wilderness Congress.[6]

Constraints imposed by México's land tenure structure, legislation defining land tenure restrictions, and the conceptualization of its protected area systems, had to be taken into consideration to develop a viable strategy for the adoption and implementation of the wilderness concept in México.

México's land tenure structure is the initial and most important constraint to the establishment of a nonvoluntary wilderness system. Almost 90 percent of the land in México is either in social or private hands, and the remaining 10 percent consists of public lands that are mostly represented by highly fragmented and scattered patches or linear properties, with the exception of the 1.5 percent[7] already included within México's protected areas.

Land Tenure Structure in Mexico[8]	Percent of total land
Social Property (communal rural landholdings)	51.6
Private Property (subject to limits on the amount that can be legally owned by any one person)	38.2
Public Property (includes federal, state, and municipal lands; freshwater and coastal water bodies; federal zones adjacent to water currents and beaches; roads right of way; and islands)	10.2
TOTAL	**100**

Article 27 of the Mexican Constitution and México's Agrarian Law also establish precise limits on the amount of land that can be held by any person or entity. In practical terms, the legislation states that no individual can hold more than 800 hectares (2,000 acres)[9] of forestlands, or the amount of land needed to raise 500 head of cattle[10] in desert lands. Up to twenty-five individuals can join together through a "forestry or cattle landholders' corporation,"[11] which in forestlands can add up to a maximum of 25,000 hectares (62,000 acres), but can result in substantially larger landholdings in desert areas. Places where foreigners are restricted from owning land—within 100 kilometers (62 miles) of international borders and within 50 kilometers (31 miles) of the coast—are further defined by article 27 of the Mexican Constitution and the Foreign Investment Law.[12]

México's federal protected areas category system already includes biosphere reserve core zones and sanctuaries as IUCN Category Ia: Strict Nature Reserves,[13] which constitute protected areas managed mainly for science. Since science is a human activity that is generally carried out to the benefit of mankind, within the context of the Constitutional framework provided by article 27, it becomes a relatively straightforward issue to justify the establishment of IUCN Category Ia status on private and social lands since "the nation holds the right to impose modalities upon its use, in order to achieve a greater public good." Establishing a IUCN Category Ib: Wilderness Area[14] as a protected area managed mainly for wilderness protection, even if basically indistinguishable on the ground from Category 1a, could also become a pragmatic tool for achieving conservation of biodiversity. Nonetheless it also represents a huge conceptual change from the current utilitarian concept behind article 27, to a new ethical/recreational paradigm implied by the words "managed so as to preserve its natural condition," which could probably be legally challenged by landowners.

The above mentioned practical and legal limitations lead to the conclusion that a voluntary system for wilderness designation would currently provide the most effective course of action in México.

Designation Process

México is developing two mechanisms for designating wilderness areas. First, through an existing official system currently being implemented by CONANP as specified in the Ecology Law,[15] which will provide government wilderness certification to private and communal land conservation efforts.[16] This will in turn provide priority access to economic incentive programs to landowners, such as payment for ecosystem services from watershed-based forest conservation, biodiversity conservation, and carbon sequestration. As a result of the INE Wilderness Seminar, conservation and academic groups approached CONANP to develop a new level of recognition as "Wilderness Zones,"[17] which will seek to promote the highest possible level of ecological integrity of the land and avoid perceivable human impacts. Wilderness zones would represent the wilderness concept within this recognition framework, and would facilitate the rewilding process of more land in the future.

Second, and from the private sector, a coalition of national and international conservation organizations and academic institutions will create a "private wilderness certification system," certifying areas as "Wildlands"[18] and thereby providing solid, verifiable, moral, and prestige-based backing either to those landowners who have already certified their lands through CONANP, or to those who prefer to certify their land as wilderness only through the private sector process.

Regulation for Wilderness to Be Included within Mexico's Official Recognition System

The current plan is to include the Wilderness Zone concept within the legal framework provided by the Protected Area Regulations,[19] where it will be defined as:

> Areas where habitats, biotic communities, and natural processes remain predominantly intact; where the footprint of industrial civilization and its infrastructure is not present; where human activities are developed without leaving evidence of their presence; and, are sufficiently ample to provide opportunities for the reconciliation of man, as a species, with nature.

Specific criteria will be provided to CONANP by the National Protected Area Council[20] in order to asses whether specific proposals conform to the definition. In addition, after CONANP's evaluation of individual proposals, the council will be consulted on the results of the evaluation.

Landowners will voluntarily commit their lands for conservation as a wilderness zone for a period of at least fifty years, refraining from developing any type of infrastructure on the land during this period. Landowners must also specify what kind of management

The El Carmen Complex. Photo by Patricio Robles Gil.

practices or programs will be implemented on the land. If needed, the landowner must also develop a "re-wilding program" that will at a minimum include: the eradication of exotic species and habitat mitigation practices until their impact to natural communities is phased out; reintroduction of extirpated native species; and the elimination of the footprint of industrial civilization in the form of structures and infrastructure.

Regulations will provide for the recognition of land involved in a re-wilding process, if those parcels at the time of submission are not deemed suitable to be recognized as wilderness zones.

Lessons Learned and Outlook for the Future

The Mexican wilderness designation jointly announced by CONANP and CEMEX in the 8th World Wilderness Congress—although somewhat premature in the sense that the regulatory framework was and currently still is not in place, and that the land to be designated has not been completely acquired[21]—generated important deliberations between governmental, academic, private, and conservation groups, which for the first time sat down to define how to conceptualize and implement the wilderness concept in México.

These deliberations have also resulted in a series of preliminary definitions on how to use México's legal system to incorporate and help protect other important voluntary protection schemes, such as sacred sites, scientific reserves, and traditional cultural landscapes that include anthropogenic-derived biodiversity.

Consensus from the INE Seminar suggests that within the context of México's fragmented land tenure system, and given the large amount of land required to create true wilderness, opportunities to develop voluntary wilderness designations will mostly develop in the arid northern part of the country—where private property is an important component of the land tenure structure—rather than in Mexico's tropical southern portion, where communal property upon which communities depend for their livelihoods will, except in a few notable exceptions, remain under multiple use schemes.

The inclusion of a wilderness management regime upon public lands within already established protected area core zones[22] can be accomplished through management programs within the existing legal and regulatory system.

Deliberations on the definition of marine wilderness were deferred to the future, once the terrestrial wilderness concept has been implemented and is working. In this case, marine property rights belong to the nation, so their designation will not include private voluntary processes, but most likely marine protected area zoning measures.

Acknowledgments

The following people contributed to the development of the wilderness concept and other important voluntary protection schemes for México as described in this document: Francisco Cantón (CONANP), Gerardo Ceballos (UNAM), Roberto de la Maza (CONANP), Rodolfo Dirzo (UNAM), Ernesto Enkerlin (CONANP), Exequiel Ezcurra (San Diego Museum of Natural History), Adrian Fernández (INE), Ana Gallardo (CONANP), Armando García (CEMEX), Arturo Gómez Pompa (CITRO), Ana Luisa Guzmán (CONABIO), Marco Lazcano (Amigos de Sian Ka'an A.C.), Gloria Portales (INE), Patricio Robles Gil (Sierra Madre A.C.), and Dan Roe (CEMEX).

The El Carmen Complex, México. Photo by Patricio Robles Gil.

Valley access to the Olivine Wilderness Area, Mt. Aspiring National Park, New Zealand. Photo by Neill Simpson. Crown Copyright. Department of Conservation, New Zealand.

CHAPTER 10

New Zealand

Jonty Somers[1]

Introduction

Public conservation land is the term used to refer to all protected terrestrial areas in New Zealand. These areas are significant, making up approximately 30 percent of the entire country, including its offshore islands. Broadly speaking, public conservation land is divided into three main categories. These are conservation areas,[2] reserves,[3] and national parks.[4] The Department of Conservation[5] is the government agency charged with responsibility for managing these areas under the Conservation Act 1987, the Reserves Act 1977, and the National Parks Act 1980, respectively. Each act makes provision for wilderness areas.[6]

Under section 18 of the Conservation Act, for example, land held under the Conservation Act for conservation purposes may, additionally, be held for one of seven specific purposes, including the purpose of a wilderness area. When this occurs, the area attains a specially protected status and must be managed in accordance with section 20 of that act. The Reserves Act sets up a reserve classification system, which includes recreation reserves, historic reserves, and nature reserves.[7] Wilderness areas are provided for not as a type of reserve, but as an overlay status that recognizes the unique qualities of that reserve.[8] The National Parks Act is similar in that a wilderness area may be established over part of a national park.[9] That area continues to be part of the park, but the overlay status requires that it be managed in a specific way.

Much of the public conservation land in New Zealand that is not formally gazetted as a wilderness area would, either in terms of the criteria specified for wilderness by the International Union of Conservation on Nature (Category 1b) or, for example by the management specifications for wilderness in the United States, be considered to be the most remote kind of wilderness. This simply reflects the ruggedness, remoteness, and level of inaccessibility of this land: there is much *de facto* wilderness in New Zealand.

Definition

Unlike the U.S. Wilderness Act of 1964, neither New Zealand's Conservation Act nor the Reserves Act define the term *wilderness area* or what is meant by *wilderness*—at least not in so many words. The National Parks Act merely provides that a wilderness area is "any part of a national park set apart as a wilderness area under section 14 of the Act."[10]

The relevant provisions in the three acts overcome this omission by laying down what may and may not be done in a wilderness area, always subject to the requirement to preserve a wilderness area's indigenous natural resources. The following are expressly proscribed:[11]

- The erection of any building or machinery;
- The construction or maintenance of any building, machinery or apparatus;
- The taking or use of animals, vehicles, motorized vessels, or aircraft (including helicopters) into or in wilderness areas; and
- The construction of roads, tracks, or trails.

In addition, under both the Reserves Act and the National Parks Act, bylaws can be gazetted for the purpose of prescribing conditions under which persons may be permitted to enter or remain in wilderness areas within reserves and national parks.[12]

The following may occur in wilderness areas:

- All forms of recreation which do not involve animals or any type of motorized transport;
- Scientific tests and studies (provided these are necessary or desirable for the preservation of the wilderness area's indigenous natural resources);
- Limited commercial activities (not involving animals or motorized transport);
- Management of introduced plants and animals;
- Search and rescue;
- Firefighting;
- Release of indigenous animals (in the case of national parks act, such release can only occur if that animal was previously present in that area);

Tramping in the remote backcountry—New Zealand's vast undesignated wilderness. Photo Crown Copyright. Department of Conservation, New Zealand.

- Any of the proscribed activities listed above provided they are in conformity with relevant statutory planning documents *and* if they are necessary or desirable for preserving the wilderness area's indigenous natural resources.

Some of the activities above require the express consent of the minister of conservation, who is the key statutory decision maker under each of the acts. The minister must make decisions that conform to the policies of statutory management planning documents[13] in effect in such areas. In some instances, the consent of the director-general of conservation may be required. The director-general[14] is the chief executive of the department and has all powers necessary to carry out the department's functions as land manager.[15]

Wilderness Policy

In 1985, the Wilderness Policy[16] was published by the then Department of Lands and Survey for the Wilderness Advisory Group, a group brought together by the government of the day to advise on wilderness issues. The policy's aim is to increase public appreciation of the value of retaining wild lands and to encourage a coordinated approach to wilderness management. The policy effectively underpins the legislation by specifying the prerequisites for wilderness areas. It identifies wilderness areas as wild lands designated for protection and managed to perpetuate their natural condition, and which appear to have been affected only by the forces of nature with any imprint of human interference substantially unnoticeable.

The policy establishes criteria for land to qualify as potentially suitable for designation as a wilderness area. A proposed wilderness area:

- Will be large enough to take at least two days' foot travel to traverse;
- Should have clearly defined topographic boundaries and be adequately buffered so as to be unaffected, except in minor ways, by human influences;

- Will not have developments such as huts, tracks, bridges, signs, or mechanized access;
- Should have a wide geographic distribution and contain diversity in landscape and recreational opportunity;
- Will preserve resources and thus options for future uses of the land; and
- Ideally should be managed in perpetuity, but the designation is not necessarily permanent in terms of the relevant statutes and can be revoked if deemed necessary.

The policy essentially promotes the notion that wilderness is personal; that it embodies remoteness, discovery, challenge, solitude, freedom, and romance; and that it fosters self-reliance and empathy with wild nature. Wilderness is therefore seen as a recreational and cultural concept that is compatible with nature conservation. It should be available to everyone. Management of large remote areas of wilderness is necessary in order to retain the widest opportunity for outdoor recreation in a variety of landscapes. The policy considers the opportunity for wilderness recreation in New Zealand to be of international significance.

In 1996, the department released its Visitors' Strategy to guide its management of recreation. The strategy confirmed that wilderness areas would be managed in accordance with the 1985 Wilderness Policy as follows:

- No facilities or services should be allowed;
- Buffer zones should be utilized;
- Access would be limited by remoteness;
- Commercial recreation should be controlled;
- Motorized access or use would be prohibited;
- Self-sufficiency would be required;
- Other development or use should be limited; and
- Management and emergency exceptions should be allowed.

Management Guidelines

Apart from the Wilderness Policy and Visitors' Strategy, both of which are forms of non-statutory policy, there is a hierarchy of statutory management documents that guides the department in its management functions and decision makers under the legislation. These documents constitute statutory policy as they are made in accordance with relevant legislation.

Statements of general policy are at the top of the hierarchy. A prime example is the General Policy for National Parks, which is made under the National Parks Act.[17] Originally adopted in 1983 by the New Zealand Conservation Authority, it was substantially reworked and adopted (or approved) in April 2005. The purpose of this general policy is to provide a management framework to implement the National Parks Act. Policy 6(p) provides that wilderness areas in national parks should be large enough and sufficiently remote and buffered to be unaffected by human influences except in minor ways.

A general policy made under the Conservation Act[18] and Reserves Act[19] in May 2005 is similar in content to the General Policy for National Parks and duplicates that policy with respect to wilderness areas.

The next level of statutory management documents in the hierarchy are conservation management strategies. These implement general policies and establish objectives for the management of reserves and for the integrated management of natural and historic resources, including any species managed by the department, and for recreation, tourism, and other conservation purposes.[20] They also establish objectives for the management of national parks and any areas within those parks.[21] Conservation management strategies must not derogate from the legislation or general policies.[22]

The department conducts its work through thirteen conservancies; each conservancy has a conservation management strategy.[23] The Mainland Southland/West Otago conservation management strategy provides that wilderness areas are designated to ensure that large natural areas retain their wilderness qualities essentially free from facility development and mechanized access. It points out that in contrast to virtually all of New Zealand's designated or proposed wilderness areas, the Waitutu area offers the opportunity of solitude and challenge without requiring mountaineering skills. The strategy stipulates that any specific proposal for a wilderness area in Southern Fiordland will require an investigation, including opportunity for public comment. Public submissions on the draft conservation management strategy demonstrated strong local opposition to certain areas being included in a wilderness area.

With reference to the proposed wilderness area in South Fiordland, Section 6.4 of the strategy provides as follows:

Opportunity Objectives

- West of the Wairaurahiri River, to provide opportunities for low impact recreation remote from high-use areas and modern facilities, managing the area in a manner that does not preclude future wilderness opportunities free of facilities and motorized transport.

Implementation

- Facilities west of Wairaurahiri River will be maintained and not upgraded nor will any further facilities be developed.
- To investigate options for a wilderness area somewhere between the west of Wairaurahiri River and Preservation Inlet, including some of the large inland lakes.

National Park management plans provide for the management of national parks in accordance with the National Parks Act, the General Policy for National Parks, and that part of a conservation management strategy that relates to a park.[24] Management plans must not derogate from conservation management strategies.[25] In usual circumstances, the lower the statutory management plan in the hierarchy, the more detailed the management objectives. This is the case with National Park management plans, which, because they relate to national parks, will be more specific than a conservation management strategy.

The Tasman wilderness area, which was gazetted in the 1990s, is a good illustration of how a National Park management plan deals with wilderness areas. It is described in the Kahurangi National Park Management Plan as providing a special recreational opportunity offering sanctuary, peace, solitude, and inspiration to wilderness seekers; and as giving visitors an opportunity to witness a truly unspoiled landscape and to experience nature on a one-to-one basis in the absence of tracks, huts, or other facilities. The policies are:

- To preserve the integrity of the Tasman wilderness area and preserve its existing boundaries; and
- To recognize the importance of the Tasman wilderness area as the only gazetted wilderness area in the top half of the South Island.

Issues include:

- Helicopter deer hunting, which occurs in accordance with section 14(4) of the National Parks Act. However, it is recognized that deer hunting has the potential to affect visitor experience. Other issues are boundary and visitor impacts.

Implementations are:

- To enforce prohibitions on helicopter landings (except for wild animal control, park management, approved scientific, or emergency purposes) in line with the National Parks Act and to review landings on its borders;
- To seek to limit the number of helicopter operators hunting deer in the Tasman wilderness area;
- To monitor the social and environmental impacts and numbers of visitors; and
- To retain the Tasman wilderness area at its present size with existing boundaries.

With respect to wilderness the Fiordland National Park management plan states:

> Although most of Fiordland is viewed by many as a wilderness now, legal designation as a wilderness area under section 14 of the National Parks Act ensures parts of the park will remain as true wilderness free from facility development for the long term. Without formal designation, incremental development over a period of 20–30 years could substantially change the traditional recreational use of the area.
>
> The intention of wilderness areas is not to lock up the land or prevent people from going there. The primary purpose is to provide recreation opportunities for highly experienced hunters, trampers and climbers seeking solitude and challenge in a natural environment free from facilities. Section 5.3.5

Designation Process

In New Zealand, the department usually takes the initiative in inventorying land to assess whether it qualifies for wilderness designation. In doing so, it will necessarily be guided by the Wilderness Policy, which establishes the various benchmarks that must be present before land can seriously be considered for special protection.

Part of the exercise will include consideration of historical views. Much of this is informed by the work of the Federated Mountain Clubs (FMC), comprising the New Zealand Alpine Club and a variety of tramping, mountaineering, and skiing clubs, which was formed in 1931 to further common aims of promoting and safeguarding mountain and forest recreation. At the 1981 Wilderness Conference, hosted by FMC as part of its Fiftieth Jubilee, it put forward proposals for ten wilderness areas that satisfied the criteria of size, remoteness, naturalness, and buffering. Most, but not all, have now been adopted; even those not yet adopted are still under active consideration.

Current views are remarkably similar to historical views, since the land under consideration for wilderness area is evaluated against criteria in the Wilderness Policy, namely naturalness of landscape, remoteness, sufficient size, adequate buffering, and the absence of recreational development or mechanical access.

Although the wilderness qualities of an area will usually be self-evident, an appraisal combining environmental and developmental assessments is usually conducted. This will include the identification of alternative resource uses for the area and a socio-economic impact study of various alternative land-use designation and management options. Thus, it could cover such issues as mining, hydrodevelopment, recreational uses, animal control issues, and the wilderness qualities of the land itself such as remoteness and naturalness. It will explore the wilderness resource itself (whether it meets the criteria in the Wilderness Policy, for example), and analyze the land-use options and likely impacts of those options. It will evaluate the costs and benefits that would flow from a wilderness area and will tackle the problem of how to value those costs and benefits, as well as considering the type of techniques that might be used.

The means by which wilderness areas are designated depends on whether they are being established under the Conservation Act, the Reserves Act, or the National Parks Act. When wilderness is designated under the Conservation Act, the minister of conservation is required to give public notice of that intention.[26] Anyone wishing to support or object to the proposal may make submissions in writing to the director general within a specified timeframe.[27] People may also accompany their submissions with a request to be heard, in which event the director-general must give those people a reasonable opportunity to appear.[28] Following receipt of submissions and on the conclusion of any hearings, the director-general must send to the minister a summary of all objections and comments received, with a recommendation as to the extent to which they should be allowed or accepted.[29] The minister then considers the recommendations and contents of this summary before deciding whether or not to proceed with the proposal.[30]

To proceed with the proposal requires the minister, by notice in the Gazette (the official journal of government), to declare the land to be held for the purpose of a wilderness area.[31] The notice must specify a name for the wilderness area.[32] Once gazetted, the area must be managed in the manner consistent with the purpose of a wilderness area.[33]

The process under the Reserves Act is similar, but not exactly the same. In New Zealand, reserves are either vested in the Crown or in administering bodies.[34] To complicate matters further, a Crown-vested reserve may be controlled and managed by an administering body.[35] The minister of conservation (in the case of a Crown reserve that has no administering body) or the administering body with the consent of the minister (where the reserve has an administering body) may, by notice in the Gazette, set apart all or part of a reserve as a wilderness area.[36] Before doing so, the administering body must give public notice of the proposal and invite interested persons to make submissions within a specified timeframe.[37] Submitters can request hearings,[38] following which the minister must give full consideration to all objections and submissions made.[39] Curiously, no provision has been made for the minister to give public notification in respect of Crown-vested reserves. This presumably is an anomaly and will require remedying.

The process is different under the National Parks Act, as there is no express statutory requirement for a public process. The minister of conservation may, by notice in the Gazette, set apart any area of a park as a wilderness area; but can only do so on the recommendation of the New Zealand Conservation Authority (which is a statutory body with general oversight powers in national parks), whose recommendation must be in accordance with a conservation management strategy or a National Park management plan.[40] This requirement ensures that the public does, in fact, have a say, since an intention to establish (or revoke, for that matter) a wilderness area will be signaled at the draft stage of a conservation management strategy and a management plan. In this event, the public will have an opportunity to comment on the proposal.

Policy 12(b)(vii) of the General Policy for National Parks 2005 provides particular direction, since it requires a management plan to identify the need and justification for any new wilderness area. It is not, therefore, enough that the department may consider it desirable formally to gazette and manage an area as a wilderness area; it must first establish a case for the proposed gazettal and ascertain the views of the public. An example of this is the current draft Fiordland National Park Management Plan, which proposes a new wilderness area in southwest Fiordland. The area is said to offer "a truly challenging wilderness experience through its isolation, size and extreme climate" and is in contrast to the alpine opportunities offered by the park's extant wilderness areas. The key objective of this part of the draft plan is to provide a range of wilderness recreation opportunities for the long term, by maintaining areas with a high degree of naturalness and where there is no evidence of human activity. The primary implementation is "to seek gazettal of the proposed South West Wilderness as a wilderness area."

The legislation described above makes provision for wilderness areas to be revoked.[41] Revocation cannot occur without public notification[42] and the probable need for hearings, and is only likely to occur when it can be established that the area no longer possesses the qualities for which it was set aside. The West Sabine wilderness area in the Nelson Lakes National Park has been revoked because it was not considered robust enough to absorb increasing visitor pressures. In 2004, the New Zealand Conservation Authority decided to recommend to the minister of conservation the revocation of Otehake, New Zealand's first wilderness area in Arthur's Pass National Park and gazetted in 1955. The authority made the recommendation on advice from the department (which had in turn sought the views of the public when it was preparing the conservation management strategy for that area) on the basis that Otehake did not meet the requirements of the Wilderness Policy because of its small size and the presence of developments such as tracks and huts. Despite the loss of wilderness status, the area will be managed as a remote experience zone in accordance with criteria specified in the recreation opportunity spectrum.

Lessons Learned

What Has Worked Well?

The proscriptive nature of New Zealand's legislation on wilderness areas cannot be underestimated. The fact that many disruptive activities including erecting huts, constructing tracks, and using machinery in wilderness areas are statutorily prohibited[43] means that wilderness areas can more easily be preserved in a natural state. Anyone who breaches the legislation will be committing an offense under it and will face penalties of up to one year's imprisonment or a maximum fine of $10,000.[44]

The Wilderness Policy that establishes the basic prerequisites of a wilderness area is also critically important. Its adoption into the various management planning documents prepared by the department enables consideration of areas for inclusion in the wilderness system and gives the public (which appears overwhelmingly supportive of wilderness areas even though the vast majority never visits them) an opportunity to voice its views.

The extreme remoteness of most of New Zealand's wilderness areas is hugely beneficial. Most (but not all) are located in rugged terrain, far removed from road heads and airports. The terrain is often difficult, the weather inhospitable, and access problematic. These factors, coupled with the complete absence of facilities, deter all but the most intrepid. Having buffer areas around the margins of wilderness areas which are managed as remote experience zones in accordance with the ROS system[45] increases the difficulty of access. Purposely not advertising the existence of wilderness areas and avoiding any form of marketing—either to New Zealanders or to overseas tourists—ensures that the number of people who seek them out remains small. Low demand pressures have been created as a result of increased facilities available to front country visitors. All of these matters are in keeping with wilderness management philosophy, which aims to preserve an area's ecological integrity for future generations. Integral to that philosophy is the idea that, although recreation and enjoyment of wilderness areas are key objectives of wilderness management in New

Zealand, they can be achieved without compromising the natural state of an area or the quality of the wilderness experience gained by those who seek it out.

What Are the Challenges to the System?

It is critical to the maintenance of wilderness areas, wherever they may be, that their ecological integrity is sustained or, depending on their condition, enhanced. Significant threats occur from red deer, fallow deer, wapiti, chamois, thar, pigs, and goats, all of which were introduced into New Zealand in the 1800s and early 1900s. They adversely affect the forest understory and contribute to substantial erosion of mountainous terrain. Fortunately, the legislation provides the ability to meet this challenge head-on by enabling restrictions on air access to be lifted temporarily for such management purposes as the control of introduced animals.[46]

Another introduced pest is the Australian brushtail possum, which has firmly established itself in New Zealand and consumes huge quantities of forest cover, so much so that trees not infrequently die from loss of foliage. Possums, in conjunction with stoats (another introduced species), are responsible for attacking the eggs of nesting birds and, as such, pose a threat to that very New Zealand icon, the kiwi. Introduced mustelids and rodents also have a devastating impact on indigenous fauna.

The natural quiet of wilderness areas is increasingly under threat, and protecting it is fast becoming a significant issue in some areas. Under New Zealand's wilderness legislation, aircraft are not allowed to land in or operate on wilderness areas unless it is for some management purpose or for search and rescue.[47] In addition, commercial flights are not allowed below 150 meters (500 feet). But currently, aircraft are not banned from flying over wilderness areas. In places such as Pembroke wilderness area, immediately to the north of Milford Sound in Fiordland, tensions are rising as those who seek a wilderness experience find the constant overflights of tourist aircraft intrusive. Civil aviation authorities have the ability to control such flights (including prohibiting them)[48] but, to date, have been reluctant to act purely to protect a human experience (there are several examples of restricting or prohibiting overflight to prevent adverse effects on fauna).

Another issue associated with aircraft is air access to wilderness areas. Although the department has in place various air access strategies to help address the issue and relies on buffer zones around wilderness areas to manage the problem, some of New Zealand's wilderness areas border the sea. The Glaisnock wilderness area, south of Milford Sound, and Pembroke wilderness area, north of Milford Sound, are two examples. Another is Tasman Wilderness area in the northwest of the South Island. Two proposed wilderness areas, South West Fiordland in Fiordland National Park and Pegasus, Tin Range in Rakiura National Park on Stewart Island will also border the sea.

The location of these wilderness areas gives rise to jurisdictional issues. While the department manages wilderness areas, regional councils have responsibility for management of the coastal marine area (which extends from mean high water springs to the nineteen-kilometer/twelve-mile limit).[49] The boundaries of most national parks (in which the majority of wilderness areas are located) are at mean high water but, unless there is a rule in a regional plan prohibiting aircraft from landing below mean high water in certain areas or requiring aircraft operators to obtain resource consent, such landings are allowed as of right (compared to all flights—recreational and commercial—on land administered by the department, which require concessions to land and take off). In the case of the two wilderness areas on either side of Milford Sound and the proposed wilderness area in Southwest Fiordland, landings in some parts of the coastal marine area are permitted subject to certain conditions, and in other parts require discretionary resource consents to land and take off. In keeping with the purpose of these adjacent areas, the purpose of the landing may also be relevant as to whether resource consents are required. For example, flights dropping off "short stop" passengers (for a stay of less than seventy-two hours) onto tourist boats require consent, whereas dropping off passengers for longer periods is permitted and does not require consent.

As a consequence of increasing tourism flights and flights associated with commercial surface water activities, the number of aircraft landings has increased exponentially. Not only has this created issues with the quality of natural quiet, it has also led to greater numbers of people accessing these wilderness areas because of the absence of a coastal buffer zone. This creates a problem that allows a small minority (with a potentially large carrying capacity) to take advantage of a flaw in the system. Once businesses establish existing use, it is extremely difficult, legally and politically, to curb or curtail such use. Left unresolved, the problem will compromise the natural values of these wilderness areas and detract from the quality of experience that the genuine wilderness seeker is after.

There are some who claim that the establishment of wilderness systems is tantamount to locking up the land and throwing away the key, that the primary aim is to keep people away from such areas, and

Wilderness route-finding in Mt. Aspiring National Park. Photo Crown Copyright, Keith Springer, Department of Conservation, New Zealand.

that the very small numbers of people who are willing to go to great lengths to obtain a wilderness experience constitute an elite. Of course, the counter argument is that within public conservation land there is a range of user profiles, including short-stop and day visitors, thrill seekers, backcountry comfort seekers, adventurers, and remoteness seekers, and that the availability of facilities and how extensive they are depends on the group being targeted. It is entirely appropriate, therefore, that the needs of different groups should be met in different ways.

Another facet of the same complaint is that more people would visit wilderness areas if access was improved or if some facilities such as huts were provided. Thus, as more people seek a backcountry experience, thereby placing pressure on certain areas, it is inevitable that wilderness areas will come increasingly under the spotlight. But three key impediments make change unlikely. First, there is the legislation itself, which is uncompromising as to what is permitted and what is prohibited. Second, there is the issue of what a wilderness area is and how it is managed. Third, there is the issue of resourcing. So long as wilderness areas meet the criteria of the Wilderness Policy and the legislation remains unchanged, there will be no resourcing made available to the department to install facilities. Amending the legislation is unlikely, given the opposition it would provoke from the very people who urged the government in the first place to establish wilderness areas. Moreover, if the majority of the population is truly in favor of wilderness areas, there may be subsequent mandate issues for any government that decides to amend the legislation.

It is conceivable that commercial interests might challenge the system. At present, anyone can apply to the minister of conservation for a concession to operate a commercial activity within a wilderness area.[50] There are significant barriers, however, acting as a check on the minister's ability to grant such concessions. If, for example, the minister is satisfied that the application does not comply with or is inconsistent with the provisions of the legislation or any relevant conservation management strategy or management plan, or if the proposed activity is contrary to the provisions of the act, the application must be declined.[52] Thus, an application to carry out commercial guiding in a wilderness area using mechanized transport would be contrary to the provisions of the legislation (which does not allow mechanized transport).[53] If, on the other hand, someone applied to carry out commercial guiding and could demonstrate that none of the prohibitions in the legislation would be breached, the fate of the application would depend on what the management plan had to say about that sort of activity and whether the number of people to be guided would likely affect adversely the area's indigenous natural resources.[54]

Wilderness areas are off-limits to hydroelectric schemes and mining.[55] However, as the need for power increases in New Zealand and as the returns on minerals may justify new mines, it is possible that pressure will be brought to bear on the government of the day by interest groups to pass special legislation to override operation of the wilderness provisions under the legislation in certain areas.

New Zealand is a signatory to the Convention on Biological Diversity, which recognizes the rights of access to traditional materials on a sustainable basis by indigenous people. This has ramifications for Maori in New Zealand. Because wilderness areas are so remote and difficult to access, some Maori have voiced opposition to the establishment of wilderness areas unless some provision is made for them to access the areas by aircraft. This, of course, is not strictly possible under the relevant legislation, which prohibits the landing of aircraft. If, however, aircraft are carrying out management work, they may land in wilderness areas. This may provide a potential practical solution to the problem of access. If aircraft are being used for management purposes, there seems no logical reason why those aircraft could not land Maori in the wilderness area at the same time.

However, the *taking* of traditional materials, such as plants from a wilderness area, will require authorization from the minister of conservation. As matters stand, it is questionable whether such authorization would be forthcoming even if a conservation management strategy or management plan provided for it, as the minister

must be satisfied that the taking of such plants is desirable or necessary for the preservation of the area's indigenous natural resources.[56]

Probably the biggest challenge facing the wilderness system is
the realization that a fair proportion of public conservation land
already meets and surpasses the IUCN classification of wilderness.
There are huge tracts of land, particularly in Fiordland, the Southern
Alps, and the central North Island that are so remote, wild, and
untouched by humans that they constitute *de facto* wilderness areas.
Other areas, such as the sub-Antarctic islands, are nature reserves and
under New Zealand legislation, they have as much protection as any
formally gazetted wilderness areas.[57]

The unexpressed fear is that without the special protection
afforded by legislation, these *de facto* wilderness areas may disappear
over time as they come under increasing pressure from commercial
interests and recreationalists. One cannot discount this possibility out
of hand. While there are imposing hurdles for such an application (the
purpose for which the land is held, significant adverse effects on natural
resources, and strong statutory management planning documents), the
reality is that the legislation for these *de facto* areas does not proscribe
activities in the way that current wilderness provisions do.

Inherent Trade-Offs?

The sorts of trade-offs inherent in the establishment of wilderness
areas are similar to any trade-offs between those who must compromise in order to achieve their goals. Areas containing significant
mineral wealth could well be excluded from a wilderness area in
return for other land being included. There is the inevitable tension,
described above, between wilderness and commercial operators. The
latter may have established a viable business in an area that is targeted
to become a wilderness area. This may lead to an alternative area of
solitude (in itself an outstanding natural area that might otherwise
not be open to aircraft) being offered to these operators.

The creation of new wilderness areas may engender strong
opposition from local communities, including those some distance

removed from the proposed wilderness area. They may raise concerns that:

- A formal designation is unnecessary because the land is already remote;
- The designation will deny access to existing recreation users;
- Removal of huts and bridges (if they already exist) will make the area unsafe;
- Access may already be limited in other areas such that further access restrictions are unnecessary; and that
- The designation will affect tourism and employment opportunities in the region.

These concerns may be countered in a number of ways. The shifting of the proposed boundaries of the wilderness area, for example, may mean that access for existing recreational use will not be affected. It is also possible that altering the boundaries may lead to exclusion of any existing huts or bridges from the proposed area or, where this is not realistic, that the huts and bridges may be removed (remembering that under the Wilderness Policy the existence of man-made structures is prohibited). Notwithstanding that access may already be limited in other parts of the region, formal designation of a proposed wilderness area will ensure long-term protection of existing recreational opportunities compatible with that type of land status. And if more intensive use and development is projected to occur in other parts of the region not too far distant from the local community, any effect on tourism and employment opportunities as a result of the designation may either be eliminated or reduced.

References

Cessford G., and P. Dingwall. 2001. Wilderness and revocation in New Zealand. *The state of wilderness in New Zealand.* Wellington, New Zealand: Department of Conservation.

Department of Conservation. 2005. Conservation general policy. Wellington, New Zealand: Department of Conservation.

Department of Conservation. 1996. Visitor strategy. Wellington, New Zealand: Department of Conservation.

Molloy, L. F. 2001. Wilderness in New Zealand: A policy searching for someone to implement it. *The state of wilderness in New Zealand.* Wellington, New Zealand: Department of Conservation.

Molloy, L. F., and M. C. Reedy. 2001. Wilderness status and associated management issues in New Zealand. *The state of wilderness in New Zealand.* Wellington, New Zealand: Department of Conservation.

New Zealand Conservation Authority. 2005. General policy for national parks. Wellington, New Zealand: Department of Conservation for New Zealand Conservation Authority.

Barguzinski Zapovednik, *Barguzin mountains near Lake Baikal, Russia.*
Photo by Boyd Norton.

CHAPTER 11

The Russian Federation

Alexander Shestakov[1] and Dmitry Kats[2]

Introduction and Overview

The term *specially protected territories* refers to all types of protected lands in Russia, including natural areas. In situ biodiversity in Russia is conserved by more than 15,500 specially protected natural areas, represented by more than 250 categories of protected area with different protection and management regimes at the federal, regional, and local levels. Most of Russia's protected wilderness falls into this broad category.

The Russian system of protected areas (PAs) has been in existence for nearly a century; the first *zapovednik*, Russia's oldest form of protected area, was established in 1916. There are now one hundred and one *zapovedniks* with a total area of 33.7 million hectares (83.3 million acres) (more than 1.56 percent of the territory of Russia), thirty-five national parks with total area of 7 million hectares (17 million acres) (0.41 percent of the territory), and sixty-nine federal state reserves with a total area of 12.5 million hectares (30.9 million acres) including 2.6 million hectares (6.4 million acres) in marine protected areas (0.58 percent of the country's area). All types of protected natural areas combined make up over 11 percent of the country and employ about 10,000 people. More than sixty protected areas in Russia have some sort of international status.

Russia is one of the few countries in the world that still possesses vast areas of wilderness and has the opportunity to protect them. Forests cover over 70 percent of the territory, and more than 25 percent of the world's old-growth forests are found in Russia. Up to 60 percent of the country's surface area (over 1.7 billion hectares, or 42 billion acres) consists of pristine or slightly modified natural landscapes and ecosystems. Russia's wilderness is not only in excellent condition, but most of it also currently exists outside of legally protected natural areas.

However, many of these areas do have special status, falling under a range of different protection regimes such as the forest law (for protected forests or intact forests that are not in commercial use),[3] water law (water protection zones),[4] land law, fishery law (special marine mammal or fishery zones), and so forth. These areas correspond roughly to IUCN Protected Area Categories IV–VI. Group I forests (protected and protective forests) are a rather efficient means for wilderness conservation in terms of landscape conservation, while allowing use of wildlife and non-timber products. Water protection zones are less effective, as they allow different uses and currently are under severe pressure from residential construction activities. Thus, to ensure full protection of wilderness, especially in developed regions, *zapovedniks* and national park are needed.

Types of Protected Area in Russia

Protected areas in Russia can be grouped into two broad categories. The first consists of the specially protected natural areas (SPNAs), and the second consists of a wide array of lands and water bodies protected by a range of environmental and land management laws. These two categories complement each other, and it is important to understand the important role played by both in nature protection generally, and wilderness protection in particular. Both categories are described briefly below.

Specially Protected Natural Areas

SPNAs in Russia are currently divided into eight main categories established by federal legislation. Many more categories—more than two hundred and fifty—are enacted at the regional and local levels.

- *Strict State Nature Reserves* (Zapovedniks) (IUCN Ia); This category applies exclusively to federal lands. *Zapovedniks* are completely withdrawn from economic use, and are established to preserve representative natural ecosystems, typical and rare landscapes, to protect gene pools for wildlife, and for research and educational purposes.
- *National parks* (IUCN II). National parks are also an exclusively federal designation. The objectives of national parks are to promote nature conservation, research, environmental education, cultural purposes, and regulated tourism.
- *Nature Reserves* (IUCN III, IV). This designation applies to both federal and regional lands. Nature reserves consist of high-value areas for protection or rehabilitation of landscapes or their components, and maintenance of ecological balance. These protected areas include protected landscapes, botanical parks, zoological parks, areas of hydrological importance, and so forth.
- *Nature parks* (IUCN II). This is a regional designation for natural landscapes and properties of high ecological and aesthetic value, and is intended for nature protection, education, and recreation;
- *Natural monuments* (IUCN III). A federal and regional designation for unique and irreplaceable natural landscapes, natural properties, and man-made structures of ecological, scientific, cultural, and aesthetic value.
- *Botanical gardens and arboreta* (IUCN V). A federal and regional designation for environmental institutions designed for the collection of plants to protect biodiversity and for research and educational activities.
- *Curative & sanative lands & resorts* (IUCN V, VI). A federal,

regional, and local designation for areas suitable for treat-
ment and prophylaxis of diseases, as well as recreation, which
has natural curative resources (mineral waters, medicinal
mud, lake brine, curative climate, beaches, inland seas, and
so forth.);
- *Territories of traditional environmental management* (IUCN
  VI). A federal, regional, and local designation for areas established for traditional resource management and for
  maintaining the traditional lifestyles of the indigenous peoples of the Russian North, Siberia, and Far East.

Zapovedniks at the federal level and nature reserves at the federal and regional levels are the PA categories that have wilderness
conservation as one of their primary objectives. Other categories
whose goals relate to wilderness conservation are national parks and
territories of traditional environmental management. Aside from the
above eight categories, each of Russia's provinces also has the right to
establish its own regional and local categories. Some of these categories also have wilderness protection as their primary objective.

Other Types of Protection for Natural Areas

The Federal Law on Environmental Conservation (No. 7-FZ of
10.01.02) states that natural areas of high conservation, scientific, cultural and historic, aesthetic, recreational, sanative, or other value are
subject to special protection. The act further states that a special legal
status, including the status of specially protected natural areas, is conferred via a range of environmental laws, natural and cultural heritage
laws, or other laws to ensure protection of natural areas, and that all
such areas constitute the Nature Reserve Fund. Other types of specially protected areas which are not regulated by the Federal Law on
Specially Protected Natural Areas (1995) (unless they are explicitly
granted the status of SPNA) include:
- Protected water bodies;
- Aquatic protection zones adjoining rivers, lakes, and reservoirs;

- Protected forest sites;
- Specially protected geological sites; and
- Protection zones and districts with regulated economic regimes.

The Russian concept of protected areas is therefore based not only on a broad regime of nature management and protection that includes SPNAs, but also on a range of forest management guidelines to protect forests (for example riparian forests or forests on steep slopes), water protection zones and shoreline protection areas, sanitary protection zones to safeguard sources of drinking water, wildlife sanctuaries, natural landscapes within cultural and historic open-air museums, reserved areas, erosion control, tree stands providing wind breaks for agricultural areas, other lands performing nature protection functions or established as nature protection areas, and so forth. The SPNAs must therefore be seen as an integral part of a much wider system of protected areas.

Higanski Zapovednik, *Amur region, Russian Far East.*
Photo by Boyd Norton.

In addition to providing biodiversity benefits in their own right, protection zones and areas with limited land use as prescribed by the environment, land, and protected area laws are an important tool for safeguarding wilderness and SPNAs generally. In accordance with existing legislation, protection zones may be established by Russian Federation regional authorities to provide buffers to SPNAs[5]. These zones have a dual function: 1) to provide additional safeguards for SPNA natural landscapes and properties, and 2) to provide for the economic and other interests of local communities. These protection zones are established without withdrawing lands included in the zone from the owners, holders, users, or tenants. In some cases, lands under the management authority of Russian Federation regions or municipalities are included in a protection zone. The management and use regime of each protection zone is specified in its charter and is based on general provisions in Russia's environmental legislation.

Wilderness and Russian Protected Areas

As noted above, Russia contains some of the most significant remaining tracts of wilderness on the planet, much of which is conserved as SPNAs or other forms of protection. However, Russian legislation does not use the term *wilderness area*. The Federal Law on Specially Protected Natural Areas (1995) instead uses the term *state strict nature reserves* (*zapovednik*), defined as:

> areas of land, water surface and the airspace above them
> where natural landscapes and properties with high conserva-
> tion, scientific, cultural, esthetical, recreational or sanative
> value are located, which are completely or partially withdrawn
> from economic use by decision of state bodies, and for which
> a special protection regime is established. Article 6.

However, as seen below, several categories of protected area contain large *de facto* wilderness areas, and seek to maintain natural areas in the wildest state possible. The strictest protection of all is provided by the state strict nature reserves, or *zapovedniks*. As the name implies, *zapovedniks* were originally intended as areas corresponding more to IUCN's Category 1a—strict nature reserves rather than Category 1b—wilderness. Their core functions have always been science-based: to provide control areas for environmental monitoring and to allow for other scientific research. However, the Federal Law on Specially Protected Natural Areas (1995) specified that environmental education was also one of the main functions of *zapovedniks*. As a result, limited eco-tourism for educational purposes in *zapovedniks* was given a degree of legitimacy it did not necessarily have prior to 1995, even though some *zapovedniks* have always had visitors.

While traditionalists argue that eco-tourism is inconsistent with the original purpose of *zapovedniks*, which by definition imply a complete withdrawal of the lands, the pressure on all Russian protected area managers to supplement their budgets with their own fundraising has created a situation where eco-tourism will likely increase. The combination of this change in legislation with the new financial pressure on protected areas as protected areas budgets were slashed has made some *zapovedniks* closer to Category 1b—wilderness areas rather than strict nature reserves. Indeed, some of Russia's leading conservationists describe *zapovedniks* as falling into both categories, depending on the particular protected area. This is an ongoing debate, and the subject of some controversy within Russia's conservation community. However, in the context of this discussion, *zapovedniks* are clearly the closest analogous entity to designated wilderness areas, though they are clearly not the only mechanism for wilderness protection in Russia.

Management of SPNAs
Management Authorities for Protected Areas
The Federal Service for Environmental Management and Control (*Rosprirodnadzor*) is the federal agency responsible for managing federal protected areas under the Federal Law on Specially Protected Natural Areas (1995), and the Federal Law on Natural Curative

Resources, Curative and Sanative Lands and Resorts (1995). Territories of traditional environmental management are established and regulated in accordance with the Federal Law on Territories of Traditional Environmental Management (2001).

Management policies as well as all regulations related to PAs are developed by the Ministry of Natural Resources. Most federal state nature reserves are managed by the Ministry of Agriculture. Management of PAs at regional and local levels are provided by the corresponding executive power bodies of regions and municipalities.

Management Guidelines for SPNAs

There are several laws that guide government authorities in their management of SPNAs generally, and provide specific statutory management criteria for SPNA categories of protected areas. Legislation related to protected areas and conservation of wildlife and wilderness in Russia has several levels. At the top of the hierarchy are:

- Federal Law on Environmental Conservation (2002);
- Federal Law on Specially Protected Natural Areas (1995);
- Land Code (2001).

These laws determine the basic principles of the management regimes for the main SPNA categories. Thus, the Federal Law on Environment Conservation (2002) prohibits:

- Withdrawal and privatization of lands from the Nature Reserve Fund, unless the withdrawal is called for under federal law;
- Economic or other activities potentially detrimental to the environment and causing degradation or destruction of protected natural properties of high conservation, scientific, cultural, historic, aesthetic, recreational, sanative, or other value; and
- Privatization of lands within protected natural properties of high conservation, scientific, cultural, historic, aesthetic, recreational, sanative, or other value.

The specifics of management are regulated by laws, generalized decrees (on specific types of activities such as tourism, education, filming, hunting, and so forth) and the charters for individual SPNAs—the statutory framework for each SPNA containing details of management regimes and zoning where appropriate for national parks and nature parks. For example, the general principles for use of natural resources in SPNAs are regulated by the Federal Act on Mineral Resources, Water Code of the Russian Federation, Forest Code of the Russian Federation, and the Federal Act on Wildlife.

State Strict Nature Reserves/Zapovedniks

The basic management requirements for State Strict Nature Reserves (SSNRs) are established by article 9 of the Federal Law on Specially Protected Natural Areas (1995) which prohibits:

- Activities at odds with the objectives and protection regime established by the charter of the SSNR; and
- The introduction of living organisms.

The same article allows:

- Conservation of natural landscapes, restoration, and prevention of changes to natural landscapes and their components caused by human-induced impact;
- Maintenance of conditions providing health and fire safety;
- Prevention of conditions that might cause disasters threatening people;
- Environmental monitoring;
- Scientific and research activities;
- Environmental education;
- Activities providing for SSNR functioning and the daily activities of people living in SSNRs in accordance with the charter of the SSNR in special areas assigned for partial economic use; and
- Visits by persons who are neither SSNR employees or officials nor employees of SSNR supervising bodies, with the permission of such bodies or SSNR managers.

The following activities contradict SSNR objectives and are thereby prohibited (Statute on State Strict Nature Reserves of the Russian Federation):

- Activities altering the hydrological regime;
- Mineral exploration, mining, damaging soil, and rock exposure;
- Large-scale logging, harvesting gum, sap, medicinal herbs, raw materials, and other uses of forest resources (excluding those specified by the statute);[6]
- Hay making; grazing; placing beehives and apiaries; harvesting wild fruits, berries, mushrooms, nuts, seeds, or flowers; and other uses of plants (excluding those specified by the statute);
- Construction and placement of industrial and agricultural enterprises, their branches or properties, house building, road building, overpass building, and so forth, excluding structures required for SSNR maintenance;
- Commercial, sport, and amateur hunting, and other kinds of wildlife use (excluding those specified by the statute);
- Use of mineral fertilizers and chemicals for plant protection;
- Wood floating, rafting;
- Driving domestic animals through SSNRs;
- Unauthorized presence in and transit through SSNRs other than on general-purpose roads and waterways;
- Making zoological, botanical, and mineral collections, excluding those specified by the SSNRs' research themes and plans;
- Flying of planes and helicopters through SSNRs lower than 2,000 meters (6,600 feet) above land or water surfaces without permission of the SSNRs or supervising environment bodies, and breaking the sonic barrier above SSNRs; and
- Other activities disturbing natural processes, threatening natural landscapes and territories, or that are not connected with SSNR objectives.

The Statute on State Strict Nature Reserves in the Russian Federation allows the following activities in some areas of SSNRs in accordance with their individual charters:

- Establishing subsidiary plots for growing food for SSNR employees and members of their families;
- Grazing cattle belonging to the SSNR or its employees, including retired and other persons living in the area;
- Granting plots of arable lands and pastures to SSNR employees, including retired employees if they live in the area;
- Harvesting fuel wood or industrial round wood to satisfy demands of the SSNR or other persons dwelling in the area;
- Gathering mushrooms, nuts, or berries by SSNR employees and other persons living in the area for their personal needs (not for sale);
- Sport fishing by SSNR employees and other persons living in the area for their personal needs (not for sale);[7]
- Conducting ecological excursions; and
- Establishing museums of SSNR nature, including open-air expositions.

National Parks

The protection regime of national parks is established by article 15 of the Federal Act on Specially Protected Natural Areas.[8] A differentiated protection regime based on natural, historic, cultural, and other conditions is established in national parks. Based on these conditions, different functional zones are set up in national parks, including:[9]

- Strictly protected zones with all economic and recreational activity prohibited;
- Protected zones with facilities for the conservation of natural landscapes and areas where strictly regulated visits are allowed;
- Zones for educational tourism intended for environmental education and sightseeing in the national park;

- Recreational zones;
- Protection zones for historic and cultural properties;
- Visitor service zones with lodging facilities, tent camps, and other amenities of tourism, including cultural, communal, and informational services for visitors;
- Economic zone where activities to maintain the functioning of the national park are carried out; and
- Zones of traditional extensive nature management (often related to indigenous peoples), where traditional activities, handicrafts, and related use of natural resources are allowed in designated areas with the approval of the NP administration.

The management regime of national park strictly protected zones is similar to the management for SSNRs. The percentage of each national park zoned for strict protection varies considerably, from 11 to 73 percent.

In national parks, any activity is prohibited if it causes damage to natural landscapes, plant or wildlife resources, cultural, or historic resources and contradicts the objectives and purposes of the national park, including:
- Exploration for and extraction of mineral resources;
- Activity causing damage to soil and rock exposures;
- Activity changing the hydrological regime;
- Assignment of land plots for summer cottages and gardens;
- Building of roads, pipelines, transmission or other communication lines, houses, and other projects unrelated to the functioning of national parks;
- Logging,[10] thinning, gum harvesting, commercial hunting and fishing, commercial harvesting of wild plants, activity disturbing plant and wildlife, making biological collections, or the introduction of living organisms for acclimatization;
- Operating or parking vehicles that are not related to the functioning of national parks; driving domestic animals

outside general-purpose roads or waterways and assigned areas; wood floating or rafting in streams and pools;

- Mass sport events and entertainment, setting up tourist camps, or lighting fires outside designated sites;[11]
- Removing items or artifacts of historical and cultural value.

Allowable uses of such lands are established by a statute endorsed by the state body supervising the national park, with the approval of executive bodies of regions of the Russian Federation.

Nature Parks

The protection regime of nature parks is established by article 21 of the Federal Act on Specially Protected Natural Areas. As in the case of national parks, different protection and use regimes are established in nature parks, depending on the environmental and recreational value of the various natural areas. The following zones are used in nature parks:

- Conservation zones;
- Recreation zones;
- Agricultural zones;
- Protection zones for historic and cultural complexes and resources; and
- Other functional zones.

Any activities with the following effects are prohibited:

- Changes to a historically formed natural landscape;
- Reduction or destruction of the environmental, aesthetic, or recreational value of nature parks; or
- Violating the maintenance regime of historic and cultural monuments.

Activities reducing the environmental, aesthetic, cultural, or recreational value of the area may be prohibited or limited in nature parks as well. Protection regimes and functional zoning are quite specific in nature parks, depending on the considerable differentiation of landscape and recreational values of the area.

The features, zoning, and regime of a nature park are established by the charter statute of the park and endorsed by the appropriate state authorities of regions of the Russian Federation, with the approval of a duly authorized environmental body of the Russian Federation and local government.

State Nature Reserves

The management regime for state nature reserves is established by the Federal Act on Specially Protected Natural Areas (article 24). In accordance with article 24, any activity in state nature reserves is prohibited—permanently or temporarily—if it contradicts the stated objectives of state nature reserves or damages natural landscapes or their components. For state nature reserves in which small indigenous communities reside, use of natural resources is permitted to allow for traditional lifestyles.

The objectives and features of the protection regime for a state nature reserve of federal importance are established by the statute endorsed by a duly authorized environmental body of the Russian Federation, with the approval of the executive bodies of the region of the Russian Federation. The objectives and features of the protection regime of a state nature reserve of regional importance are established by the state body of the region of the Russian Federation that has taken the decision to establish the state nature reserve.

In accordance with the Statutory Framework on State Nature Reserves in the Russian Federation (endorsed by the Russian Federation Ministry of Environment, No. 20 of January 16, 1996), activities prohibited or limited in state nature reserves include:

- Agriculture;
- Logging[12] and other kinds of cutting; gum harvesting; hay making; grazing; harvesting and gathering of mushrooms, berries, nuts, fruits, seeds, herbs, or other plants; and other kinds of plant use;

- Commercial, sport, and amateur hunting; fishing and catching of non-game animals; and other kinds of wildlife use;
- Making zoological, botanical, or mineralogical collections; collecting cultural or archaeological artifacts;
- Assigning plots for buildings, summer cottages, and gardens;
- Hydrological melioration and irrigation works, geological exploration, mining;
- Building of structures, roads, pipelines, transmission, or other communication lines;
- Using chemicals, mineral fertilizers, chemical means of plant protection, and plant growth stimulants;
- Wood floating or rafting;
- Blasting;
- Operating or parking vehicles, anchoring ships or other vessels, tourist camps and fires, other kinds of public recreation; and
- Other activities, including economic, recreational or other

Higanski Zapovednik, *Amur region, Russian Far East.*
Photo by Boyd Norton.

use of natural resources which hamper the protection, restoration, and regeneration of natural landscapes or their components.

Designation Process

The process by which wilderness areas are designated as SPNAs varies depending on the protected area classification. The designation process for all categories is prescribed by the Federal Law on Specially Protected Natural Areas (1995).

The establishment of a new SPNA usually includes the following series of steps:

- Identification of the ecologically important area (usually by a scientific body or interested NGO);
- Submission of a proposal to the appropriate state authorities;
- Inclusion in the plan of protected areas network development (federal or regional government);
- Setting aside of land by government authorities;
- Preparation of documentation;
- Initiation of the SPNA establishment procedure;
- Submission of all supporting documentation for state environmental review (following requirements of the Federal Law on Ecological Expertise, 1995); and
- Decision by the designated authority (federal government for federal SPNA, or regional/local legislative/executive body depending on regional PA legislation).

The Russian Federation's plans to develop the federal protected areas system envisage increasing the number of *zapovedniks* and national parks. Unfortunately, other categories of SPNAs are not really covered by long-term plans. The Russian Federation endorsed a proposal for establishing nine new *zapovedniks* and twelve national parks (Executive Order 725-r of May 23, 2001) between 2001 and 2010, though to date only one *zapovednik* from that list has been established. Regions of the Russian Federation have their own plans and strategies for SPNA development, which are valid primarily for SPNAs of regional and local importance.

Article 2 of the Federal Law on Specially Protected Natural Areas and the Land Code of the Russian Federation specifies that authorities of Russian Federation regions may set aside lands for the future establishment or expansion of SPNAs, and may restrict economic activities in those areas. The law also states that the decision to set aside lands shall be based on endorsed SPNA development plans or territorial nature conservation strategies. However, the mechanisms for such actions have not been detailed, which makes it difficult to apply this norm. Nevertheless, there are successful precedents for this in several Russian Federation regions.

Designation of State Strict Natural Reserves (Zapovedniks)

In accordance with the Federal Law on Specially Protected Natural Areas, *zapovedniks* are established by decision of the Russian Federation (with the consent of a region to the transfer of its area to federal status). The decision is made based on the submission of the authorities of an RF region and duly authorized federal environment body (the same procedure is applied for territorial expansion). The commitment by the regional authorities is preceded by decisions by local authorities based on consultations with users and owners of lands to be withdrawn.

Methodological Instructions for the Preparation of a State Strict Nature Reserve Design (1994) provides general directions for preliminary outlines, recommendations on project sections, and pre-project justification of a *zapovednik's* establishment. The executive bodies of Russian Federation regions establish SSNR protection zones with the consent of local authorities, land users, owners, or tenants whose parcels of land are expected to be included in the protection zones. They also approve the statutes of protection zones.

Designation of National Parks

National parks are established by decision of the government of the Russian Federation, after the Russian Federation region has agreed to convey its area to federal property. The decision is authorized by Russia's federal environment agency (currently the Ministry of Natural Resources) as a result of a submission by the regional authorities. Prior to submission, the regional executive body makes a decision with the consent of local authorities, land owners, users, or tenants whose lands will be included in the national park. The same procedure is applied for expanding a national park. Currently twenty-two of thirty-five existing national parks include third-party lands (sometimes as much as 48 to 58 percent).

Designation of Nature Parks

In accordance with the Federal Law on Specially Protected Natural Areas, nature parks are established by state bodies of Russian Federation regions after submission by the duly authorized federal environment bodies, with the consent of local authorities. The establishment of nature parks and the setting aside of lands is accomplished by the decision of a region with the approval of the Russian Federation. It can also be done on behalf of the federal government by a designated federal agency, usually the Ministry of Natural Resources.

The particular features, zoning, and regime of a nature park are set up by the state body that has established the park with approval of the duly authorized federal environment body and local authorities.

Designation of State Nature Reserves

State nature reserves of federal importance are established by the Russian Federation based on the submission by the executive bodies of Russian Federation regions and duly authorized federal environment bodies (currently the Ministry of Natural Resources or Ministry of Agriculture). State nature reserves of regional importance are established by the executive bodies of the Russian

Federation regions with the consent of local government. The statutes of state nature reserves are endorsed by respective supervising bodies. Most state nature reserves belong to the system of the Ministry of Agriculture; they were initially established as game reserves, which are traditionally part of Ministry of Agriculture's authority.

The Land Code of the Russian Federation specifies that a state nature reserve is established—either with withdrawal of land (with compensation) or without withdrawal from land owners, holders, or users. The boundaries of state nature reserves are marked by warning and informational signs.

Lessons Learned
What Has Worked Well?
The Russian *zapovedniks* and national park systems have a long history of strong legal protection; their large territories are withdrawn from economic use and their ecosystems are well protected. As a result, Russian PAs have become an important and effective tool for wilderness conservation. In addition to providing vital biodiversity protection, Russia's PAs function as:

- Large islands of intact wilderness that provide the core base for the development of ecological networks in Russia;
- Centers for scientific research, providing an invaluable source of long-term environmental data about intact ecosystems and anthropogenic effects on those systems, with long-standing traditions in the theory and practice of nature conservation;
- Places where experiments can be made in developing technologies for sustaining natural resources, or developing new approaches for wilderness conservation; and
- "Incubators" for new conservation ideas and centers for ecological education and public awareness.

The Russian legal system bans withdrawal of PA lands (article 58 of the Federal Act on Environment Conservation and article 95 of the Land Code) for purposes that are not related to SPNA activities and objectives. This principle is an important part of the legal foundation of SPNAs, and should not be subject to the revisions proposed by various industrial lobbies.

What Are the Challenges to the System?

- Delineation of federal/regional powers and authorities. Existing legislation (including the Constitution, Land Code, Act on Environmental Conservation, Act on Delimitation of State Land Ownership, and so forth) specifies that SPNAs are under the jurisdiction of the Russian Federation, the Russian Federation regions, and local government. This provision is central to the creation of an effective SPNA system in the country, and the legislation should therefore preserve this three-level system. Following the principle of federalism, and to ensure greater uniformity, the legislation should provide the necessary rights and powers to the Russian Federation regions to establish and manage their own SPNAs, so that all new categories are created under Russian Federation law, and not by executive bodies or regional laws on an ad hoc basis. The establishment of regional or local SPNAs should be coordinated with a duly authorized federal environment body and, if prescribed by law, the government of the Russian Federation. The system should not undermine the rights of Russian Federation regions, or restrict their rights to joint jurisdiction on SPNAs.
- Special attention should be paid to establishment of new marine protected areas following decisions made at the World Summit on Sustainable Development in 2002 and the Convention on Biological Diversity's Conference of the Parties in 2004. The government of the Russian Federation should set up a special procedure for their establishment.

- Russian legislation does not identify a state authority responsible for the establishment, functioning, and protection of World Heritage sites, or other international designations, such as Wetlands of International Importance (Ramsar sites). As a result, some protected areas with international status remain as regional-level territories. Federal legislation should include a procedure for establishing protected areas of international importance and create a state commission for reviewing such sites.

- Provisions should be adopted to transform the Russian protected areas system from a series of individual sites or natural islands to an integrated national ecological network which is linked to the Pan-European Ecological Network (part of the Pan-European Biological and Landscape Strategy joined by Russia in 1995). Linking Russia's PA system to regional ecological networks increases the PA system's ability to adapt to possible social changes and natural transformations (such as climate change) and helps promote more effective wilderness protection.

- It is necessary to improve PA management and the effectiveness of the PA system generally, to make it a more effective tool for global long-term biodiversity conservation. The first general assessment of the effectiveness of Russian federal protected areas was made by the World Wildlife Fund in 2002–2003, and provides a number of useful recommendations.

- There are often conflicts between protected areas and local communities. It is essential to work with key stakeholders, to convey the importance of PA ecosystem services, and to ensure that they share in the economic benefits of the PA.

- The state budget for protected areas is highly limited and inadequate, especially with respect to infrastructure development and for training personnel.

- There is insufficient societal support, especially organized support, for conservation ideas and activities. In many other countries, nature protection has strong public support, which guarantees the future of existing protected areas and the establishment of new protected areas. In Russia, the main "insurance" for protected areas is wilderness legislation. Given the present-day political situation in Russia, ill-advised decisions by authorities could easily damage the PA system. Bitter past experience (for example, Stalin's orders eliminating 88 of the country's 128 reserves) shows it is easy to destroy the system and extremely difficult to restore it.

- The modern Russian economy is strongly focused on extraction and use of natural resources. As a result, there is constant pressure to eliminate protected areas, weaken protective management regimes, water down environmental legislation, etc. The industrial lobby views PAs as an annoying barrier to economic development.

- There is a lack of enforcement capacity for wilderness protection, and no clear strategy for policing Russia's protected areas.

- Probable forest land privatization threatens the existence and development of the protected areas system, and complicates setting aside prospective territories for establishing new PAs. It is necessary to develop legislation making it easier to set aside lands for future PAs of different categories. It is extremely important to change the approach to establishing PAs where possible, and to begin developing the system in critical areas.

- Continuous efforts to weaken the protected areas regime and legislation to allow more types of economic activities and to convert natural lands currently under protection into some economic developments (private villas, mass recreational facilities, engineering and transport infrastructure, mining, forestry, and so forth). A number of new amendments seriously affecting the status of protected areas in Russia were adopted in December 2006.

Conclusion

There is much debate about the historical and modern role of SPNAs and their future. But there is consensus that the main achievement of the PA system has been the long-term protection of very large intact territories. And despite serious threats to withdraw large areas of the PA system in recent years, there is a low probability of a dismantling of the PA system (although the real effectiveness of the PA system could decline). The PA system has passed through very hard times and has repeatedly demonstrated its ability to survive.

A recent decision of the Russian government to establish a number of new federal PAs gives certain optimism: a new *zapovednik* (the 101st) will be created. There seems to be increasing understanding in society and governmental institutions of the benefits of PAs' ecosystem services (particularly due to market mechanisms like the Kyoto Protocol, increasing regional budget income because of tourism created by PAs, and so forth). PA strategies and modern approaches are

Kamchatka Peninsula, Russian Far East.
Photo by Vance G. Martin.

also actively being developed within the conservation community, and greater international cooperation could help promote the system within Russia, saving it from development in the future.

However, it is also true that there is a negative trend with respect to PAs. For example, preparation for the 2014 Winter Olympics has led to the opening up of several areas to the kind of development for mass sporting events that were previously prohibited. The prohibition to enlarge or build facilities on national park lands that have not been withdrawn from economic activities has also been revoked. Buffer zones are under threat. The authority of park administrators over their lands has been reduced. While efforts at significantly reducing the extent of the PA system have been successfully resisted, the challenge today is to ensure that the ability to manage the system effectively is not eroded to the point where PAs are unable to provide their full range of services and maintain their ecological integrity.

References

Blagovidov A., D. Ochagov, and A. Ptichnivov. 2002. Conservation of forest biodiversity in Russia: input from specially protected natural areas and group I forests. IUCN Office for Russia and CIS.

Dejkin V. V., and V. V. Snakin. 2003. Territorial conservation: terminological explanatory dictionary-manual with commentaries. NIA-Nature, Moscow.

Federal law. 1995. On specially protected natural areas. March 14, 1995.

Federal law. 2001. On territories of traditional land-use practice of small indigenous nationalities of the North, Siberia and Far East of the Russian Federation. May 7, 2001.

Federal law. 2002. On environmental conservation. January 10, 2002.

Land Code of the Russian Federation. 2001. October 25, 2001.

Larin V., R. Mnatsakanyan, I. Chestin, and E. Shvarts. 2003. Environmental conservation in Russia: from Gorbachev to Putin. Moscow: KMK Scientific Press Ltd.

Ochagov, D. M., N. A. Potapova., L. S. Isaeva-Petrova, et al., eds. 2001. Consolidated list of specially protected natural areas of the Russian Federation. Moscow: VNIIlesresurs.

Stepanitsky, V.B. 2001. Article-by-article commentary to the federal law of the Russian Federation "On specially protected natural areas." Moscow: Biodiversity Conservation Centre.

Stepanitsky V. B., and M. L. Krendlin. 2004. The Russian state *Zapovedniks* and the national parks: threats, setbacks, and lost opportunities. (In Russian.) Moscow: Greenpeace.

Shestakov A. S., ed. 2001. Legislation of the Russian federation on biodiversity use and conservation. Analytical review. Federal legislation. Moscow: GEOS.

Shestakov A. S., ed. 2003. Protected areas in Russia: legal regulations. An overview of federal laws. Moscow: KMK Scientific Press Ltd.

Drakensberg Mountains, South Africa.
Photo by Vance G. Martin.

CHAPTER 12

South Africa

W. R. Bainbridge and I. Lax[1]

Introduction

Although Africa still retains some of the planet's largest remaining wilderness areas, South Africa has been developed to a greater extent than much of the rest of the continent, particularly in the past fifty years. During this period, landscape transformation has made major inroads into South Africa's once ubiquitous wilderness resources.

South Africa began to address its high rate of wildlands conservation in the latter part of the nineteenth century. Since then, South Africa has played a leading role in the establishment and management of protected areas (PAs). The first PAs on the African continent were proclaimed by the colonial government of Zululand in 1895, including the first designated African wilderness area, iMfolozi Wilderness Area, which was set aside by administrative arrangement by the Natal Parks Board in 1958.[2]

Despite these early efforts, the total PA system of the country at present consists of just over four hundred individual reserves, totaling about 6.7 million hectares (16.6 million acres), or just under 6 percent of South Africa's land surface, and about 5 percent of its marine and coastal environments.[3] The terrestrial PAs include eleven proclaimed wilderness areas, which have the distinction of being the first legally proclaimed wildernesses on the continent. However, they total just under 300,000 hectares (741,000 acres), or only 0.5 percent of the terrestrial PA system.[4] (The government has publicly stated its intention of increasing the extent of the PA system to the generally accepted international norm about 10 percent of the land surface[5] and also plans to significantly increase the extent of the national wilderness system.)

As with other continents, the characteristic landscapes and biodiversity resources of Africa (especially its big game) are unique to it. South African wilderness is also unique in its own right, and its natural environment differs in many respects from that of the rest of the continent. In fact, South Africa is the only country worldwide that contains an entire floral kingdom (the Cape Floral Kingdom, one of six globally) within its national borders.[6] It also contains all or part of three different biodiversity hot spots and several globally important wilderness areas. South Africa is also a pioneer in transboundary conservation.

Definition and Policy Considerations

The National Environmental Management: Protected Areas Act, No. 57 of 2003 (NEM:PAA) defines a wilderness area as:

> An area designated in terms of section 22 or 26 for the
> purpose of retaining an intrinsically wild appearance and
> character, or capable of being restored to such and which is
> undeveloped and roadless, without permanent improvements
> or human habitation.

Wilderness protected areas in South Africa can be created in a number of ways:

- By designation as a protected area or as a part thereof under the law;
- By classification under the zonation and management regime within an existing state protected area;
- By classification under the zonation and land use management

regime within a private or communal protected area; and
- By agreement and classification under special conditions registered against the title of a private protected area.

Sections 22 and 26 of the NEM:PAA state that the designation of any national park or nature reserve, or part thereof, as a wilderness area may only be issued:

a. to protect and maintain the natural character of the environment, biodiversity, associated natural and cultural resources and the provision of environmental goods and services;
b. to provide outstanding opportunities for solitude;
c. to control access which, if allowed, may only be by non-mechanized means.

NEM:PAA does not prescribe a minimum area for a wilderness area, but states that one of the purposes of South Africa's protected areas generally is "to protect ecologically viable areas representative of South Africa's biological diversity."[7] Accordingly, it may be inferred that individual protected areas must be of sufficient size to satisfy this requirement, though what constitutes an area of sufficient size is not specified, and has not to date been tested in the courts.

Wilderness Values

Biodiversity

Chapter 1, section 6 of NEM:PAA states that the act must be read, interpreted and implemented in conjunction with the Biodiversity Act, No. 10 of 2004 (NEM:BA). Chapter 3, section 17 of the NEM:PAA further specifies that the national protected area system (including wilderness areas) must protect ecological integrity and conserve biodiversity resources, protect areas representative of all ecosystems, habitats, and species in the country, and protect threatened and rare species. NEM:PAA (section 1) also specifies that wilderness areas are to be managed "to retain an intrinsically wild appearance and character or capable of being restored to such," and section 26 states that the purpose of designating a nature reserve as a wilderness area is "to protect and maintain the natural character of the environment, biodiversity, associated natural and cultural resources, and the provision of environmental goods and services."

The designated wildernesses play a significant role in biodiversity conservation in South Africa. Five proclaimed wildernesses (and a candidate wilderness) protect the unique biodiversity resources of the Cape Floral Kingdom.[8] Four designated wilderness areas occur in protected areas which conserve portions of two internationally recognized biodiversity "hot spots".[9] Included are the wilderness areas that protect portions of the Drakensberg Alpine Region, CPD Site Af82[10] within the Ukhahlamba-Drakensberg Park World Heritage Site. Four wilderness zones are scheduled for designation in the Greater St. Lucia Wetland Park World Heritage Site, which protect portions of the Maputaland-Pondoland Region, Site Af59.[11]

Ecosystem Services

Section 1 of the NEM:PAA also discusses the importance of protecting ecosystem services. The NEM:PAA defines ecosystem services in much the same way as the Millennium Ecosystem Assessment, 2003 (MEA)— that is, as the benefits people derive from ecosystems—with the notable exception that water is not included in the NEM:PAA definition.

All eleven wilderness areas play an important role in the provision of ecosystem services, particularly in relation to watershed protection and the sustained yield of high-quality water. South Africa is generally an arid country, and water supplies are a limiting factor to the national economy. These areas were all proclaimed under the National Forest Act, in state forests located in mountain environments, which were originally set aside for protection of the mountain catchments that form the sources of some of the most important rivers of the country.

With respect to cultural services, the act[12] states that wilderness areas provide outstanding opportunities for solitude, considered in many countries to be an essential component of wilderness experience. Most of the mountain wilderness areas also protect important archaeological sites, including the world-renowned San or Bushman rock art. The rock art present in the three Drakensberg wilderness areas in KwaZulu-Natal Province forms part of the cultural resource that was one of the primary attributes for which the Ukhahlamba-Drakensberg Park was awarded World Heritage status. These sites are considered sacred sites by the descendants of the people who once inhabited these areas and whose master artists created the art.

Allowed Uses

The uses permitted within designated wilderness areas are largely of a nonconsumptive nature, including access for nature-based recreation (and by inference, wilderness experience), and ecological goods and services, as above. Section 23 of the NEM:PAA states that a nature reserve (and consequently a wilderness area designated in part or an entire nature reserve) may be set aside to meet the needs for a sustained flow of natural products and services. However, uses that are not permitted include prospecting and mining (without specific permission from the environment minister and the cabinet member responsible for mineral and energy affairs), hunting, and access by vehicle.

No specific protection is given against low flying by aircraft over wilderness areas, though the NEM:PAA states that aircraft must stay 760 meters (2,500 feet) above the highest point of a nature reserve, national park, or World Heritage Site (and therefore any designated wilderness areas included within), unless they are taking off or landing from an approved airstrip.

Relevant South African Environmental Law

Sections 22 and 26 of the NEM:PAA provide explicit statutory guidance with respect to the establishment of wilderness protected areas in National Parks and Nature Reserves. However, these provisions do not address the creation of wilderness zones within protected areas through zonation or management regimes. Moreover, the NEM:PAA is intended to be applied in conjunction with other supplementary or complementary legislation. As a result, a complete understanding of wilderness protected areas in South Africa requires a brief review of the broader framework of protected areas and related legislation.

The Constitution

The Constitution of the Republic of South Africa, Act 108 of 1996 provides for three spheres of government: national, provincial, and municipal. Schedule 4 to the constitution provides for functional areas of concurrent national and provincial legislative competence. The environment is one such area, as are the administration of indigenous forests; animal control and diseases; nature conservation (excluding national parks, national botanical gardens, and marine resources); pollution control; regional planning and development; soil conservation; tourism; and urban and rural development. As a result, both the national and the provincial legislatures may pass laws dealing with the environment and related matters that can affect wilderness.

Section 146 of the constitution establishes the framework for resolving conflicts between national legislation and provincial legislation that fall within a functional area listed in schedule 4, while schedule 5 to the constitution provides for functional areas of exclusive provincial legislative competence. Areas that may affect wilderness include provincial planning; provincial cultural matters (many cultural sites are located in wilderness areas); provincial recreation and amenities; and provincial sport.

Finally, the constitution includes a Bill of Rights[13] that provides for the right to a healthy environment. All other environmental legislation must be consistent with this right. In particular, the National Environmental Management Act, 107 of 1998 (NEMA) outlines a set of environmental management principles applicable to all state agencies.

Statutes Affecting the Management of Wilderness

The following national statutes all have a bearing on the definition, application of law and management of wilderness in South Africa:

- National Environmental Management Act, 107 of 1998;

- World Heritage Convention Act, No. 49 of 1999;
- Environment Conservation Act, No. 73 of 1998;
- National Heritage Resources Act, No. 25 of 1999;
- National Environmental Management: Protected Areas Act, No. 57 of 2003; and
- National Forests Act, No. 84 of 1998.

A range of provincial nature conservation legislation is also applicable to wilderness management, but is outside the scope of this chapter.

National Environmental Management
Act, 107 of 1998 (NEMA)

NEMA is South Africa's national umbrella legislation for environmental management, and section 2 of NEMA contains a broad set of national environmental management principles, applicable throughout the country to the actions of all state agencies that may significantly affect the environment. A number of laws have been promulgated under the NEMA framework, including NEM:PAA and NEM:BA.

National Environmental Management:
Protected Areas Act, No. 57 of 2003 (NEM:PAA)

The objectives of NEM:PAA include the declaration, protection, conservation, and management of ecologically viable areas representative of South Africa's biological diversity and its natural landscapes and seascapes on state land, private land, and communal land. It also seeks to promote sustainable utilization of protected areas for the benefit of people, in a manner that would preserve the ecological character of such areas.[14] The provisions of NEM:PAA must be interpreted and applied in accordance with the national environmental management principles and other applicable provisions of NEMA.[15]

The act provides for the following kinds of protected areas:

- special nature reserves, national parks, nature reserves, and protected environments;

- World Heritage Sites;
- marine protected areas;
- specially protected forest areas, forest nature reserves, and forest wilderness areas declared in terms of the National Forests Act, No. 84 of 1998; and
- mountain catchment areas declared in terms of the Mountain Catchment Areas Act, No. 63 of 1970.[16]

As noted above, both national parks and nature reserves, in whole or in part, may be designated as wilderness. In addition, some of these areas, although not explicitly designated as wilderness, under the law may nevertheless contain wilderness zones managed as such in terms of the management plan for the protected area concerned. The act also makes provision for the declaration of private land as one of the categories discussed below, at the request of the owner[17] and the consequent endorsement of the title deeds of the land in question by the registrar of deeds.[18]

World Heritage Convention Act,
No. 49 of 1999 (WHCA)
This statute facilitates the incorporation of the World Heritage Convention into South African law. It provides, among other things, for the establishment, powers, and duties of authorities whose functions include the administration and safeguarding the integrity of World Heritage Sites.

The NEMA principles are explicitly adopted into this statute[19] and then restated in the text and in some cases elaborated upon.[20] Chapter 4 of the act provides for the preparation and implementation of integrated management plans by the relevant authority. Some of the World Heritage Sites in South Africa contain wilderness areas, either as protected areas in their own right or as wilderness zones, and are subject to appropriate management prescriptions in the respective integrated management plans. An important consideration relates to the requirement that such plans must have due regard for, and seek to integrate and harmonize the requirements of, the Convention and the Operational Guidelines, and with applicable national, provincial, local, and existing organizational planning and development plans.[21]

NEM:PAA makes the provisions of chapters 1 and 2 of that act applicable to World Heritage Sites.[22] This means that the provisions of the WHCA must be read and interpreted in the light of the definitions and other provisions of these chapters of NEM:PAA. This is particularly important as the WHCA is silent about the definition of wilderness or the broader objectives of such protection and NEM:PAA thus adds these aspects to the application of the WHCA.

National Heritage Resources Act,
No. 25 of 1999 (NHRA)
This act lays down general principles for governing the management of national heritage resources, and states that

> The heritage resources of South Africa which are of cultural significance or other special value for the present community and for future generations must be considered part of the national estate and fall within the sphere of operations of heritage resources authorities.[23]

The national estate may include:
- places to which oral traditions are attached or that are associated with living heritage;
- landscapes and natural features of cultural significance;
- geological sites of scientific or cultural importance;
- archaeological and paleontological sites; or
- graves and burial grounds.[24]

All of the above considerations may be relevant to wilderness, and would thus make the NHRA applicable to wilderness areas or zones in such places.

National Forests Act, No. 84 of 1998 (NFA)

The NFA primarily addresses the management and sustainable utilization of natural and plantation forests, but also provides mechanisms for the declaration of natural forest areas as protected areas including forest wilderness. The NFA provides a set of principles that govern its implementation and make it applicable to the activities of all state agencies. Some of the relevant principles include:

- natural forests must not be destroyed save in exceptional circumstances; and
- forests must be developed and managed so as to:
  - conserve biological diversity, ecosystems, and habitats;
  - sustain the potential yield of their economic, social, and environmental benefits
  - promote the fair distribution of their economic, social, health, and environmental benefits;
  - conserve natural resources, especially soil and water; and
  - conserve heritage resources and promote aesthetic, cultural, and spiritual values.[25]

The act empowers the minister to declare certain forests as protected forest areas in one of the following categories: a forest nature reserve; a forest wilderness area; or any other type of protected area that is recognized in international law or practice. This can only be done if the minister is of the opinion that the area is not already adequately protected by other legislation.[26] NEM:PAA makes the provisions of chapters 1 and 2 of that act applicable to protected forest areas,[27] which is particularly important as the NFA is also silent regarding the definition of wilderness or the broader objectives of such protection.

The minister is required to manage the protected area in a manner that is consistent with the purpose for which it was established, and to make rules for the management of the protected area to achieve such purpose.[28] The decision to declare a protected area may not be revoked, nor may a protected area that is state forest be sold or encumbered without the minister following the same procedure as that required for declaring the protected area and the approval by resolution of Parliament.[29] All of South Africa's early wilderness areas were declared through forest legislation.

NEM:PAA Protected Area Categories

National Parks

The minister may declare national parks for the following purposes:

a. [to] protect—
   1. the area if the area is of national or international biodiversity importance or is or contains a viable, representative sample of South Africa's natural systems, scenic areas, or cultural heritage sites; or
   2. the ecological integrity of one or more ecosystems in the area;
b. [to] prevent exploitation or occupation inconsistent with the protection of the ecological integrity of the area;
c. [to] provide spiritual, scientific, educational, recreational, and tourism opportunities that are environmentally compatible; and
d. contribute to economic development, where feasible.[30]

The act specifically provides for the designation of a national park, in whole or in part, as a wilderness area. The minister may issue such designation only after consulting the park management authority. The designation must also seek:

a. to protect and maintain the natural character of the environment, biodiversity, associated natural and cultural resources, and the provision of environmental goods and services;
b. to provide outstanding opportunities for solitude;
c. to control access which, if allowed, may only be by non-mechanized means.[31]

Wilderness zones are presently being planned in at least one national park (see below).

Nature Reserves

The minister may declare nature reserves for the following purposes:

    a. to supplement the system of national parks in South Africa;

    b. to protect the area if the area—

        1. has significant natural features or biodiversity;

        2. is of scientific, cultural, historical, or archaeological interest; or

        3. is in need of long-term protection for the maintenance of its biodiversity or for the provision of environmental goods and services;

    c. to provide for a sustainable flow of natural products and services to meet the needs of a local community;

    d. to enable the continuation of such traditional consumptive uses as are sustainable; or

    e. to provide for nature-based recreation and tourism opportunities.[32]

The act specifically provides for the designation of a nature reserve or part thereof as a wilderness area by the national or relevant provincial minister or member of the Executive Council of a province (MEC) in almost identical terms to those dealing with national parks,[33] except that provision is made for notice of the declaration by the relevant provincial minister being given to the national minister.[34]

As with national parks, wilderness zones are presently being planned in a number of nature reserves.

Special Nature Reserves

The minister may declare special nature reserves for the following purposes: to protect highly sensitive outstanding ecosystems, species, or geological or physical features in the area; and to make the area primarily available for scientific research or environmental monitoring.[35] No candidate or wilderness zones have so far been designated within a special nature reserve.

Protected Environments

The national minister or relevant MEC may declare an area as a protected environment for the following purposes:

 a. to regulate the area as a buffer zone for the protection of a special nature reserve, national park, World Heritage Site, or nature reserve;
 b. to enable owners of land to take collective action to conserve biodiversity on their land and to seek legal recognition therefore;
 c. to protect the area if the area is sensitive to development due to its—
    1. biological diversity;
    2. natural characteristics;
    3. scientific, cultural, historical, archeological, or geological value;
    4. scenic and landscape value; or
    5. provision of environmental goods and services;
 d. to protect a specific ecosystem outside of a special nature reserve, national park, World Heritage Site, or nature reserve;
 e. to ensure that the use of natural resources in the area is sustainable; or
 f. to control change in land use in the area if the area is earmarked for declaration as, or inclusion in, a national park or nature reserve.[36]

We have included this category in this discussion because these provisions are consistent with wilderness objectives and offer a useful mechanism for provisional designation and protection of candidate wilderness areas. In addition, the provision for using this designation to facilitate buffer zones is crucial to the protection and conservation of wilderness. No wilderness zones have yet been designated within declared protected environments.

World Heritage Sites

NEM:PAA provides that chapters 1 and 2 (sections 1 to 16) apply to World Heritage Sites, but that the other provisions of the act do not apply except where expressly or by necessary implication provided for.[37]

Marine Protected Areas

Similar to World Heritage Sites, provisions incorporating parts of the NEM:PAA apply to marine protected areas, except that section 48 dealing with restrictions on commercial prospecting or mining activities applies to marine protected areas. In addition, the act provides that if a marine protected area has been included in a special nature reserve, national park, or nature reserve, the area must be managed and regulated as part of that entity in terms of the act.[38] An example of a proposal to designate a marine wilderness zone is given below in the section on the Greater St. Lucia Wetland Park World Heritage Site.

Specially Protected Forest Areas,
Forest Nature Reserves, and Forest Wilderness Areas

As with World Heritage Sites and marine protected areas, parts of the NEM:PAA apply especially to protected forest areas, forest nature reserves, and forest wilderness areas. Also, if any such area has been declared as or included in a special nature reserve, national park, or nature reserve, the area must be managed in accordance with an agreement concluded between the minister and the Cabinet member responsible for forestry.[39] Several wilderness zones in state forests are proposed for designation. As discussed above, all existing wilderness areas were proclaimed under then Forest Act, No. 72 of 1968.

Mountain Catchment Areas

Parts of the NEM:PAA are also applied to mountain catchment areas.[40] No candidate or wilderness areas have been identified within the proclaimed mountain catchment area system.

NEM:PAA Management Authorities and Management Plans

Management Authorities

The minister must assign the management of a special nature reserve or a nature reserve to a suitable person, organization, or organ of state; and management of a national park to South African National Parks or another suitable person, organization, or organ of state. The minister may also assign the management of a protected environment to a suitable person, organization, or state agency.

Similarly, the relevant MEC must assign the management of a nature reserve to a suitable person, organization, or organ of state and may assign the management of a protected environment to a suitable person, organization, or organ of state.

This assignment must be in writing and the minister or the MEC must give notice to all landowners or other parties whose rights may be affected by the declaration. The party to whom the assignment is made becomes the management authority of the area in question.[41] The concurrence of the prospective management authority is also a key requirement.[42] Within twelve months of the assignment, the management authority must submit a management plan for the protected area to the minister or the MEC.[43]

Management Plans

The object of a management plan is to ensure the protection, conservation, and management of the protected area concerned in a manner consistent with the objectives of NEM:PAA.[44] A management plan must contain the following:

 a. the terms and conditions of any applicable biodiversity management plan;

 b. a coordinated policy framework;

 c. such planning measures, controls and performance criteria as may be prescribed;

 d. a programme for the implementation of the plan and its costing;

   e. procedures for public participation, including participation by the owner (if applicable), any local community or other interested party;

   f. where appropriate, the implementation of community-based natural resource management; and

   g. a zoning of the area indicating what activities may take place in different sections of the area, and the conservation objectives of those sections.[45]

A management plan may contain the following:

   a. development of economic opportunities within and adjacent to the protected area in terms of the integrated development plan framework;

   b. development of local management capacity and knowledge exchange;

   c. financial and other support to ensure effective administration and implementation of the co-management agreement; and

   d. any other relevant matter.[46]

Some of these aspects are not directly relevant to the management of wilderness, but we note them as they reflect the broader goals of NEM:PAA, which places protected area management in the context of the significant development needs in South Africa, and the need to strike a balance between conservation and sustainable development.

In this context the notion of co-management of protected areas—particularly with local communities—is important. The NEM:PAA provides for co-management agreements with a state agency, a local community, an individual, or other party, provided that such co-management does not lead to fragmentation or duplication of management functions.[47]

The NEM:PAA also provides for the minister or relevant MEC to establish indicators for monitoring management performance of national protected areas, provincial protected areas, and local protected areas, and the conservation of biodiversity in those areas. The management authority is required to manage in accordance with such indicators and to report annually on its performance against them. Provision is made for the external auditing of such performance.[48] Where performance is not up to standard, the minister or relevant MEC is required to notify the management authority accordingly and indicate corrective measures. Continued failure to perform adequately can result in the management authority losing its mandate.[49]

Access and Use

NEM:PAA provides for the regulation of access to all protected areas and sets requirements for permits, depending on the category of area concerned.[50]

Use of Aircraft

The act provides that a special nature reserve, national park, or World Heritage Site includes the air space above the reserve, park, or site to a level of 760 meters (2,500 feet) above the area's highest point. No one may fly below this level, except as needed to land or take off under conditions determined by the management authority. These restrictions do not apply to emergencies or to a person acting on the instructions of the management authority. In addition, the minister, acting with the concurrence of the Cabinet member responsible for civil aviation, may prescribe further reasonable restrictions on flying over protected areas.[51] This offers the potential for increased protection against this intrusive noise and visual pollution.

Restrictions

No person may conduct commercial prospecting or mining activities in any of the protected areas categories except a protected environment, in which case the written permission of the minister and the Cabinet member responsible for minerals and energy affairs is required. The minister, after consulting the Cabinet member, is required to review all mining activities that were lawfully conducted in protected areas prior to the implementation of the act. Provision is made for such activities to continue, subject to conditions, and the minister must take into account the interests of local communities and the environmental principles referred to in section 2 of NEMA.[52]

Provision is made for activities in protected areas to be regulated or restricted by national or provincial regulations. Despite such regulations, but subject to the management plan, a management authority may carry out or allow a commercial activity or an activity aimed at raising revenue in the park, reserve, or site. The management authority may also enter into a written agreement with a local community inside or adjacent to the park, reserve, or site to allow members of the community to use biological resources in the area in a sustainable manner. The act provides for such activities on the condition that they do not negatively affect the survival of any species or significantly disrupt the integrity of the ecological systems of the area, and that the management authority must monitor such activities.[54]

Designation of Wilderness Areas

Prior to passage of the NEM:PAA, it was only possible to designate wilderness areas on state forest land—which form a part of the public lands—in the third category above. The eleven proclaimed areas are all situated on this form of land. However, in 2003, a wilderness zone of 2,915 hectares (7,287 acres) was proclaimed in a private reserve (Shamwari Game Reserve) in the Eastern Cape Province, on freehold land by title deed entailment. A second 15,000-hectare (37,050-acre) area was proclaimed by the same landowner on the Sanbona Wildlife Reserve in the Western Cape Province.

As far as we are aware, inventories of wilderness resources have been undertaken by—at least—South African National Parks, KwaZulu-Natal Nature Conservation Service, and the Eastern Cape Department of Economic Affairs, Environment and Tourism. Inventories have been conducted at the national as well as at provincial levels with the objective of identifying areas of wilderness character within existing protected areas, in order to provide permanent protection of the remaining wilderness resources that have not been compromised by development such as road construction or tourism infrastructure. Some of the most important of these are the following.

Wilderness Resources in the Kruger National Park

The Kruger National Park, in the custody of South African National Parks, is just under 1.9 million hectares (4.7 million acres)—one of the largest protected areas on the subcontinent. Over the past few years, a planning process has been undertaken to identify portions of the park with relatively unmodified wilderness character, or areas that may be restored to wild state, through a zoning system identified for the purpose.[55] Buffer zones were delineated by a geographical information system (GIS) along the permanent road system and around permanent developments such as tourist camps and management installations. A number of firebreaks—many of which were navigable by four-wheel-drive vehicles—previously employed for fire management purposes have been permanently closed and rehabilitated.

This exercise has resulted in the delineation of a suite of wilderness zones, each of which exceeds 1,000 hectares (2,470 acres). The total area of candidate wilderness zones identified is slightly less than 1 million hectares (2.47 million acres), or just under half the total extent of the park. Investigations are currently underway to determine the most effective means of protecting this wilderness resource. It is likely that one of the options considered will be proclamation of these individual zones under the provisions of the NEM:PAA.[56]

The Baviaanskloof Mountains

This important protected area, just under 190,000 hectares (469,000 acres), was formerly a state forest. In 2005, it was proclaimed a component of the Cape Floristic Region World Heritage Site. It has long been known for its wilderness resources, and following a recent planning exercise, a candidate wilderness zone of approximately 106,000 hectares (262,000 acres) has been identified and proposed for permanent protection under the provisions of the NEM:PAA. This wilderness, which was not previously specifically protected by law, now represents an addition to the national wilderness system.

Another component of the World Heritage Site, Groendal Nature Reserve, formally Groendal Wilderness Area (proclaimed under the Forestry Act, No. 122 of 1984) has also been re-proclaimed as a provincial nature reserve. This contains a wilderness zone of about 27,000 hectares (67,000 acres) to be proclaimed under the NEM:PAA.[57]

The Ukhahlamba-Drakensberg World Heritage Site

This important area conserves portions of the Drakensberg Mountain system. It received World Heritage status because of its globally significant biodiversity resources in an international biodiversity hotspot and its cultural resources, including world-famous San rock art. It is an Important Bird Area and a wetland of international importance proclaimed under the Ramsar Convention.[58]

Four wilderness areas were designated under the Forest Act more than forty years ago—the Mdedelelo, Mlambonja, Mkhomazi and Mzimkhulu Wilderness Areas (WAs). They were subsequently incorporated into the Ukhahlamba-Drakensberg Park World Heritage Site and currently make up just under half the total extent of the park. Subsequently, a planning exercise was conducted similar to that employed in the Kruger National Park, based in Recreation Opportunity Spectrum[59] and Wilderness Opportunity Spectrum.[60] The planning exercise has identified a number of possible candidate wildernesses within the park, the most important of which is an area in the upper mountainous portions of the Giants Castle component of the WHS, just over 41,000 hectares (101,000 acres), which it is intended be proclaimed under the provisions of the NEM:PAA. The areas proposed for proclamation will increase the area of wilderness to approximately two-thirds of the World Heritage Site.[61]

The Greater Santa Lucia Wetland Park World Heritage Site

This is also an important protected area that conserves the biodiversity and cultural resources in a portion of the Maputaland Coastal Plain. It is an internationally recognized biodiversity hotspot, containing two wetlands of international importance proclaimed under the Ramsar Convention and is recognized as an Important Bird Area for migratory birds.[62] Two wilderness zones are proposed within the site. The first includes portions of the world-famous Lake St. Lucia and associated terrestrial areas and wetlands, and is approximately 53,500 hectares (132,100 acres). The second comprises coastal and marine environments of the Indian Ocean, including extensive areas of Maputaland rock coral beds. This will be the first coastal marine wilderness on the African continent.[63]

Transfrontier Wilderness

Promoting transfrontier conservation areas (TFCAs) has been a major focus of the conservation community in southern Africa in the past decade. Six transfrontier initiatives have been launched, involving all of South Africa's immediate neighboring countries—Namibia, Botswana, Zimbabwe, Mozambique, Swaziland, and Lesotho.

Two of the major South African protected areas that will form components of two TFCAs contain wilderness zones or candidate wilderness zones. These are the Kruger National Park, which will form a component of the Great Limpopo Transfrontier Park, discussed above, which borders on Zimbabwe and Mozambique; and the Ukhahlamba-Drakensberg Park World Heritage Site, a component of the Maloti-Drakensberg TFCA. The Drakensberg wilderness area lies along the international boundary between Lesotho and South Africa. So to this extent, transfrontier wilderness is already a reality in South Africa, and may also become a reality in some of its neighboring countries.

In a recent review of transfrontier parks and TFCAs in the southern African region, van Riet[64] noted that in addition to the original six TFCA areas, sixteen further TFCAs are currently being investigated in the Southern African Development Community region. The expected area of TFCAs in the region, should these become a reality, would increase to approximately 120 million hectares (296 million acres), with an increase in the extent of protected areas in the region and a possible corresponding increase in the extent of its core wilderness areas.

Principal Threats
to Wilderness in South Africa

Lack of Awareness of Wilderness Values

A high proportion of South Africans are ignorant of the wilderness concept, are apathetic to it, or consider wilderness a waste of valuable land. This emphasizes the urgent need to expand and supplement awareness and environmental education programs, especially to decision makers and to youth, to promote wilderness values.

Lack of Capacity of Conservation Agencies and Inadequate Government Funding

Transformation programs have had significant impacts on the capacity of nature conservation agencies. The financial support provided by the national treasury to nature conservation has been in decline for a number of years, and has placed the agencies responsible for wilderness conservation in the country under considerable pressure in their attempts to meet wilderness conservation goals. Apart from a range of other competing demands on the national treasury—given South Africa's immense underdevelopment flowing from the legacy of apartheid and colonialism—the misguided notion that "parks should be able to pay for themselves," either through cross-subsidization or self-funding, has been a primary driver of this situation.

Nonconforming and Non-Sympathetic Development in the Protected Area Systems and Peripheries

A range of types of development, mainly tourism-related, has taken place or is planned, both within the protected area system and in its peripheries. Much of this has the potential to negatively affect wilderness resources, or has already exerted some negative impact. This requires vigilance and considerable energy on the part of wilderness advocates to oppose inappropriate development proposals that might threaten the wilderness resource.

Alien Invasive Plants

A range of alien invasive plant species occur in many protected areas or are present in the peripheries and have the potential to threaten native biodiversity resources. Some of the infestations pose a major threat to both biodiversity and water resources, because of the greater evapo-transpiration potential of some of the alien species. Many of the problem plants listed below are persistent and difficult or almost impossible to eradicate, and control measures pose a major drain on the financial resources of the nature conservation agencies. Fortunately, the Departments of Water Affairs and Forestry and of Agriculture have introduced special programs to control alien and invasive vegetation nationwide.

Among the most serious of the problem species are wattle (*Acacia* species of Australian origin), *Hakea* (also Australian), *Chromalaena* and *Lantana* (South American), and *Rubus* (North American bramble). The new NEM:BA has been introduced to, among other things, address the threats posed by alien and invasive plant species to the biodiversity resources. Among the proposals are measures to reduce the importation of potential invasive plants into the country.

Low Flying by Aircraft

Air tourism and demands by tourists to appreciate protected areas from the vantage of low-flying aircraft—which may in turn cause unacceptable levels of noise and visual pollution for conventional tourists—is becoming a major threat to the protected-area system generally. This activity poses a particular threat to the appreciation of solitude by wilderness users.

The NEM:PAA affords protection against the use of aircraft flying at low altitudes over the air space above wilderness zones in special nature reserves, national parks, and World Heritage Sites, but not in other forms of protected areas.

Land Claims

A number of legal claims for restitution of rights have been lodged by previously disadvantaged communities who once occupied areas now designated as protected. Some designated wilderness areas are included in the areas over which claims have been made. However, due to the policies and methods of settling such claims, no changes to the boundaries or area of any of the designated wildernesses have been made. It is not known whether some changes may be required in future. NEM:PAA in particular provides that sections 45 (access to special nature reserve), 46 (access to national park, nature reserve, and World Heritage Site), 49 (regulation or restriction of activities in protected areas), 50 (commercial and community activities in national park, nature reserve, and world heritage site), 51 (regulation or restriction of development and other activities in protected environment), or 52 (internal rules) may not be applied in a manner that would obstruct the resolution of issues relating to land rights (claims) dealt with in terms of the Restitution of Land Rights Act, No. 22 of 1994.[65]

Lessons Learned

The Importance of Legal Protection

The eleven designated wilderness areas set aside some forty-odd years ago have persisted without serious incursion and currently receive standards of wilderness management that vary from acceptable to excellent. In most instances, wilderness areas have not only maintained their quality, but in a number of instances their wild character has improved as a result of protection. Despite fears to the contrary, public awareness, while not optimal, has at least not declined significantly. One of the most important steps taken to conserve the national wilderness resources has been the introduction of laws to protect wilderness areas permanently. The most important of these was the recent promulgation of the NEM:PAA. In contrast, experience has shown that unless wilderness resources are afforded protection by law, there is a strong possibility that development of one form or another will in due course result in the diminishment of wild character over time.

The Importance of Awareness of Wilderness Values

Awareness of the value to society in maintaining wilderness areas for posterity is far from ideal in South Africa. However, the combined effects of initiatives by local and international wilderness-oriented wilderness NGOs, together with the fact that wilderness use is traditional in parts of the country, especially in mountainous areas such as in the Western Cape and KwaZulu-Natal (in which most of the existing designated wildernesses are located), have contributed to ensuring that support is maintained by some key champions.

The fact that provision for the proclamation of wilderness areas on all forms of land (not just state forest land as in the past) has been included in the NEM:PAA, and that several official conservation agencies are currently engaged in programs to extend wilderness zones within existing protected areas, is testimony to the levels of awareness that exist in official circles. This is in no small way related to official policies and strategies to conserve biodiversity resources (especially in biodiversity hotspots) and ecosystem services. That said, there is an urgent need for conservation agencies and NGOs to continue and intensify their interpretive programs and to heighten wilderness awareness programs.

Summary and Conclusions

It has become traditional in the past half-century in South Africa to maintain wilderness areas as part of the national protected area system. The first wilderness areas to be proclaimed on the African continent were designated in this country. However, the first legislation for the designation of wilderness areas was contained in the then Forest Act, No. 72 of 1968, and while it was considered a significant conservation milestone at the time, it had the disadvantage of applying only to state forests and limited the extent of designated wildernesses areas.

Nevertheless, the eleven areas proclaimed over thirty years have been well managed and are in good to excellent condition.

The recent promulgation of NEM:PAA has been an extremely important development for wilderness conservation. It provides opportunities for the designation of wildernesses or wilderness zones in all the protected area categories listed in the act, on all forms of land tenure in the country, and in both terrestrial and marine ecosystems. As a result of this statute, the extent of designated wilderness will increase significantly if present plans to proclaim wilderness zones in a number of existing protected areas are realized. The proposal to designate the first coastal marine wilderness zone in the Greater St. Lucia Wetland Park World Heritage Site, which will be the first marine wilderness on the African continent, is especially noteworthy.

However, while the promulgation of NEM:PAA is a notable milestone, the official designation of protected areas as wilderness is not strongly entrenched. Furthermore, the act is in the early stages of implementation and is largely untested. It remains to be seen if the optimism its promulgation has elicited is borne out over time.

Acknowledgments

The authors acknowledge with thanks the contributions made to this paper by Mr. Cormac Cullinan through his presentation made to the Roundtable on International Wilderness Law and Policy, in Washington, DC, United States, in November 2004, which forms a part of the source material on which this paper is based. Information was also provided by Drs. F. Venter and S. Freitag-Ronaldson of South African National Parks; Ms. S. Kreuger of Ezemvelo KwaZulu-Natal Wildlife; Mr. A. Skownow of WILD South Africa; and Mr. Peter Hartley of the Greater St. Lucia Wetland Park World Heritage Site Management Authority. The kind assistance of The WILD Foundation for funding the attendance of two delegates to the round table in 2004 is also acknowledged.

References

Bainbridge, W. R. 2001. An update on wilderness conservation in the new South Africa. *International Journal of Wilderness* 7 (3).

————. 2002. Wilderness in South Africa. In *Wilderness Management: Stewardship and Protection of Resources and Values, Third Edition*, John C. Hendee and Chad P. Dawson. Golden, CO: Fulcrum Publishing.

Barnes, K. N., ed. 1998. *The important bird areas of southern Africa.* Johannesburg, South Africa: BirdLife South Africa.

Christ C., O. Hillell, S. Matus, and J. Sweeting. 2003. *Tourism and biodiversity: mapping tourism's global footprint.* Washington, DC: Conservation International.

Clark, R. N., and G. Stankey. 1979. The recreation opportunity spectrum: a framework for planning, management and research. Gen.Tech.Rep. PNW-98. Portland, OR: USDA, Forest Service, Pacific Northwest Forest and Range Experiment Service.

Cowling, R. M., and C. Hilton-Taylor. 1994. Patterns of plant diversity and endemism in southern Africa: an overview. In *Botanical Diversity in Southern Africa (Strelitzia)*, ed. B. Huntley. South Africa: National Botanical Institute. 31–52.

Department of Environmental Affairs and Tourism. 2002. A bioregional approach to South Africa's protected areas. Mimeo. Pretoria, South Africa: Department of Environmental Affairs and Tourism.

Geddes-Page, J. T. 1979. Natal Parks Board and Wilderness. In *Voices of the wilderness: proceedings of the first world wilderness congress 1997*, ed. I. Player. Capetown, South Africa: Jonathan Ball Publishers. 240–245.

Haas, G. E., B.L. Driver, P.J. Brown, and R. G. Lucas. 1987. Wilderness management zoning. *Journal of Forestry* (December).

Myers, N., R. Mittermeier, C. Mittermeier, G. Fonesca, and J. Kent. 2000. Biodiversity hotspots for conservation priorities. *Nature* 403: 853–858.

Ramsar Convention Bureau. 1990. *Directory of wetlands of international importance—sites.* Gland, Switzerland: Ramsar Convention Bureau.

Van Wyk, A. 1994. Drakensberg Alpine Region, Lesotho and South Africa. In *Centres of plant diversity: a guide and strategy for their conservation, vol. 1*, ed. S. D. Davis, et al. Gland Switzerland: World Conservation Union.

————. 1994. Maputaland-Pondoland Region, Mozambique and South Africa. In *Centres of plant diversity: a guide and strategy for their conservation, vol. 1*, eds. S. D. Davis, et al. Gland Switzerland: World Conservation Union.

Van Riet, W. 2004. Transfrontier (Peace) Parks. In *The Enviropaedia*, ed. D. Parry–Davies. Cape Town, South Africa: Ecologic Publishing.

Sinharaja Natural Heritage Wilderness Area, Sri Lanka.
Photo by Patricio Robles Gil.

CHAPTER 13

Sri Lanka

Cyril F. Kormos[1]

Introduction

Sri Lanka has an ancient tradition of respect for nature and wildlife and of nature conservation. The first wildlife sanctuary was established by King Devanampiyatissa in the Third century BC, which coincided with the introduction of Buddhism to Sri Lanka.[2] Several of Sri Lanka's remaining forest tracts benefited from royal protection as sanctuaries over the centuries. Legal protections for Sri Lanka's flora and fauna began in the late nineteenth century, and today Sri Lanka's biodiversity is protected by two departments: the Department of Wildlife and Conservation and the Forest Department. Most of Sri Lanka's protected areas fall under the Department of Wildlife and Conservation. These include strict nature reserves, national parks, jungle corridors, refuges, marine reserves, buffer zones, and sanctuaries. However, the Forest Department manages forest lands, and because Sri Lanka's forest ordinances did not adequately address conservation,[3] the National Heritage Wilderness Areas Act, No. 3 was passed in 1988.[4] Unfortunately, the act has not been used to a great extent, though it has been applied to a section of the Sinharaja forest, which is one of the largest and most biologically significant forests in Sri Lanka.

Conservation is a significant challenge in Sri Lanka. Sri Lanka is a small island nation whose population has jumped from approximately

3.5 million in 1900 to over 20 million today,[5] putting great pressure on the country's remaining wild lands. At the same time, Sri Lanka is a biodiversity hotspot with very high rates of endemism, making it a global conservation priority.[6]

Passage of the National Heritage Wilderness Areas Act in 1988 was a significant step forward because the act was immediately applied to the Sinharaja Forest Reserve. The reserve, which includes roughly half of the remaining lowland rainforest in Sri Lanka, contains 270 species of vertebrates and about half of Sri Lanka's endemic mammals, and over 60 percent of Sri Lanka's endemic plant species. Passage of the act strengthened protection of the forest, which had been a reserve since 1875 under the Waste Lands Ordinance.[7] The current size of national heritage wilderness area is 7,648 hectares (18,899 acres). The reserve also became a Biosphere Reserve and World Heritage Site in 1988, further adding to its protection.[8] The area covered by this designation covers 8,864 hectares (22,000 acres).

One other protected area uses the term *wilderness* in its title in Sri Lanka—the Peak Wilderness Sanctuary (surrounding Sri Pada or Adam's Peak mountain). This area was not designated under the National Wilderness Heritage Areas Act, though it does protect a significant area of tropical forest.

Definition of Wilderness and Allowed Uses
Definition
Section 2 of the act states that national heritage wilderness areas are established:

> For the purpose of preserving in their natural state, unique
> ecosystems, genetic resources; or physical and biological
> formations and precisely delineated areas which constitute the
> habitat of threatened species of animals and plants of out-
> standing universal value from the point of view of science or
> conservation; for enhancing the natural beauty of the

wilderness of Sri Lanka, and for promoting the scientific
study and enjoyment thereof by the public.

Sri Lanka's definition of wilderness is therefore broad-based. It begins with a strong biodiversity emphasis, citing "unique ecosystems" and "genetic resources" as well as threatened species of "outstanding universal value." The definition then lists three additional purposes: enhancing the natural beauty of Sri Lanka, promoting scientific study, and allowing for enjoyment by the public.

Allowed Uses

In addition to the broad legislative purposes cited in section 2 and listed above, section 4(1)(a)-(r) of the act lists prohibited activities. This section contains broad bans on any form of disturbance to the forest, plants, or wildlife, and bans the sale of any forest or wildlife products. It also bans grazing and grass cutting, hunting, water pollution, road building, and disturbance to boundary markers. Section (4)(2) provides a single exception, stating that management authorities may erect and occupy any building within national heritage wilderness areas if "for the purposes of this Act." Violations and a resulting conviction by a magistrate can result in a fine, imprisonment, or both (section 12).

Designation

Section 2 also provides the mechanism for wilderness designations. The act states that national heritage wilderness areas may be created by order of the minister of lands and development and published in the *Gazette*. However, the minister must do so only after consultation with the ministers of the environment, wildlife conservation, fisheries, agriculture, cultural affairs, and indigenous medicine. In addition to these extensive consultations, the minister's order does not take effect until approved by the president and confirmed by Parliament, and approval and confirmation is also published in the *Gazette*.

Thus, approval of a wilderness in Sri Lanka requires many layers of high-level review and approval before an area can be established. However, given the provisions in section 5(4) requiring that every regulation be approved by Parliament, revoking wilderness status also requires high-level approval. In addition, once established, the act's powers are extensive given that it takes precedence over any other Sri Lankan law with the exception of the constitution (section 11).

Conclusion

Protecting biodiversity in a small island nation with a large population is difficult. On the other hand, perhaps because of its long tradition of respect for nature and wildlife, Sri Lanka has established a network of protected areas covering almost 14 percent of its total land area, and IUCN is working with international partners such as the United Nations to design and implement management plans for regions of conservation importance that are not yet protected, both in the wet and dry zones of the country. While additional national heritage wilderness areas have not yet been created, Sri Lanka remains a pioneer in wilderness legislation in Asia.[9]

Painted Desert Wilderness, Petrified Forest National Park, Arizona, U.S.A.
Photo courtesy of the U.S. National Park Service.

Point Reyes National Sea Shore, California, U.S.A.
Photo by Michael J. Painter,
Californians for Western Wilderness.

Untrammeled Wilderness Character and the Challenges of Wilderness Preservation in the United States

Douglas W. Scott[1] and Jeff Jarvis[2]

The wilderness that has come to us from
the eternity of the past we have the boldness to project into
the eternity of the future.

—Howard Zahniser,
Architect of the Wilderness Act

Background:
A Growing System of Protected Areas

As of February 15, 2007, the National Wilderness Preservation System in the United States comprises 43,496,616 hectares (107,436,642 acres) in 702 units in forty-four of the fifty states.[3] The Wilderness Act of 1964 protects these diverse wildlands to secure for "present and future generations the benefits of an enduring resource of wilderness,"[4] and they are protected by the strongest legal mechanism available in the American system of government—statutory law. These preserved wildlands amount to 4.7 percent of all the land in all ownerships in the U.S.

This record of accomplishment contrasts sharply with the record of federal wilderness preservation before the Wilderness Act became law. Most of the agencies that administer portions of America's federal lands had taken little if any initiative to preserve wilderness areas. The U.S. Forest Service pioneered the establishment of wilderness areas by agency administrative order in the 1920s and 1930s. However, over the twenty-five years prior to the signing of the Wilderness Act on September 3, 1964, the total acreage protected by this means increased by just 2 percent, to a modest 5,915,477 hectares (14,617,461 acres; see Table 1). And these original areas were protected only by agency administrative orders, which could easily be altered by the agency, rather than by statutory designation.

With enactment of the Wilderness Act, Congress immediately gave the much stronger protection of statutory law to a portion of those earlier, administratively protected areas—3,698,714 hectares (9,139,721 acres). Since then, Congress has passed more than 125 additional wilderness designation laws, adding 39,866,673 hectares (98,470,683 acres) to the national wilderness system—nearly twelve times as much!

And as the table below indicates, the wilderness system of the United States continues to grow. The most recent addition was approximately 200,000 hectares (over 500,000 acres) of wilderness areas added by the White Pine County Conservation, Recreation and Development Act of 2006, signed by President George W. Bush on December 20, 2006.

Table 1
Historic Progress of Wilderness Protection
in the United States

Agency	As of January 1940	As of September 1964	As of February Feb 15, 2007
U.S. Forest Service: **Wilderness areas** (administratively designated before 9/64; statutory after)	0	9,139,721	35,372,522
Primitive areas for study (given interim statutory protection by Wilderness Act)	14,235,414	5,477,740	173,762
U.S. Forest Service—Total	14,235,414	14,617,461	35,546,284
National Park Service	0	0	43,536,647
U.S. Fish and Wildlife Service	0	0	20,730,636
Bureau of Land Management	0	0	7,796,837
Total Acres Statutorily Protected (wilderness *and* primitive areas)	0	14,617,461	107,610,404
Number of States with Areas	13	13	44
Boundary Changes Can be Made	By administrative decision	Only by act of Congress	Only by act of Congress

Notes and Data Sources

Primitive area acreage from U.S. Forest Service. These received statutory interim protection in the Wilderness Act, so are counted here as statutorily protected only after September 1964. Only the Arizona portion of the Blue Range Primitive Area remains under this interim statutory protection. February 2007 data from www.wilderness. net (except Blue Range primitive area, from Web site of Apache-Sitgreaves National Forest.) Millions of acres of lands in all four agency jurisdictions are pending in presidential recommendations not yet acted upon by Congress, or are in official wilderness study areas, and these categories are not counted in this table.

Why the Wilderness Act?

The United States has the good fortune to possess a very large expanse of public lands remaining in the custody of the federal government—one-third of the entire country. Despite incursions from advancing human use, a significant portion of these public lands remains substantially unroaded and wild. The pioneering thinkers of the American wilderness movement sought to protect some of these still-wild lands as wilderness areas—and to find the means of doing so that would most securely protect them as wilderness in perpetuity.

This line of thinking began with Aldo Leopold during his career in the U.S. Forest Service, where he envisioned a system of wilderness areas encompassing several categories of federal lands—the wild portions of national parks and national forests, among others. He proposed that such areas be established by agency administrative order. His efforts led to the first such designation—the Gila Wilderness in 1924. In the 1930s, Bob Marshall, also a forester and, like Leopold, a cofounder of The Wilderness Society, took up Leopold's idea, advocating for protection of more lands and stronger protective policies. Working as officials within federal land management agencies, it was natural that both men initially urged protection by means of agency administrative orders.

However, changing priorities and politics within these agencies could—and soon did—lead to cutting back of earlier administrative wilderness designations to make way for development. Given their goal of preserving wilderness areas in perpetuity, it became increasingly evident to wilderness protection advocates that reliance on agency administrative orders would not—and could not—assure that the protected areas would remain so.

By the mid-1930s, Leopold, Marshall, and other leaders came to doubt whether federal land management agencies could be relied upon to honor these preservation decisions over a sustained time period.[5] One leading conservationist published the stark conclusion that, regarding both wilderness within national parks and national forests:

There is no assurance that any one of them, or all of them, might not be abolished as they were created—by administrative decree. They exist by sufferance and administrative policy—not by law.[6]

Through the 1940s, the idea for a wilderness preservation law— an act of Congress—evolved from this growing disenchantment with reliance on protection promised by agency administrative orders. In the American governmental system, a law enacted by Congress offered a stronger guarantee, both that the protective policies would be sustained and that the boundaries of individual wilderness areas, once established, would not be likely to be reduced. Drafted by leading nongovernmental wilderness advocates, this legislation was first introduced in Congress in 1956 and became law in 1964.

The Definition of Wilderness: "Purity" and the Wilderness Act

How "pure" must an area be to be considered for designation as a wilderness area? Must the ecosystem itself have been untouched by man? Howard Zahniser and his fellow designers of the Wilderness Act followed the guidance of Aldo Leopold, who wrote in *A Sand County Almanac* that "many of the diverse wildernesses out of which we have hammered America are already gone; hence in any practical program the unit areas to be preserved must vary greatly in size and in degree of wildness."[7]

And how did the Wilderness Act deal with this question? Many miss the fact that subsection 2(c), the definition of wilderness, comprises two sentences:

A wilderness, in contrast with those areas where man and his own works dominate the landscape, is hereby recognized as an area where the earth and its community of life are untrammeled by man, where man himself is a visitor who does not remain. An area of wilderness is further defined to mean in this Act an area of undeveloped Federal land retaining its primeval character and influence, without permanent improvements or human habitation, which is protected and managed so as to preserve its natural conditions and which (1) generally appears to have been affected primarily by the forces of nature, with the imprint of man's work substantially unnoticeable; (2) has outstanding opportunities for solitude or a primitive and unconfined type of recreation; (3) has at least [two thousand hectares or] five thousand acres of land or is of sufficient size as to make practicable its preservation and use in an unimpaired condition; and (4) may also contain ecological, geological, or other features of scientific, educational, scenic, or historical value.[8]

The first sentence is an ideal characterization, while the second gives a deliberately more practical definition. There was a vitally important legislative intent behind this arrangement, an intent of Congress carefully explained in 1961 by Senator Clinton P. Anderson (D-NM), who was speaking authoritatively both as the lead sponsor of the legislation and as chairman of the Senate committee that had the Wilderness Act under consideration. In opening hearings on the bill that year, Chairman Anderson definitively explained his legislative intent in these two definitions:

The first sentence is a definition of pure wilderness areas, where "the earth and its community of life are untrammeled by man. ..." It states the ideal.

The second sentence defines the meaning or nature of an area of wilderness as used in the proposed act: A substantial area retaining its primeval character, without permanent improvements, which is to be protected and managed so man's works are "substantially unnoticeable."

The second of these definitions of the term, giving the meaning used in the act, is somewhat less "severe" or "pure" than the first.[9]

Commenting on the two-part structure of the definition during the final Senate hearing on the Wilderness Act in 1963, Zahniser noted that:

> In this definition the first sentence is definitive of the
> meaning of the concept of wilderness, its essence, its essential
> nature—a definition that makes plain the character of lands
> with which the bill deals, the ideal. The second sentence is
> descriptive of the areas to which this definition applies—a
> listing of the specifications of wilderness areas; it sets forth
> the distinguishing features of areas that have the character of
> wilderness.
>
> The first sentence defines the character of wilderness, the
> second describes the characteristics of an area of wilderness.[10]

The practical effect of this distinction, as repeatedly under-scored by Congress as it shaped and explained subsequent wilderness designation laws, is that "impure" lands showing the impact of human uses, such as past human settlement, are not barred from protection under the Wilderness Act.[11]

Designation of Wilderness Areas
The Key to Preservation in Perpetuity: Statutory Protection

Acts of Congress are very difficult to enact. The Founding Fathers deliberately designed the American legislative process with an inherent inertia, requiring success at every one of many procedural steps and thus giving an advantage to opponents of proposed legislation. For just this reason, the Wilderness Act, which was strongly opposed by development interests, took eight years to become law. Howard Zahniser, observed that an:

> outstanding characteristic that I have learned to emphasize in
> our Congressional government—in our whole government—
> that is this: it is very difficult for anybody in our form of
> government to get anything done that anybody doesn't want

done. Now you can see right away, that's a pretty good
characteristic of a large democratic government established by
a people who have learned to fear tyranny and to fear over-
government.[11]

Under the Wilderness Act, a new act of Congress is required to
add any land to extend its protection to additional land. This places
the burden on those who advocate wilderness protection for additional areas. Yet, that very burden is the single most important fact
about American wilderness preservation policy, for the Wilderness
Act also specifies that the boundary of a wilderness area can only be
changed by another act of Congress. Thus, once an area has been protected by Congress, the burden of the inherent legislative inertia shifts
to those who might seek to weaken its protection or alter its
boundary. Such changes have occurred about a dozen times over
forty-one years, but all have been minor and in most cases involved
correction of errors in the original boundary.[12] [BOOK: 15–18]

The Politics of Wilderness Preservation

The authors of the Wilderness Act did not come from the federal
agencies or Congress, but from the citizen conservation movement.
Indeed, both Leopold and Marshall were founders of The Wilderness
Society, for they understood the need for strong advocacy from outside the government. In 1947, this organization resolved to initiate a
campaign for a nationwide system of wilderness area, to be protected
by a wilderness law. They also understood that the nature of
Congressional politics carried with it inherent implications:

- Legislation will best progress if it has broad and bipartisan
  support within Congress.
- Congress is moved by many forces, but strong grassroots citizen advocacy from across the country is essential.
- Congress does not enact sweepingly visionary legislation, but
  acts incrementally, through "the art of the possible."
- Where legislation primarily impacts one state or locality,

other members of Congress strongly tend to defer on the details to the members of that state's Congressional delegation. Absent support from a state's congressional delegation, a wilderness designation bill introduced by others is highly unlikely to make any headway, including hearings and committee consideration.

· The essential lubricant which allows any law to be enacted by a diverse legislative body is accommodation and compromise.

These are immutable pragmatic realities of American legislative politics. [BOOK: 114–122] They have come into play with every one of the more than 125 laws Congress has enacted over four decades to add lands to the National Wilderness Preservation System. And they came into play in the design and details of the original Wilderness Act itself. It is by working within this system that wilderness advocates have made such progress in preserving more of America's wilderness heritage year after year.

To some wilderness enthusiasts, the very idea of compromise is anathema. They have a very pure ecological and ideological vision of wilderness and, in many cases, strong distaste for the realities of legislative politics. Fortunately, those who conceived and drafted the Wilderness Act—led by Howard Zahniser—took a more practical approach. In this, they continued a fundamental pragmatism that was always central in the thinking of Leopold, Marshall, and the other pioneers of the wilderness preservation movement. This is exemplified by the fact that the Wilderness Act itself embraced compromises that were essential to its successful enactment. Notable among these was the acceptance of certain nonconforming uses such as domestic grazing in those areas where these uses were already established. Indeed, in acknowledgement of political realities, Zahniser included the accommodation for established grazing in his handwritten first draft of the Wilderness Act.

Wilderness Management
Stewardship for a Perpetual Wilderness System: The "Non-Degradation Principle"

The goal of projecting wilderness into the eternity of the future requires more than a congressional decision to designate areas, of course; it takes great care by the agencies administering these special places. As one close confidant of Zahniser's wrote:

> At the same time that wilderness boundaries are being
> established and protected by Acts of Congress, attention must
> be given to the quality of wilderness within these boundaries,
> or we may be preserving empty shells.[13]

The practical challenges of preserving wilderness character are today the work of thousands of devoted employees of the four federal land management agencies—administrators, planners, experts in diverse resource fields, and on-the-ground wilderness rangers. The Wilderness Act sets out one overarching directive for these wilderness stewards regardless of which agency is involved:

> Except as otherwise provided in this Act, each agency admin-
> istering any area designated as wilderness shall be responsible
> for preserving the wilderness character of the area and shall
> so administer such area for such other purposes for which it
> may have been established as also to preserve its wilderness
> character.[14]

Zahniser linked this fundamental command to the ideal concept in the first sentence of the act's definition, which would otherwise have no function in the act, an assumption not allowed by the rules of statutory interpretation.[15] As Zahniser told Congress, the ideal definition makes plain the character of lands with which the bill deals and thus functions to give meaning to the act's command that administrators preserve "wilderness character."

The allowance or prohibition of various uses within wilderness areas is central to the protections of the Wilderness Act. A subsection

of the law captioned "Prohibition of Certain Uses" carefully distin-
guishes uses that are flatly prohibited—commercial enterprises and
permanent roads—from others that may be allowed for agency personnel under very limited circumstances, including the use of
chainsaws, motorized equipment and vehicles, among other things.
The agency discretion to use these tools is limited in one of the most
delicate of Zahniser's phrasings:

> Except as necessary to meet minimum requirements for the
> administration of the area for the purpose of this Act
> (including measures required in emergencies involving the
> health and safety of persons within the area), there shall be no
> temporary road, no use of motor vehicles, motorized equip-
> ment or motorboats, no landing of aircraft, no other form of
> mechanical transport, and no structure or installation within
> any such area.[16]

Senator Frank Church (D-ID), a leader in passing the
Wilderness Act, explained the rationale for this provision:

> We intend to permit the managing agencies a reasonable and
> necessary latitude in such activities within wilderness where
> the purpose is to protect the wilderness, its resources and the
> public visitors within the area—all of which are consistent
> with 'the purpose of the Act.' ... The issue is not whether
> necessary management facilities and activities are prohibited;
> they are not—the test is whether they are in fact necessary.[17]

The elegance of this so-called minimum requirement language
lies in its two-part test for allowing exceptions for use of normally prohibited tools by agency personnel themselves. First, is the proposed
exceptional activity necessary and, second, if so, is the means proposed
the minimum tool to achieve that purpose? The federal training center
for wilderness stewards, the Arthur Carhart National Wilderness
Training Center, provides a detailed "Minimum Requirement Decision
Guide" to equip wilderness stewards with instructions and worksheets

to apply this minimum requirement analysis to proposed actions, projects, and activities in wilderness areas.[18]

Taking the command to preserve wilderness character and the two-part wilderness definition together, the result is a non-degradation directive to wilderness stewards. Congress may—and does—designate lands that are less than pure, lands with some fading imprints of man's work or existing nonconforming uses, for these are within the meaning of what Senator Clinton Anderson called the "somewhat less 'severe' or 'pure'" second definition in the Act.

The point of the non-degradation principle is that whatever an area's past history of human impact, once a wilderness area has been designated the goal for stewardship is to manage that area toward the ideal concept of the first definition, so that "the earth and its community of life are untrammeled by man," so that the wilderness is to the greatest extent possible what the etymology of the word suggests: self-willed land.[19]

The Practical Reality of Nonconforming Uses

From the inception of deliberate establishment of wilderness areas, it was perfectly obvious to Leopold and his colleagues that they were seeking to apply this protection to lands on which other, sometimes conflicting uses had already been long established and practiced. As Leopold wrote in 1925:

> An incredible number of complications and obstacles ... arise
> from the fact that the wilderness idea was born after, rather
> than before, the normal course of commercial development
> had begun. The existence of these complications is nobody's
> fault. But it will be everybody's fault if they do not serve as a
> warning against delaying immediate inauguration of a compre-
> hensive system of wilderness areas.[20]

Similarly, Bob Marshall understood that "certain infringements on the concept of an unsullied wilderness will be unavoidable in almost all instances," observing that "almost all the disadvantages of the wilderness can be minimized by forethought and some compromise."[21] The architect of the legislation, Howard Zahniser, executive director of The Wilderness Society, followed this line of thinking. As he explained,

> Where considerations of expediency or recognition of existing
> practices have permitted inconsistent wilderness use—such,
> for example, as domestic stock grazing within designated
> wilderness areas in the national forest system—such uses
> should be recognized as nonconforming and looked upon as
> subject to termination as soon as this can be done and done
> equitably for those immediately concerned. Such noncon-
> forming uses should be permitted only when their temporary
> sufferance appears to be a means of insuring future values of
> the area.[22]

The assertion is sometimes made that if the law designating a wilderness area includes special management provisions allowing nonconforming uses, Congress is allowing activities that degrade that wilderness area. However, when Congress designates a new wilderness area, the act of Congress it passes does not cause those nonconforming uses. Rather, they already exist as physical realities on the ground—and as political realities, too. [BOOK: 130–131]

As he introduced the first version of the Wilderness Act in 1956, Senator Hubert H. Humphrey (D-MN) explained the philosophy that guided the approach to this problem in the legislation:

> Existing uses and privileges are respected in this bill, and
> private rights are protected. … this is not essentially a reform
> measure but rather a measure to insure the preservation of a
> status quo which fortunately includes a great resource of
> wilderness. …
>
> Special provision is made for the protection of existing
> rights and privileges on any areas involved. Grazing within
> the national forest areas is provided for as at present, and
> existing uses authorized or provided for in [national wildlife]

refuges are also permitted. The termination of nonconforming uses is provided for whenever this is agreeable to
those making the uses.[23]

Nonconforming Uses Allowed by the Wilderness Act
Within all wilderness areas:

- Such measures may be taken as may be necessary in the control of fire, insects, and diseases, subject to such conditions as
the administrator may deem desirable (paragraph 4[d][1]).
- Use of aircraft or motorboats may be permitted to continue,
subject to such restrictions as the administrator deems desirable (paragraph 4[d][1]).

Within wilderness areas on those lands administered by the
U.S. Forest Service and the Bureau of Land Management:

- Grazing by domestic livestock under agency permit shall be
permitted to continue, subject to such reasonable regulations
as are deemed necessary by the administrator (paragraph
4[d][4][2]).
- Nothing in the Wilderness Act shall prevent any activity,
including prospecting, for the purpose of gathering information about mineral or other resources, if such activity is
carried on in a manner compatible with the preservation of
the wilderness environment (paragraph 4[d][4][2]).[24]
- The President may authorize prospecting for water resources,
the establishment and maintenance of reservoirs, water-con-
servation works, power projects, transmission lines, and
other facilities needed in the public interest, including the
road construction and maintenance essential to development
and use thereof, upon his determination that such use or uses
in the specific area will better serve the interests of the United
States and the people thereof than will its denial (paragraph
4[d][4]).

In a 2004 report, researchers at the University of Colorado School of Law analyzed the provisions for nonconforming uses that have appeared in wilderness designation laws since 1964. They concluded that

> the principal determinant for which special uses ... Congress addresses in a wilderness bill is the scope and intensity of a particular use (or uses) occurring in a proposed wilderness area prior to designation. For example, there are many instances where the same Congress that insisted on specifically dealing with a special use or a water project in one wilderness bill was silent on the same issue in a different wilderness bill. We infer from that consistent pattern that the composition and predilections of the congressional delegations for the state in which wilderness is being designated also is a critical factor in determining how specific uses will be accommodated.[25]

Conclusions and Lessons Learned

Over four decades have passed since the U.S. Congress established the National Wilderness Preservation System (NWPS) through the Wilderness Act of 1964. One obvious measure of the act's success is that Congress has steadily expanded the NWPS over the years. But what, more specifically, have been the lessons learned from both the passage of the law and its administration over time? How have the agencies responsible for managing the national wilderness resource continued to adjust to the evolving challenges of wilderness management? This section reviews ten key lessons learned over the past forty years.

1. **The Wilderness Act of 1964 worked.** The national policy embedded in the Wilderness Act of 1964 to preserve wilderness worked. It is clearly possible to preserve and protect the wilderness resource. Millions of acres of public lands remain in their natural state as testimony to the success of the act. The public supports wilderness, Congress

will designate additional wilderness, and the agencies can manage wilderness.

The corollary is that the act has not worked for all deserving lands. Our legislative process is designed to be difficult, and many areas have not survived the entire legislative process. For example, Montana is one of two states that has not had a statewide U.S. Forest Service wilderness bill. Montana wilderness bills had been introduced for over two decades, and one bill passed both the House and Senate before being vetoed by the president. 2.4 million hectares (6 million acres) of U.S. Forest Service roadless areas in Montana still await Congressional attention.

2. **The definition of *wilderness* in the act provided a uniform standard.** It is necessary to have a national definition of *wilderness*. In defining the term, the simple beauty in the language of the act has stood the test of time. The act defines *wilderness* a number of ways:

   • In the Ideal: Where earth and its community of life are untrammeled by man ...
   • By Wilderness Criteria: Natural, outstanding opportunities for solitude or a primitive and unconfined

Sangre de Cristo Wilderness Area, Colorado, U.S.A.
Photo courtesy of the USDA Forest Service.

recreation, at least [2,000 hectares or] 5,000 acres or of sufficient size to make practicable its preservation, and may have special values. The criteria are a set of practical standards that can be used on the ground to determine if an area qualifies for designation.

- By Protective Management Criteria: No commercial enterprise, no roads, no use of motor vehicles, no motorized equipment, no landing of aircraft or other forms of mechanical transport, and no structures or installations. These criteria provide a broad understandable wilderness management standard.

- By Exceptions to Protective Management: Established grazing and aircraft and motorboat use can continue. Mining on valid claims can continue. Commercial activities are permitted if they are needed to realize wilderness purposes. These exceptions to the protective management criteria were needed to clarify that Congress intended that these uses could continue within designated wilderness. Without this direction, a variety of users of the public land would have successfully opposed the protection of some areas that have been designated wilderness. The National Wilderness Preservation System would not include more than 40 million hectares (100 million acres) without these assurances.

- With Designated Areas: Wilderness is a real place, with a map and a boundary. Congress creates a new definition of wilderness with each new designation by saying a specific place is wilderness. Wilderness is the legendary Bob Marshall in Montana and the Sequoia-Kings Canyon in California. It is also the lesser known Bisti/De-Na-Zin in New Mexico and the Great Swamp in New Jersey. Ultimately, wilderness is defined by those places that are designated wilderness.

Together, these definitions are very functional. The criteria for size are an excellent example of Zahniser's brilliance as principal architect of the act. Although areas should generally be at least 2,000 hectares (5,000 acres) of federal land, there is no absolute minimum size limit and smaller areas can be designated if they are practicable to manage. Congress has chosen to designate almost 100 wilderness areas that are less than 5,000 acres. The smallest, Pelican Island, is a 2-hectare (5-acre) island managed by the U.S. Fish and Wildlife Service.

The definition also acknowledges that wilderness is not limited to pristine, untouched lands. Rather, to be considered for wilderness designation, lands must appear to be natural with the work of man substantially unnoticeable. This allows wilderness supporters, agencies, and Congress to consider wilderness designation of lands that have had limited human influences. The protective management criteria are successful in part because the direction was written broadly. Nobody anticipated the explosion of all-terrain vehicle use when the act was written. The broad prohibition of motorized equipment and mechanical transport makes it clear that vehicles are incompatible with wilderness, and the broad language of the act has kept wilderness free from the impacts of these vehicles. This definition directs the agencies to exclude activities that are incompatible with wilderness preservation (such as mountain bikes, wheeled big-game carriers, or motorized rock drills) while allowing activities that do not affect the resource (like modern pack stock equipment, watches, and cameras).

In combination, these definitions have been a major success of the act. They provide a clear understanding of what wilderness is and how it is managed. The definitions are broad enough to cover unanticipated uses and specific enough to address on-the-ground issues. Directing that wilderness can only be used in ways that leave it unimpaired for future use and enjoyment establishes a clear management standard and priority of protection of the wilderness resource.

One shortcoming of the definition is the lack of emphasis on biological values. Although biological diversity and ecosystem services are among the many benefits provided by a well-managed wilderness system, the definition of wilderness does not explicitly emphasize these values. As a result, the areas considered for and designated wilderness do not represent the entire biological diversity of the United States. Some species have benefited directly from wilderness designation. Wilderness is one of the key tools that protects the habitat needed by grizzly bears to forage, den, and reproduce successfully. The Marjory Stoneman Douglas Wilderness in Everglades National Park protects the watery habitat of alligators, bottle-nosed dolphins, sea turtles, manatees, flamingos, roseate spoonbills, and hundreds of other colorful birds. The Otay Wilderness in southern California was designated in part to protect a long list of unique and sensitive plant species. These examples and many more demonstrate that wilderness has been a successful tool in protecting the habitat of a wide variety of species. But wilderness designations do not include all ecosystems. Underrepresented ecosystems include America's great prairies, the hardwood forests of the Midwest, and wetlands along the Eastern seaboard.

3. **The act allows for flexibility.** If one of the great strengths of the act was its clarity in providing management guidelines and standards to ensure an integrated national system, an equally important aspect is the act's inherent flexibility. The fact that each wilderness designation requires an act of Congress means that each wilderness designation is carefully debated and reviewed, and that compromises are ultimately reached to facilitate protection of wilderness in that particular place. While individuals or organizations may disagree

with the particular compromises reached as a result of any particular wilderness designation, generally speaking this approach ensures that wilderness legislation is tailored to adapt to realities on the ground while at the same time preserving wilderness values. Perhaps the best example of this flexibility is the Alaska National Interest Lands Conservation Act of 1980,[26] which designated 22.7 million hectares (56 million acres) of wilderness in Alaska, much of it in very pristine condition. This act recognized that, contrary to other parts of the United States, many rural and indigenous users still depended to a significant degree on subsistence use of the land and allowed for these uses to continue. The act also recognized that significant numbers of Alaska's inhabitants still lived in wilderness and allowed for about 324,000 hectares (800,000 acres) of inholdings. The flexibility of the Wilderness Act of 1964, combined with its clear standards, contributes to the act's effectiveness and continued use.

4. **Wilderness reviews are required**. The act established clear requirements for conducting wilderness reviews, including holding public hearings. The act set a deadline for these initial wilderness reviews. This direction was needed to ensure that the agencies completed the reviews in a timely manner. Congress anticipated that even though there is a legal requirement for wilderness review, a congressional deadline to complete the initial wilderness was needed to encourage the agencies to add the wilderness issue to land-use plans. An additional benefit of this direction from the act is that when the wilderness review is completed in a land-use plan, the public has an opportunity to participate in planning for how the public lands should be managed.

Although the act is commonly interpreted to direct that wilderness reviews are continuous and ongoing, the act itself is not in fact clear on this. In 2003, the Bureau of Land Management interpreted the wilderness review responsibility identified in Federal Land Policy and Management Act of 1976 (FLPMA)[27] as a one-time authority that had expired in 1993. This new interpretation has been litigated and is currently being reviewed by the courts. This issue could have been avoided if the act had been more specific and clarified that either agencies have a continuous wilderness review responsibility, or that there is a statutory deadline that ends the agencies' authority to complete a wilderness review.

The act was also not clear on how areas will be managed during the time between a wilderness review and consideration for wilderness designation by Congress. Absent specific direction for management, agencies have wide discretion in how areas are managed while waiting for Congressional attention. In some areas, wilderness values have been lost in the time between a wilderness review and consideration for wilderness designation by Congress. For the Bureau of Land Management, this issue was resolved by FLPMA, which specifically directs that lands with wilderness character must be managed to protect those values until Congress either designates the areas as wilderness or releases them for other uses.

5. **The Act created a National Wilderness Preservation System.** The act directs that wilderness management is the responsibility of each agency and that wilderness areas are managed as part of the National Wilderness Preservation System. The act prohibited the creation of a separate agency for the management of wilderness. This approach to managing wilderness as a system and managing wilderness as a part of each agency's mission has many benefits:
   - Wilderness is managed as a resource, equal to the other resources that each agency is responsible for.
   - The prohibition of a separate agency for the management of wilderness allows the existing land-management agencies to embrace wilderness management as a part of

their mission. If a separate wilderness management agency had been created, each agency would view a potential wilderness designation as a diminishment of its responsibility and would resent transferring the most beautiful wild landscapes to other agencies. Agencies generally oppose actions that reduce their responsibilities, and the agencies would oppose wilderness designation if this designation would lead to the transfer of their lands to another entity.

- Agencies cooperate with and learn from each other. The U.S. Forest Service has a long history of leadership in the use of primitive tools. The National Park Service excels in visitor management. The Fish and Wildlife Service is an innovative manager of wildlife resources. In the last several years, the Bureau of Land Management has become a leader in restoration. Each agency can learn from the successes of the others and strive to manage at equally high standards. In addition, agencies—like businesses—compete to be the best. Interagency cooperation mixed with a little competition results in a stronger national system.

- At the local level, the system promotes consistency in the way wilderness areas are managed. Far from being just an odd assortment of unrelated pieces, wilderness brings agencies together as they work to manage these areas seamlessly. Clark County, Nevada, for example, demonstrates consistent management across agency boundaries. Here, a complex of wilderness managed by different agencies has been designated. The Bureau of Land Management, the U.S. Forest Service, and the National Park Service are working together, with their partners, to write individual management plans for wilderness areas managed by multiple agencies.

- At the national level, the system promotes cooperation

and consistency between the agencies. To improve coordination and communication, the agencies formed an interagency Wilderness Policy Council and an interagency Wilderness Steering Committee. The Wilderness Policy Council is made up of the agencies' senior managers with wilderness responsibilities. The Wilderness Steering Committee is made up of the agencies' senior wilderness staff. These committees discuss issues of mutual interest, coordinate on development of policy, share information, and agree on cooperative approaches to new priorities. Together, the committees work to insure that the individual wilderness areas are managed as part of the National Wilderness Preservation System.

• Finally, management as a system across agency boundaries increases the biological values that flow from a well-managed wilderness system. For example, the patchwork of wilderness areas in southern California together protects a representative sample of the different ecosystems in this biologically diverse region. Another example occurs in Arizona with the Kofa Wilderness managed by the U.S. Fish and Wildlife Service and the contiguous New Water Wilderness managed by the Bureau of Land Management. The Kofa Wilderness, part of the larger Kofa National Wilderness Refuge, provides habitat for approximately 800 desert bighorn sheep. At 209,000 hectares (516,000 acres), the Kofa Wilderness is one of the larger wilderness areas in Arizona, though it does not include the entire habitat used by the bighorn. One of the prime lambing areas for the sheep is located in the adjacent New Water Mountains Wilderness. Together, these two wilderness areas, managed by different agencies, ensure protection of critical desert bighorn sheep habitat.

6. **The act provides standard legislative direction.** Over the years, Congress has developed a set of standard legislative direction or legislative language to guide wilderness management. The appendix in this chapter is a list of this standard language based on the California Desert Protection Act of 1994 (Public Law 103-433) and the Arizona Desert Wilderness Act of 1990 (Public Law 101-628). Most wilderness bills either rely on the legislative direction from the act or on this standard legislative language. Standard language covers diverse topics including designation, management, maps and legal descriptions, livestock management, fish and wildlife, management of acquired lands, withdrawal, and release. The use of this standard language allows a shared common understanding of how wilderness is managed, strengthens management of wilderness as part of a larger system, and helps ensure that future wilderness bills will continue to provide the types of protection universally applied to existing wilderness.

7. **Wilderness fosters partnerships**. Wilderness designation and management require partnerships. Both call for cooperation and coordination with a number of groups and individuals with different points of view, including the presidential administration, governors, public-lands users, and conservation groups. At no time is designation and management simply the job of the agencies.

   Conservation groups in particular are essential for a diverse and healthy National Wilderness Preservation System. Conservation groups educate the public about the wilderness resource and advocate for the resource. National conservation organizations including The Wilderness Society and the Sierra Club provide national leadership in support of the National Wilderness Preservation System. Local organizations like the Idaho Conservation League, the Colorado Environmental Coalition, and the Friends of the

Nevada Wilderness develop and support local wilderness bills, and, after designation, support management of these areas. Organizations such as Wilderness Watch advocate for the use of wilderness-appropriate tools and projects within designated wilderness. The Trust for Public Lands and the Wilderness Land Trust work with agencies and private land owners to acquire private land inholdings after wilderness designation. Education organizations such as The National Outdoor Leadership School, Outward Bound, and Leave No Trace Incorporated teach the public appropriate uses of wilderness. Volunteer organizations such as The Student Conservation Association and Backcountry Horseman assist agencies on the ground to restore wilderness or complete needed wilderness projects. International organizations such as the The WILD Foundation or The Wilderness Society-Australia use the lessons learned from around the world to promote the wilderness concept internationally. Working together, these conservation groups and many others make designation of wilderness and long-term protection of the wilderness resource possible.

8. **Agencies need a support system.** The agencies found that an interagency wilderness support system was needed to ensure long-term protection of the wilderness resource. This support system would focus attention on wilderness science and research, provide wilderness training and education, and improve internal and external communication. In response, the agencies created organizations to address each of these needs.

To help create a foundation of science to inform wilderness management decisions, the agencies formed the Aldo Wilderness Research Institute (http://leopold.wilderness.net). The Institute concentrates on developing wilderness-related science. For example, there have been tremendous global ecological changes since passage of the Wilderness Act. Most of the public lands and most of the wilderness areas are increasingly under pressures from threats as diverse as species extinction, exotic species invasions, global climate change, and unnatural build-up of fuels that may create catastrophic wildfires. The Act did not specifically anticipate these challenges. The institute therefore supports research to help the agencies and the public better manage wilderness in light of these and other significant challenges.

To improve wilderness-related training and education, the agencies formed the Arthur Carhart Wilderness Training Center (http://leopold.wilderness.net). The center trains agency personnel with state-of-the-art information on wilderness management, planning, restoration, and a number of other topics. The center also educates the public on issues related to wilderness.

To improve internal and external wilderness information, an interagency wilderness Web site was developed (www.wilderness.net). This site is an Internet-based tool connecting the natural resource workforce, scientists, educators, and the public to their wilderness heritage through ready access to current wilderness information.

In addition, the *International Journal of Wilderness* (www.ijw.org) evolved as a way to improve communication among wilderness professionals, scientists, educators, environmentalists, and interested citizens worldwide. The journal has grown into a forum for discussing wilderness ideas and events; strategies for planning, management, and allocation; education and research; and other aspects of wilderness stewardship.

9. **Wilderness is one option.** There are many national designations available to protect natural resources. Other protective designations include national parks (National Park Service), national wildlife refuges (U.S. Fish and Wildlife Service), national monuments (any federal agency), and national

conservation areas (Bureau of Land Management). Each of these designations and many others offer different forms of protection and are applied for different reasons. As the highest level of protection available to public lands, wilderness designation is not suitable for all public lands deserving special designation or attention. Wilderness is one of many designations that can be used to achieve different levels of protection of natural resources.

10. **Wilderness possesses diverse values.** There is much to learn about the various values of wilderness. Although wilderness has long been valued as a recreation resource, it is much more than that. Wilderness, for example, plays a large role in maintaining ecological health. Early supporters of wilderness understood this. Aldo Leopold wrote, "A science of land health needs, first of all, a base datum of normality, a picture of how healthy land maintains itself as an organism." Wilderness has become an increasingly important laboratory for the study of land health. More work is needed to better understand the role of wilderness in the protection of habitat for rare plants and animals.

Maroon Bells—Snowmass Wilderness, Colorado, U.S.A.
Photo courtesy of the USDA Forest Service.

Wilderness areas also protect the headwaters of many of the nation's major river systems. Many of the large cities in the United States including Los Angeles, San Francisco, Salt Lake City, Tucson, Seattle, and Denver rely in part on clean water that flows from wilderness areas. Research is needed to better understand the ecological and economic benefits that flow from the clean water provided by wilderness.

Wilderness is increasingly being used as a source for healing, vision quests, and teaching personal responsibility to youth at risk. This is a little-understood but growing use that may have more importance as urban areas continue to expand.

Finally, wilderness is growing in economic significance. It is increasingly apparent that wilderness forms part of the foundation for a higher quality of life that attracts new business as well as the growing benefits of tourists, outfitters, hunters, and fisherman. Additional work is needed to define and quantify the economic benefit of these uses.

Wilderness must be managed. Wilderness designation by itself is not enough. To enjoy the numerous benefits that derive from the National Wilderness Preservation System, wilderness must also be managed. Agencies, local governments, the public, and other partners must continually invest in wilderness stewardship.

On the other hand, deepening ecological sophistication brings ever greater challenges in stewardship of wilderness. For example, the issue of invasive non-native species poses conundrums regarding how far, if at all, wilderness stewards should go in intervening to manipulate the environment toward the goal of restoring what we perceive to be more natural conditions. Yet, in a world warming under the impact of global climate change, that and other man-caused ecological change occur so pervasively that sorting man-caused change from natural ecological progression may in some cases even prove impossible.

The very fact that our ecological sophistication is growing could tempt us, at any given moment, to conclude that we have enough wisdom to know what well-intentioned manipulation is best to achieve some preconceived wilderness ideal. However, this temptation conflicts at the most fundamental level with the self-restraint and ecological humility bound up in the very idea of wilderness. Zahniser believed that well-intentioned manipulation of wilderness could pose a serious threat to the wilderness concept itself, leading to "rationalization of projects to carry out certain current concepts of ... management" conflicting with "the wilderness philosophy of protecting areas at their boundaries and trying to let natural forces operate within the wilderness untrammeled by man." As the ideal, he said, wilderness areas "should be managed so as to be left unmanaged," and that with respect to these areas "we should be guardians not gardeners."[28]

Appendix

Standard Wilderness Language from the California Desert Protection Act of 1994 (Public Law 103-433) and the Arizona Desert Wilderness Act of 1990 (Public Law 101-628).

1. **Designation**. In furtherance of the purposes of the Wilderness Act, the following public lands are hereby designated as wilderness and therefore, as components of the National Wilderness Preservation System:

   a. certain lands in _____ county, _____ (state), which comprise approximately _____ acres, as generally depicted on a map entitled "_____ Wilderness" and dated _____, and which shall be known as the _____ Wilderness. (Section 101(a) Arizona Desert Wilderness Act of 1990)

2. **Management**. Subject to valid existing rights, each wilderness area designated under section _____ shall be administered by the Secretary of the Interior (hereinafter in this Act referred to as the "Secretary") or the Secretary of

Agriculture, as appropriate, in accordance with the provisions of the Wilderness Act, except that any reference in such provisions to the effective date of the Wilderness Act shall be deemed to be a reference to the effective date of this title and any reference to the Secretary of Agriculture shall be deemed to be a reference to the Secretary who has administrative jurisdiction over the area. (Section 103 (c) California Desert Protection Act of 1994)

3. **Maps and Legal Description**. As soon as practicable after the date of enactment of section _____, the Secretary concerned shall file a map and a legal description of each wilderness area designated under this title with the Committee on Energy and Natural Resources of the United States Senate and the committee on Natural Resources of the United States House of Representatives. Each such map and description shall have the same force and effect as if included in this title, except that the Secretary or the Secretary of Agriculture, as appropriate, may correct clerical and typographical errors in such legal description and map. Each such map and legal description shall be on file and available for public inspection in the Office of the Director of the Bureau of Land Management, Department of the Interior, or the Chief of the Forest Service, Department of Agriculture, as appropriate. (Section 103 (b) California Desert Protection Act of 1994)

4. **Livestock**. Within the wilderness areas designated under section _____, the grazing of livestock, where established prior to the date of enactment of this Act, shall be permitted to continue subject to such reasonable regulations, policies, and practices as the Secretary deems necessary, as long as such regulations, policies, and practices fully conform with and implement the intent of Congress regarding grazing in such areas as such intent is expressed in the Wilderness Act and section 101(f) of Public Law 101-628. (Sec 103 (c) California Desert Protection Act of 1994)

5. **Fish and Wildlife**. As provided in section 4(d) (7) of the Wilderness Act, nothing in this title shall be construed as affecting the jurisdiction of the State of _____ with respect to wildlife and fish on the public lands located in that State. (Section 103 (e) California Desert Protection Act of 1994)

6. **Management of Newly Acquired Lands**. Any lands within the boundaries of a wilderness area designated under this Act which are acquired by the Federal government, shall become part of the wilderness area within which they are located and shall be managed in accordance with all provisions of this Act and other laws applicable to such wilderness area. (Section 704 California Desert Protection Act of 1994)

7. **Withdrawal**. Subject to valid existing rights, the Federal lands referred to in _____ are hereby withdrawn from all forms of entry, appropriation, of disposal under the public land laws; and from location, entry, and patent under the United States mining laws; and from disposition under all laws pertaining to mineral and geothermal leasing, and mineral materials, and all amendments thereto. (Section 104(c) California Desert Protection Act of 1994)

8. **Authorizations and Appropriations**. There is authorized to be appropriated such sums as may be necessary to carry out this title. (Section 1208 California Desert Protection Act of 1994)

9. **No Buffer Zones.** The Congress does not intend for the designation of wilderness areas in section _____ of this title to lead to the creation of protective perimeters or buffer zones around any such wilderness area. The fact that nonwilderness activities or uses can be seen or heard from areas within a wilderness area 103 shall not, of itself, preclude such activities or uses up to the boundary of the

wilderness area. (Section 103 (d) California Desert Protection Act of 1994)

10. **Release.** The Congress hereby finds and directs that lands in the _____ , not designated as wilderness by this Act have been adequately studied for wilderness designation pursuant to section 603 (c) of the Federal Land Policy and Management Act of 1976, and are no longer subject to the requirement of section 603 (c) of the Federal Land Policy and Management Act of 1976 pertaining to the management of wilderness study areas in a manner that does not impair the suitability of such areas for preservation as wilderness. (Section 104 (a) California Desert Protection Act of 1994 modified to remove reference to the designation of Wilderness Study Areas)

   a. **Overflights.** Nothing in this Act, the Wilderness Act, of other land management laws generally applicable to the new units of the National Wilderness Preservation System (or any additions to existing units) designated by this Act, shall restrict or preclude low-level overflights of military aircraft over such units, including military over-flights that can be seen or heard within such units. (Section 802 (a) California Desert Protection Act of 1994 modified to remove reference to the National Parks)

Part III

Non-Statutory
Wilderness Designations

Wilderness Zone, Serengeti National Park, Tanzania.
Photo by Boyd Norton.

Note from the Editor for
Chapters 15–17

The preceding chapters consist of case studies of countries that have a national law creating a separate wilderness protected area category, or, in the alternative, a national law allowing for wilderness zones to be established within other categories of protected areas. In South Africa, the law allows for both mechanisms (see Chapter 12).

However, a number of countries use the term *wilderness* without any explicit statutory authority—for example as a zoning mechanism within management plans for protected areas, as a management guideline based on directives in government policy statements, or for wilderness designations made at lower levels of government—such as designations by regional or municipal management authorities without statutory backing from regional or national legislatures. As discussed in Chapter 1, these areas therefore correspond to Class III designations.

In addition to the wilderness laws enacted by Finland and Iceland, and discussed in Part II, Europe also provides many examples of Class III uses of wilderness designations. Sweden, for instance, does not designate wilderness areas and does not have a wilderness law. However, a joint publication by the National Board of Forestry and the Swedish Environmental Protection Agency entitled *Protecting the Forests of Sweden, Legal Protection in the Form of National Parks, Nature Reserves, Habitat Protection Areas and Nature Conservation Agreements* states that 3,328,000 hectares (8,220,160 acres) are managed according to IUCN's Category 1b-Wilderness. Norway has land-use planning policies that seek to preserve "wilderness-like" countryside (defined as places that are at least five kilometers (three miles) away from major infrastructure developments) and areas without infrastructure development that are one to five kilometers (0.6 to three miles) away from major infrastructure development. The Svalbard Environmental Protection Act, in force since 2002, specifically seeks to protect the archipelago's wilderness qualities. A visitor's brochure for the Hohe Tauern National Park in Austria makes mention of the wilderness values being protected in the park. Italy does not have a federal wilderness law, but numerous wilderness areas have been established by municipal authorities or regional forestry authorities, or on private lands (see Chapter 16). Ukraine has developed a national wilderness policy (see Chapter 17), and Scotland has a wild lands policy that shares many characteristics with wilderness policy.

The wilderness concept is also being championed by several NGOs at the European level, including by PAN Parks, an NGO founded by a private sector NGO partnership between the Dutch tour company Molecaten and the World Wildlife Fund, and which was established to provide certification for well managed European national parks. PAN Parks places a strong emphasis on wilderness, defining wilderness areas as those "lands that have been least modified by man" and that "represent the most intact and undisturbed expanse of Europe's remaining natural landscapes" (see http://www.panparks. org/introduction/vision/wildernessconcept). Several other NGOs have been working to increase interest levels in wilderness policy both at the national and European level, including Wild Europe, the Wilderness Associazione Italiana, the Wilderness Foundation (UK), and the Wilderness Foundation (Germany).

In Asia, the law governing protected areas in the Philippines (Republic Act No. 7586, An Act Providing for the Establishment of a National Integrated Protected Areas System (NIPAS), Defining its Scope and Coverage, and for Other Purposes Act of 1992) does not list wilderness as a protected category. However, the definition of a National Park in Section 4(e) does refer to "a forest reservation of natural wilderness character."

The Philippines also previously had a number of wilderness area designations established under a range of presidential proclamations and based on two letters of instruction (LOI 917, 917-A). Most of these were small islands, with the notable exception of two large areas in the Sierra Madre mountains. These wilderness designations were designed to protect special forest types, establishing as wilderness areas: "all mangrove forests essentially needed in foreshore marine life, including special forests which are exclusive habitats of rare and endangered Philippine flora and fauna" as well as "certain areas including critical watersheds and proclaimed watershed reservations" (LOI 917). These areas were removed from all forms of exploitation. Many of these areas, including the Palanan Wilderness Area, have been incorporated into new protected areas under the NIPAS system. Palanan has been incorporated into the Northern Sierra Madre Natural Park, and several of the island areas have been incorporated into the protected landscapes and seascapes. The remaining wilderness areas will ultimately be incorporated into the NIPAS system as well.

Southern and Eastern Africa have at least seven countries with Class III wilderness areas: Botswana, Kenya, Namibia, Tanzania, Uganda, Zambia, and Zimbabwe. The protected areas in Southern and Eastern Africa benefiting from wilderness zones are some of the largest and most iconic parks in Africa, including the Serengeti National Park in Tanzania, the Moremi Game Reserve in Botswana, the Sperrgebiet and Waterberg Plateau National Parks in Namibia, and Kafue National Park in Zambia.

The following chapters summarize some of these non-statutory uses of wilderness, focusing on four countries in two regions where these alternative usages of wilderness are most significant: Southern and Eastern Africa (Tanzania and Zimbabwe) and Europe (Italy and Ukraine).

Nogahabara Sand Dunes, Koyukuk Wilderness Area,
Koyukuk National Wildlife Refuge, Alaska, U.S.A.
Photo courtesy of the U.S. Fish and Wildlife Service.

Wilderness Zone, Serengeti National Park, Tanzania.
Photo by Boyd Norton.

CHAPTER 15

Southern and Eastern Africa

Cyril F. Kormos[1] and Vance G. Martin[2]

Introduction

Much wilderness is protected *de facto* in large protected areas throughout Southern and Eastern Africa, and the region has also been a world leader in developing transboundary protected areas to protect ecosystems, and to facilitate the migration and ranges of large mammals.[3] South Africa also has passed wilderness legislation and has a number of wilderness protected areas (see Chapter 12).

At least seven other countries—Botswana, Kenya Namibia, Tanzania, Uganda, Zambia and Zimbabwe—have either designated wilderness protected areas or have established wilderness zones within protected areas. None of these have done so by statute, however, either creating wilderness zones in protected area management plans or using local designations by Rural District Councils to confer wilderness status. Nevertheless, the protected areas in Southern and Eastern Africa benefiting from wilderness zones are also some of the most iconic parks in Africa, including the Serengeti National Park in Tanzania, the Moremi Game Reserve in Botswana, the Sperrgebiet and Waterberg Plateau National Parks in Namibia, and Kafue National Park in Zambia. Two of these countries are discussed in more detail below: Tanzania, because of its wide use of wilderness zones in its national parks, and

Zimbabwe, because of the innovative use of a wilderness designation by rural tribal authorities.

Tanzania

Tanzania has made a remarkable commitment to nature conservation generally, setting aside over a third of its territory in national parks, game reserves, forest reserves, and other types of protected areas, a far greater percentage than many of the wealthiest countries in the world.[4] In the process of doing so, Tanzania has created some of the largest protected areas in Africa. Because of its strong focus on protecting its biodiversity, Tanzania is pursuing a sustainable, low-impact and carefully managed tourism policy,[5] and wilderness zoning in national parks is an important component in this tourism strategy.

Responsibility for the management of Tanzania's remarkable national parks lies with the Tanzanian National Parks Authority (TANAPA), a parastatal organization entrusted with management

Wilderness Zone, Serengeti National Park, Tanzania.
Photo by Boyd Norton.

responsibility by the Ministry of Natural Resources and Tourism.[6] In 1990, TANAPA established a Park Planning Unit to facilitate management planning and establish guidelines for drafting management plans. TANAPA's mandate is to:

> Manage and regulate the use of areas designated as national parks by such means and measures to preserve the country's heritage, encompassing natural and cultural resources, both tangible and intangible resource values, including the fauna and flora, wildlife habitat, natural processes, wilderness quality, and scenery therein. The park resources should provide for human benefit and enjoyment of the same in such manner and by such means as will leave them unimpaired for future generations.[7]

As a result of these measures, most of Tanzania's national parks now have wilderness zones, and many of these areas are extremely large. The wilderness zone in Tanzania's largest national park, Serengeti National Park, covers 35 percent of the park, or roughly 517,000 hectares (1.28 million acres).[8] The Serengeti National Park's latest management plan emphasizes wilderness values, stating that "large areas of the Park are very remote and form extensive wilderness areas" and that "access to many of these areas is very difficult in the wet season due to impassable 'black cotton' soils."[9] The plan also states that the "wilderness areas have been purposefully underutilized in terms of tourism in order to retain their conservation value."[10]

The wilderness zone in Tanzania's second largest national park, the Ruaha National Park, is even more extensive, at over 600,000 hectares (1.5 million acres),[11] which is 59 percent of the park's total area. The area is not only extremely large, but the park's location in the convergence zone between northern and southern eastern African species, as well as the fact that the wilderness zone encompasses the Isunkaviula Plateau, an isolated area rising to 1,800 meters (5,900 feet) above sea level, makes this wilderness area extremely rich in biodiversity.[12]

Zimbabwe

Zimbabwe's sole official wilderness designation is the Mavuradona Wilderness Area, an area protected and managed by tribal authorities pursuant to Zimbabwe's Communal Areas Management Program For Indigenous Resources (CAMPFIRE) program.[13] The Mavuradona Wilderness Area is therefore of particular interest given its hybrid status as a conservation initiative sanctioned at the national level, but designated and managed at the communal and tribal level through the Mzaribani Rural District Council. As a result of the designation by the Rural District Council, the wilderness area is labeled as such on official Zimbabwean maps.[14]

The Mavuradona wilderness is a mountainous and rugged 50,000-hectare (123,500-acre) area in the escarpment area of the

Olifants River, Kruger National Park, South Africa.
Photo by Patricio Robles Gil.

Zambezi Valley, which is bisected by one road. In Shona, the word *mavuradona* translates to "land of falling waters." The area was established in 1988 and was initially intended as a safari hunting area, but has since emphasized eco-tourism and other wilderness values when safari hunting revenues proved lower than expected. No hunting takes place in the area.[15] Although two other Rural District Councils (Plum Tree and Tjolotjo) have considered following the Mavuradona model,[16] to date there have not been any new wilderness designations by Rural District Councils.

Zimbabwe does have two smaller areas that are informally referred to as wilderness, though they do not appear as such on national maps and have not been formally designated by the relevant Rural District Councils: the Nyatana Wilderness and the Umfurudzi Wilderness Area, which is also referred to as the Umfurudzi Safari Area. Both are safari areas on the Mazowe River in northeastern Zimbabwe, and both are roughly 74,000 hectares (183,000 acres). Nyatana has the potential to be expanded to roughly 100,000 hectares (247,000 acres), and, if linked with areas across the border in Mozambique, could ultimately reach 200,000 hectares (494,000 acres) in extent. Hunting is allowed in both areas, with private safari operators operating with leases. Of these two areas, the Umfurudzi is more threatened, with mining, quarrying, and associated infrastructure, including a right of way for a power line.[17]

Gola del Fiume Rapido Area Wilderness, Italy.
Photo courtesy of Associazione Italiana
per la Wilderness.

CHAPTER 16

Italy

Franco Zunino[1]

Introduction

Promoting wilderness conservation in Italy, a country with a long history of civilization and settlement, is a significant challenge. Few very large areas remain, and almost all of them are impacted by human activity. Moreover, there is no obvious Italian equivalent to the word *wilderness* and no deeply ingrained wilderness culture as there is in countries such as the United States or Canada. Nonetheless, finding a way forward for a wilderness conservation strategy is a high priority in Italy—in particular the Alps in the northern part of the country, in the central Appennini Mountains, and on the island of Sardinia, where critical habitat exists for bears, wolves, lynx, vultures, and other large mammals and raptors. Italy is also an integral part of the Mediterranean Hotspot, and has many endemics—and unfortunately many species on IUCN's redlist: 12 of 39 threatened European mammal species, 15 of the 29 threatened bird species, and 4 of the 14 threatened reptile species.[2] Despite its relatively small size, Italy contains over one-third of all European fauna.[3]

Despite the obvious challenges, Italy has many rural areas throughout the country that still contain wild lands, and in some cases local populations have a deep appreciation for these areas. As a result, there is in fact a strong basis for wild lands conservation in

Italy, and it has been possible to implement a gradual but highly effective strategy to start securing some of Italy's remaining wild areas and, just as important, to develop a wilderness conservation ethic. This has led to the establishment of a number of wilderness areas over the last fifteen years.

Many of the wilderness areas that have been established in Italy are small by international conservation standards, and certainly some of these units might not qualify as wilderness in other countries. However, despite their small size, many of these areas can be expanded over time, as they are part of larger wild complexes. As such, they are in many respects building blocks, providing a foundation for larger wilderness areas to be assembled in the years to come, or, just as importantly, serving as a tool for developing a wilderness conservation culture in Italy.

For a highly populated country that does not have a culture of wilderness conservation, an incremental approach to wilderness protection is necessary. The wilderness ethic must be nurtured, and a wilderness network must be established gradually as awareness, understanding, and acceptance of the concept grow. The good news is that this incremental approach is producing results: new wilderness areas are being established on a regular basis in Italy, providing a model that can followed not only in new areas throughout the country, but throughout the European Union as well.

Background

Origins of the Wilderness Movement in Italy

Italy's wilderness movement began with a booklet written by the author (then an expert naturalist on the staff of the Abruzzo National Park) and published by the former National Department of Agriculture and Forests (which today is divided between the Department of Agriculture and the Department of the Environment) in 1980 entitled *Wilderness, a New Necessity for the Preservation of Natural Areas.*[4] The booklet briefly illustrated the American history of the wilderness philosophy and concept, the importance of wilderness areas, and the history of the U.S. Wilderness Act of 1964. The booklet also illustrated the first proposal for wilderness areas in Italy, as well as criteria for future European wilderness areas.

In 1981, the author began publishing and distributing a newsletter entitled *Documenti Wilderness* ("Wilderness Papers"), designed to raise awareness among Italian environmentalists of both the wilderness philosophy and the broad parameters of wilderness conservation and management. At the 3rd World Wilderness Congress in Scotland in 1983, the author presented "A wilderness concept for Europe" during the Congress's plenary sessions, which was later included in the Congress's proceedings.[5] Momentum from the 3rd World Wilderness Congress inspired the author and several friends and colleagues to found an Italian wilderness society: *Associazione Italiana per la Wilderness* (AIW), which then began working to establish wilderness areas in Italy.

Wilderness Areas in Italy

By December of 2006, there were forty-two wilderness areas covering over 29,000 hectares (71,600 acres) in seven regions of Italy and

Monte Maggiore Area Wilderness, Italy. Photo courtesy of Associazione Italiana per la Wilderness.

fifteen provinces—from the Alps to the coast to the central-southern
Appenine mountains. The very first Italian wilderness area was Fosso
del Capanno, established in 1988, now covering 760 hectares (1,877
acres). This area was first established by a management agreement with
a private foundation covering 118 hectares (283 acres). The area was
expanded when the Regional Forest Authority classified an additional
259 hectares (622 acres), and then expanded again when the
Municipality of Bagno di Romagna added another 383 hectares (919
acres).[6] The largest wilderness area is the Ausoni Wilderness Area
4,230 hectares (10,338 acres). The smallest is Brizzulera, at 0.3 hectares

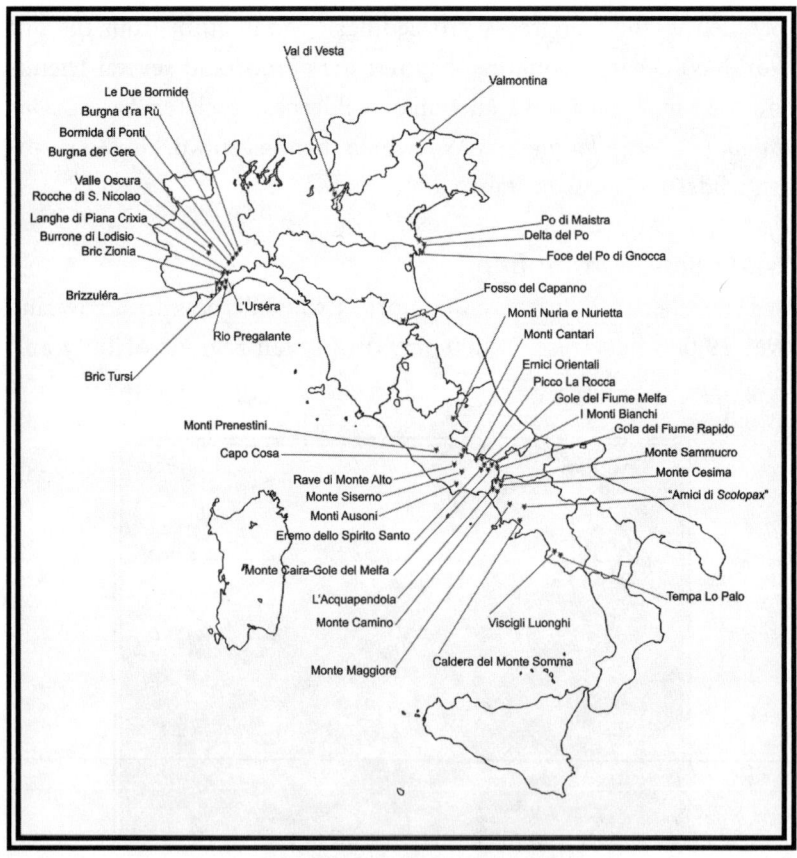

Wilderness Areas of Italy.
Map courtesy of Associazione Italiana per la Wilderness.

(0.741 acres). Most of these areas are protected by municipalities, regional forestry authorities, or private landowners, including, in some cases, AIW. Only one designation is by a national park authority (Vesuvio). The largest *de facto* roadless wild area in Italy is in the Val Grande Mountains (over 30,000 hectares [74,100 acres]), partly protected in a National Park of 14,700 hectares (36,300 acres). AIW played a key role in the protection of the first 11,700 hectares (29,000 acres) of this park, an effort that was strongly supported by several World Wilderness Congress resolutions.

Definition of Wilderness and Allowed Uses

AIW defines a wilderness area as an area with no roads or other industrial infrastructure, no houses or permanent buildings, no ski resorts, no wind-power mills, no industrial artifacts, and no motorized use of the land. AIW therefore adopts strict protection measures to preserve the territorial integrity of the areas. However, AIW is generally open to a sustainable use of renewable natural resources, such as hunting, fishing, gathering forest products, some logging, and grazing. With respect to logging, AIW generally does not allow any cutting in wilderness areas managed by the regional forest authorities, on lands for which AIW holds an easement, or for lands that AIW acquires directly. For municipal wilderness areas, however, only some parts of the forest are completely protected: coppice clear-cutting is permitted, and mature forests may also be logged, though only very selectively. Grazing also generally has low impact and in some cases is useful from a biodiversity perspective. Hunting is generally permitted in municipal wilderness areas, but not in wilderness areas inside parks or other forms of protected areas.

These criteria take into account the fact that in Italy, local people are often favorable to the idea of preserving their wild lands if protection does not mean a strict no-use policy of renewable natural resources, as it does in national parks, regional parks, or nature reserves.

This approach of respecting traditional resource use is consistent with the approach taken by many countries around the world, from Finland to México, to achieve a balance between wilderness values and local uses. However, AIW always requests of the authorities who designate wilderness areas that at least part of the area be preserved as a core area without any logging or other loss of habitat, and that at least some portion of the wilderness area also be closed to hunting.

Designation Process

Italy's wilderness areas have not been created by legislation, but rather by internal administrative initiatives of the authorities that manage municipal, regional, or domain lands. As a result, most designations are therefore made by decrees, drafted in partnership with AIW based on the criteria above, and issued by municipalities or regional forestry authorities. In some instances, wilderness areas designated by municipal councils are then added to town-planning guidelines and regulations.

Bric Zionia Area Wilderness, Italy.
Photo courtesy of Associazione Italiana per la Wilderness.

There are of course some exceptions to this rule: some wilderness areas are established entirely privately by easements held by AIW or by private philanthropies, or in a few cases through direct land acquisition by AIW of wooded areas. As mentioned above, only one wilderness area was established by a national park (two are established inside national parks and five in regional parks, but by forestry or municipalities authorities only).

Direct land acquisitions and wilderness areas created by easement are permanent. Designations by municipal councils or regional authorities are ideally permanent, though their status could in principle be revoked. In practice however, this almost never happens. Almost all the wilderness areas have been approved unanimously, with support from both the majority and minority parties on the municipal councils. To date, only one municipality has ever revoked a wilderness designation (to attempt to build a wind farm) though AIW successfully intervened to prevent this from happening.

In a very positive development, a regional wilderness act was proposed in the Lazio Region, which has the highest number of wilderness areas. Because of a change in government, the Lazio Region has not yet acted on this proposal, though AIW has hopes that this could be the first step toward regional legislation, and ultimately perhaps a national law. Another possibility for legislation is emerging in the Friuli Venezia Giulia Region, where in December 2006 a decree[7] was passed to authorize a program for the designation of regional wilderness areas, and which identified nine areas for a total of 4,103 hectares (10,134 acres). These areas may be the most similar to U.S. wilderness areas. They would be the first designations made by a regional government (rather than a regional land management authority), and therefore this initiative would represent the highest legislative point reached in Italy to date.

Conclusion

Thirty years ago, there was almost no dialogue in Europe about wilderness. Certainly there was no discussion of any sort about wilderness in Italy, and very few people knew the term even existed. Today, every environmentalist in Italy is familiar with the term, a literature on the wilderness concept is developing, and experiential wilderness trail programs are gaining in popularity. In 2005, the Italian government officially recognized the AIW as an official environmental preservation association through a decree from the Department of the Environment. And some organizations are even beginning to speak about the necessity of a wilderness areas concept supported by national law.

There is much work yet to do, both at the policy level and in terms of designating new wilderness areas in Italy. Nonetheless, it is important to take stock of the successes to date and of the fact that we have successfully adopted the philosophy of Aldo Leopold, who referred to a wilderness area as "A continuous stretch of country preserved in its natural state, open to lawful hunting and fishing, devoid of roads, artificial trails, cottages, or other works of man."[8]

Nogahabara Sand Dunes, Koyukuk Wilderness Area, Koyukuk
National Wildlife Refuge, Alaska, U.S.A.
Photo courtesy of the U.S. Fish and Wildlife Service.

Carpathian Biosphere Reserve, Ukraine. Photo courtesy of
Carpathian Biosphere Reserve, http://cbr.nature.org.ua/.

CHAPTER 17

Ukraine

Anatoliy V. Podobaylo[1] and Anna B. Pidgorna[2]

Introduction

Ukraine is a country with history of land use dating back to 4,000–6,000 years BC. Nearly 70 percent of Ukraine's territory is currently under agricultural use, with 57 percent of the nation's territory used as cropland. Large areas of the country are covered with settlements, industrial sites, and transportation infrastructure. As a result, there is a strong incentive to be strategic about remaining natural areas, and in particular to conserve all areas still left in their pristine state without exception.

The concept of *wilderness* was only introduced recently in Ukraine, when the writings of Aldo Leopold, Bob Marshall, and other wilderness proponents were translated and published. In 2001, Ukrainian conservationists also took part in their first wilderness congress—the 7th World Wilderness Congress held by The WILD Foundation in South Africa. This Congress was an important driver for including wilderness views in Ukraine's nature protection policy.

Ukraine's Protected Areas Fund

The Protected Areas Fund (PAF) of Ukraine includes all lands set aside to be managed in their natural state. As of December 2005,

4.7 percent of the territory of the country was in protected areas. The Protected Areas Fund, as defined in the Nature Conservation Act of 1991[3] and in the Protected Areas Fund Act of 1992,[4] includes land and water that have conservation, scientific, aesthetic, recreational, or other values. These areas were set aside to preserve ecosystem diversity, the genetic diversity of plants and animals, to maintain environmental balance, and to monitor the state of the environment. The status of land within the PAF is determined by the Protected Areas Fund Act and by the Land Code of Ukraine[5] (2001).

Protected areas within the PAF are established and managed by the State Protected Areas Agency, within the Ministry for Environmental Protection of Ukraine. Ukrainian legislation identifies seven categories of protected areas for conservation within the PAF: biosphere reserves, nature reserves, national nature parks, regional landscape parks, natural landmark reserves (*zapovidne urochyshche*), natural monuments, and wildlife refuges (*zakaznyks*). Each category of protected areas has its own set of management guidelines and a specific management regime, which determine the area's legal status, its purpose, the extent of allowed anthropogenic activities, and which provide a plan for conserving, using, and restoring the ecosystems within the protected area. An individual management plan is created for each protected area within the PAF. This management plan includes specific individual management requirements for the protected area, drawn within the framework of applicable legislature.

Wilderness Policy

There is currently no legislative definition of wilderness in Ukraine's protected areas classification system. However Ukraine is developing several policy mechanisms to facilitate wilderness protection.

The 2003 Policy Statement: The Conceptual Foundation of Development of Nature Protection in Ukraine

A recent policy document developed by the State Protected Areas

Agency and the Kiev Ecological and Cultural Center, and approved by the State Protected Areas Agency on December 26, 2003, formally introduced wilderness policy to Ukraine. This document, entitled *The Conceptual Foundation of Development of Nature Protection in Ukraine*, establishes two key principles:

- Areas that are biologically intact, or close to intact, should be protected; and
- Areas that have historic, cultural, religious, or aesthetic value should be protected.

The Cabinet of Ministers of Ukraine also approved this policy document in 2006. This policy is being used as a baseline for the State Nature Protection Program, which will guide all state nature protection efforts in Ukraine through 2020.

Select articles of the Protected Areas Fund Act also include statements that are relevant to the principles of wilderness conservation. For example, the following actions are prohibited within the PAF:

- Construction of buildings;
- Construction of roads and all other transportation and/or communication routes;
- Movement of heavy machinery;
- Passage of airplanes and/or helicopters at an elevation below 2,000 meters (6,600 feet);
- Breaking the sound barrier over a protected area;
- Mining, logging, disturbance of the topsoil, and destruction of geological formations;
- Hunting, fishing, or the introduction of exotic plants or animals;

Fire prevention activities, scientific research, and environmental education activities are permitted within the PAF.

Amendments to the Protected Areas Fund Act of 1992

The State Protected Areas Agency and the Kiev Ecological and Cultural Center have developed proposed amendments to the

Protected Areas Fund Act (1992), which include several wilderness provisions. Two of the most important new provisions include the creation of a new registry of wilderness areas and the establishment of two new subcategories of protected areas—wilderness *zakaznyks* and sacred nature monuments.

The State Wilderness Registry

The State registry of areas within the PAF of Ukraine is a database of information on areas that contain entire natural ecosystems or parts of natural ecosystems mainly unaltered by anthropogenic activities, whether or not they are included in the PAF of Ukraine. This registry will be supplemented by the state registry of wilderness areas, which will include information on geographic location, ownership, qualitative

Carpathian Biosphere Reserve, Ukraine.
Photo courtesy of Carpathian Biosphere
Reserve, http://cbr.nature.org.ua/.

and quantitative characteristics of these areas, management guidelines and legal status, and their conservation, environmental, scientific, educational, and other values. The state registry of wilderness areas will be maintained with the purpose of preserving all areas that contain wilderness and to sustain in perpetuity the fundamental components of the biosphere, natural evolutionary processes, and biodiversity. The registry will also be used for educational purposes, to conduct environmental monitoring, and to support eco-tourism, ethnic, and traditional uses.

The proposed amendment has been approved by the Commission on Environmental Policy of the Verhovna Rada (Parliament)[6] of Ukraine and was included in the hearings during a session of the Verhovna Rada. However, the unstable political situation at the time of the hearings prevented the Verhovna Rada from taking the proposed amendment under advisement within the allocated timeframe. The amendments will be resubmitted at the earliest opportunity.

Wilderness Zakaznyks

The Kiev Ecological and Cultural Center and recommended the introduction of a new subcategory of protected areas, wilderness *zakaznyks*, which would be included in the proposed registry of wilderness areas and then in the PAF. *Zakaznyks* are one of the most common categories of protected areas in Ukraine and play an important role in the PAF. The total area within *zakaznyks* amounts to 40 percent or close to 1.1 million hectares (2.7 million acres) of the PAF. The size of existing individual *zakaznyks* ranges widely, from one hectare to tens of thousands of hectares. The largest *zakaznyk*, with an area of 31,161.3 hectares (76,968.4 acres), is the Zhulyanskyj Landscape *Zakaznyk* located in central Ukraine. Depending on their conservation, environmental, scientific, and other values, *zakaznyks* can be of state or local importance.

The management regime of an individual *zakaznyk* is derived from an assessment of the area and scientific substantiation. The specifics of a management regime are determined using a number of criteria, including the conservation goal, the state of natural ecosystems, external impacts, possible threats, and so forth. As a result, the management regimes of *zakaznyks* can be very different from each other. The requirements of the *zakaznyk's* management regime are included in the *zakaznyk's* management plan, approved by the State Protected Areas Agency or by the regional branch of the Ministry for Environmental Protection of Ukraine. All anthropogenic uses that interfere with the protection of the conservation target(s) (that is, with the purposes and goals of the *zakaznyk*) are either limited or completely suspended. Uses that do not negatively affect the conservation target(s) are permitted. For example, the wilderness *zakaznyk's* management regime would permit limited tourism (excluding motorized access) while at the same time prohibiting the construction of buildings and roads.

Because *zakaznyks* can be designated without appropriation from private landowners or current land users, they are not considered separate legal entities. As a result, however, they do not have management or conservation staff (Protected Areas Fund Act, 1992). This makes the process of designating new *zakaznyks* simpler and much cheaper, which is important given Ukraine's limited state budget. On the other hand, landowners and land users are entrusted with upholding the conservation management regime of a protected area, which can lead to problems. If a *zakaznyk* does not have regular land users, the area becomes the responsibility of local regional governments. The staff of a nature reserve closest to a *zakaznyk* is entrusted with the responsibility to coordinate and conduct scientific research in the *zakaznyk*.

The Kiev Ecological and Cultural Center has proposed a set of criteria to define wilderness (*zakaznyks*) areas in Ukraine:

- The wilderness site must be at least 1,000 hectares (2,470 acres);
- The wilderness site must be comprised of a single parcel of land and/or water;

- No anthropogenic activities are permitted within the wilderness site; and
- Native vegetation must cover at least 90 percent of the wilderness site.

Designation Process

The procedure for designating new protected areas within the PAF is defined by articles 51–53 of the Protected Areas Fund Act. Several articles of the Land Code and the Local Self-Government Act of Ukraine (1997)[7] also impact the designation of new protected areas. *Zakaznyks* of state importance are designated by the president's executive order. The Oblasna Rada[8] designates *zakaznyks* of local importance.

The designation process can be initiated by a number of entities: the local offices of the Ministry for Environmental Protection of Ukraine, educational institutions, NGOs, and individual citizens. To designate a new protected area, the initiator must complete a series of steps, including gathering scientific substantiation and preparing a map with proposed boundaries. Furthermore, the initiator must obtain written permission from all land users whose lands will become part of the proposed protected area, as well as permission from rural and regional local governments. If a *zakaznyk* of state importance is being designated, permission from the Oblasna Rada is also required. This stage of the designation process is the most difficult, especially given the ongoing land reforms in the country.

The next step—the preparation of a proposal for a new protected area—is done by the Ministry for Environmental Protection. This proposal, when approved by responsible agencies, is then submitted for review to the Oblasna Rada (for a protected area of local importance) or to the Office of the President (for a protected area of State importance). If the proposal for designating a new protected area is approved, the next stage is the completion of a management plan for that protected area, demarcated by state-issued signs.

The Protected Areas Fund Act also has a provision for reserving areas, which may be designated as protected in the future. This type of area reservation is performed by the Oblasna Rada and does not require undergoing the same lengthy procedure as the actual designation of new protected areas. Therefore, this type of area reservation is more of a declaration of intent, rather than actual conservation.

Lessons Learned and the Outlook for the Future

Nature conservation in Ukraine developed under the Soviet regime, and thus incorporated all the strengths and weaknesses of the Soviet system of nature conservation. The greatest strength of that system, which was passed on to Ukraine, is a combination of a relatively large number of protected areas representative of the local biota with a strict regime of protection. However, due to changes in the political system, an ongoing economic crisis, and current land reforms, a new nature conservation system is required. For example, there was no private land ownership under the Soviet regime, which made the process of designating and managing protected areas much easier. The introduction of private land ownership has significantly complicated the process of designating new protected areas and increased the risk of losing the remaining wilderness areas. A wilderness approach to nature conservation and the creation of a state registry of wilderness sites will increase the rate of new protected areas designations. The proposed status of a wilderness *zakaznyk* will provide not only an adequate level of nature protection, but will also have low execution costs—a win-win situation in the current economic crisis.

Unfortunately, the designation of wilderness *zakaznyks* will present a number of difficulties. One is the lengthy process of obtaining permission from land users during the designation procedure. For example, individuals engaged in logging are often reluctant to forego logging and give permission to designate a new protected area. Local governments, which play an important role in approving the designation, often include hunters and fisherman, who are also reluctant to give up their hunting and fishing sites.

Another cause for concern is the inability to maintain the conservation regime of a *zakaznyk*. Since *zakaznyks* are not staffed, they are especially vulnerable to poachers, illegal logging, mushroom gatherers, and so forth. This threat is even higher today in light of the extreme poverty of Ukraine's rural population. Ukraine's environmental inspectors are undermanned and cannot monitor *zakaznyks* effectively.

There is also the possibility that a *zakaznyk* may lose its protected status if a valuable mineral or other resource is discovered on its territory. The procedure for revoking a protected status is rather difficult from a bureaucratic standpoint and involves taking the same steps as the designation of a new *zakaznyk*, only in reverse. However, from 2003 to 2005, Ukraine has seen precedents for this procedure.

Finally, there is a real threat that lands will be illegally removed from the PAF with support from corrupt government officials. Such activities were fairly common from 2000 to 2004 and caused substantial damage to protected areas around Kiev and in the Crimea region. For example, there were recorded instances when lands were illegally

Carpathian Biosphere Reserve, Ukraine. Photo
courtesy of Carpathian Biosphere Reserve,
http://cbr.nature.org.ua/.

removed from botanical gardens and assigned to private ownership. The war on corruption that began several years ago has somewhat alleviated this risk, but the threat remains.

It is difficult to predict the future outlook of Ukraine's conservation lands and the role, if any, that wilderness will play in the PAF. Right now, Ukraine is standing at a crossroads between allying itself with the West (the European Union) and the East (Russia), and the direction it chooses today will most likely shape its conservation future. Although some poorer nations do have their priorities closely tied to nature conservation (such as Costa Rica), it is usually more common for conservation awareness to rise only when the economy becomes stable and the people have a more or less adequate standard of living. Until that happens, most of the protected areas in Ukraine will remain at risk. Nonetheless, the past decade has witnessed a growing number of environmental NGOs and an increase in the number of environmental projects, which could indicate a rise of national-level conservation awareness and thus allow Ukrainians to look forward to a more conservation-friendly future.

Part IV

New Directions for Wilderness Law and Policy and Conclusions

Florida panther, Everglades National Park, Florida, U.S.A. Photo by Rodney Cammauf, courtesy of the U.S. National Park Service.

Meeting of Kayapó Chiefs, southern Amazon, Brazil.
Photo by Vance G. Martin.

CHAPTER 18

New Directions
in Wilderness Designation

Cyril F. Kormos[1], Vance G. Martin[2], Brad Barr[3]

Introduction

Wilderness law and policy is evolving. Countries are assessing how to draft new laws and existing laws are being updated. At the same time, entirely new designation types—by indigenous groups and the private sector—are emerging and are being used more frequently. Work is also continuing on defining how wilderness designations might apply in a marine protected areas context, an area where the need is as great as the potential, but where progress has often proven elusive. This chapter provides a brief review of these emerging areas.

Indigenous Wilderness Designations

Indigenous groups control hundreds of millions of hectares around the world, and many groups protect and manage large wilderness areas on their tribal lands: for example, the Deh Cho in Canada's Northwest Territories,[4] the Kayapó tribe in the southern Amazon in Brazil's states of Pará and Mato Grosso,[5] and The Wind River Indian Tribes in Wyoming, U.S.A.[6] Indigenous groups are therefore an essential constituency for protecting wilderness resources globally, and many tribes are explicit in their desire to protect wilderness—protecting wild nature means protecting their way of life, and in some cases, ensuring their very survival. The Kayapó tribe in Brazil offers a particularly good example of indigenous wilderness stewardship. With a population of roughly 7,000 tribe members, the Kayapó have been able to secure the integrity of their 11.3 million-hectare (28 million-acre) homeland, despite enormous pressure from agricultural expansion all around them.

Of course, the most important consideration in this context is the safeguarding of wild lands and the protection of traditional cultures. The specific use of the term *wilderness* in indigenous conservation is a secondary concern. However, use of the term does present a range of benefits. First, it can be instrumental in communicating the management objectives for the protected area—it becomes immediately clear that the area is withdrawn from industrial activity, is probably roadless and has a high degree of ecological integrity. This clarity regarding management objectives in turn can facilitate technical cooperation with other tribes, government agencies, or other

The Native Lands and Wilderness Council at the
8th World Wilderness Congress. Photo by Vance G. Martin.

potential partners. Use of the term *wilderness* also provides a clear indication of the protected status of the land both for future generations of tribal members, as well as for members of the public who might be interested in wilderness ecotourism. Finally, few words convey an image of wild, unconstrained land more effectively than the term *wilderness*. As a result, there is real value in use of the word.

There are, however, objections to applying the term *wilderness* in an indigenous context. These include the fact that contrary to western societies, indigenous cultures do not view wilderness as something separate. Wilderness for indigenous cultures is not an escape or a refuge from modern civilization: it is the foundation of their civilization, and their home. In our view, however, and as stated in the introduction, indigenous and Western views of wilderness are not incompatible. Though they differ in some respects, they share some essential characteristics: respect for wild nature, a desire to meet wild nature on its own terms, and the realization that wilderness areas are the cornerstones of a healthy society.

Wilderness designations on indigenous lands seem to be growing in use in the United States. The 30,300-hectare (75,000-acre) Mission Mountains Tribal Wilderness Area established by the Confederated Salish and Kootenai Tribes (CS&KT) on reservation lands in Montana in 1975 (see Chapter 5) is one example of this use. Another is the InterTribal Sinkyone Wilderness Council, founded in 1986, which established the 1,557-hectare (3,845-acre) InterTribal Sinkyone Wilderness in the Lost Coast region of Northern California to preserve and restore traditionally important coastal forests and salmon runs.[7] At least three other tribal authorities in the United States have established wilderness zoning mechanisms, including the Tlingit and Haida Indian Tribes of Alaska,[8] the Confederated Tribes of the Warm Springs Reservation of Oregon,[9] and the Great Lakes Indian Fish & Wildlife Commission in Wisconsin.[10]

Several wilderness laws passed since the U.S. Wilderness Act of 1964 have also recognized tribal use of wilderness resources on federal lands. For example, two previously designated wilderness areas were returned to tribal authorities—the Taos Pueblo in New Mexico and the Yakama tribe in Washington.[11] Passage of the Alaska National Interest Lands Conservation Act in 1980 also recognized and allowed for continued local and indigenous subsistence use of designated wilderness areas.[12]

There are few examples of explicit wilderness designations internationally, though Finland's wilderness legislation passed in 1991 (see Chapter 6), which was passed with the express intent of protecting traditional Lapp culture, is an important example. The Mavuradona Wilderness Area in Zimbabwe was also established by tribal authorities (see Chapter 15).

The Native Lands and Wilderness Council (NLWC), which convened for the first time at the 8th World Wilderness (8th WWC) Congress in Anchorage, Alaska, in 2005, may help generate more interest in indigenous wilderness designations. Given the North American location of 8th WWC, the NLWC was chaired by Terry Tanner of the Confederated Salish and Kootenai Tribes (Flathead Reservation, Montana, U.S.A.), Grand Chief Herb Norwegian of the Deh Cho First Nations in Canada, and Larry Merculief, Deputy Director, Alaska Native Science Commission (and an Aleut who coordinates the Bering Sea Council of Elders). The first meeting of the NLWC was an important event at the 8th World Wilderness Congress. It involved approximately 100 representatives from twenty-five indigenous groups from around the world and specifically focused on indigenous-led wilderness conservation initiatives on lands owned and managed by indigenous groups. Participants discussed the appropriateness of the term *wilderness* in an indigenous context, the importance of wilderness conservation to their efforts to maintain their social and cultural integrity, and the value of wilderness as a source of income.

Participants emerged from the NLWC with great enthusiasm, and the CS&KT are now working with The WILD Foundation on three follow-up activities: (a) a compendium of case studies emerging from the first meeting of the NLWC, (b) an interim regional meeting of the NLWC in North America in 2008, in anticipation of a second global meeting of the NLWC at the 9th World Wilderness Congress potentially in 2009, and (c) developing a network of indigenous groups around the world that have taken the lead in establishing wilderness conservation areas on their lands. Wilderness designations are a potentially useful tool for indigenous conservation initiatives, and one that may see much more use in coming years. As with government protected areas, wilderness may be protected *de facto* in other ways, but the additional strength provided by the designation is nonetheless a valuable asset.

Private Sector
Wilderness Designations

Large-scale industries, especially in the extractive sector, are often criticized for their negative impacts on the environment. But it is also true that the corporate sector in general, as well as private land holders whose wealth derives from the corporate sector, have often played an important role in safeguarding wild areas around the world. There are many examples of *de facto* wilderness conservation by corporate and other private landowners in many different countries:

- American philanthropists Doug and Kristine Tompkins, whose work in Chile and Argentina has protected almost 800,000 hectares (2 million acres) through several foundations they established (The Foundation for Deep Ecology, The Conservation Land Trust, and *Conservación Patagonica*);[13]
- The late Dutch philanthropist Paul Fentener van Vlissingen, who founded the African Parks Foundation to finance park management in Africa (which now helps manage seven protected areas in Africa), and who purchased land in four African countries (South Africa, Malawi, Zambia, and Ethiopia), as well as in Scotland;[14]
- The recent purchase of 162,000 hectares (400,000 acres) of Amazon rainforest in Brazil by Swedish businessman

Johan Eliasch;[15]
- The transfer of over 272,000 hectares (680,000 acres) of land in Tierra del Fuego owned by Goldman Sachs to the Wildlife Conservation Society.[16]

In the United States, there are significant achievements across the country, such as those in privately owned forests in the Northeast and on vast private ranches in the West. One of the best examples of private conservation efforts involves the 2.4 million-hectare (6 million-acre) Adirondack Park in New York State, half of which is privately held.[17] An overview of the role of private philanthropy in conserving wildlands was presented at the 8th WWC by Tom Butler and is summarized in that Congress's proceedings.[18]

These efforts however, have usually been implemented through partnerships with governments, grant-making foundations, and NGOs, with relatively little in the way of practical wildlands conservation on lands still owned and managed by corporations. Encouraging direct private sector stewardship, with appropriate oversight or certification, therefore represents a significant area of potential growth for wilderness conservation.

From a private-sector perspective, significant benefits accrue to the corporate brand by engaging in wilderness conservation, particularly in light of growing public recognition of environmental problems. Furthermore, employee morale is often boosted through corporate commitment to wilderness, especially when corporate lands are also used for team building and outdoor leadership exercises.

In the context of the private-sector's use of the term *wilderness*, it is important to ensure that the term is being used with a real wilderness ethic, in other words, that it reflects a genuine interest and an actual, long-term commitment by the landowner in promoting and conserving wilderness values (ecological, social, and cultural). Simply creating a hunting preserve or a tourism destination, or using the term artificially to enhance a brand or corporate reputation, is not sufficient. Second, the landowner must develop a management plan that is suited to conserving (and where possible, enhancing) these wilderness values. This also entails restoring the wilderness character by removing fences or structures, closing roads, and "re-wilding" as much as possible, including ecologically appropriate re-introduction of wildlife or vegetation and control measures for alien invasive species. Finally, the landowner should utilize some sort of legal mechanism, such as an easement or servitude, in partnership with a conservation NGO or government agency, to secure the area's wilderness values for as many years as possible, if not permanently.

WILD has been promoting the idea of private sector wilderness designations for several years in particular in South Africa. South Africa proved a fertile area in which to start for several reasons. First, it is a country of unique biodiversity. For example, it is the only nation that contains within its borders an entire floral kingdom (Cape Floristic). The nation as a whole also has a historic and strong commitment to private-sector conservation, with 75 percent of the country's wildlands under private ownership. South Africa also has a clear commitment to wilderness conservation, as well as a history of innovation in environmental protection (for example in transfrontier conservation).

In partnership with our closest collaborator, the Wilderness Foundation (South Africa), WILD worked with Adrian Gardiner, owner and operator of the Shamwari Game Reserve, a private game reserve in Eastern Cape Province, South Africa, many times voted the Outstanding Ecotourism Destination in South Africa. Shamwari is well known and respected for its commitment to restoring wildland values to degraded farmlands. Working with the Wilderness Foundation, Shamwari went even further and developed a management plan that zoned the reserve into four areas—wilderness, roaded natural, rural, and breeding centers.

This collaboration resulted in the first ever wilderness designation on private lands in Africa (announced at the 7th WWC in Port Elizabeth, South Africa, in 2001), in which 18 percent of the reserve (2,915 hectares or 7,287 acres) is now managed as wilderness under legal servitude with the Wilderness Foundation. Based on the success of this model, a second 15,000-hectare area (45,000 acres), this time in the Sanbona Wildlife Reserve, Western Cape province, South Africa, and also owned by the Adrian Gardiner, was announced at the 8th WWC in Anchorage, Alaska.

Based on this precedent, WILD is now working with *Agrupación Sierra Madre*, Conservation International, The Nature Conservancy, and other NGO partners to establish a certification mechanism for wilderness areas on private lands in Mexico. At the same time, this NGO coalition is working with the government of Mexico to establish a wilderness designation for public lands, which will constitute the first official wilderness protected area classification in Latin America (see chapter 9).

The first actual designation of wilderness in Latin America was in Mexico, on private-sector land owned by CEMEX Inc., one of the world's largest cement producers. The wilderness area is the core 30,000 hectares (75,000 acres) on CEMEX's El Carmen complex in northern Mexico, located in the far north of the eastern Sierra Madre mountain range. From an original area of 74,000 hectares (175,000 acres), CEMEX owns a total of almost 121,000 hectares (300,000 acres) in this area, and continues to purchase parcels extending into south Texas, adjacent to the Big Bend National Park and Black Gap Wildlife Management Area (State of Texas). The region includes numerous and spectacular "sky islands," mountains rising steeply from desert to high mountain tops covered in temperate forest, making the region very rich in biodiversity. It has five hundred plant species, four hundred bird species, seventy mammal species, and fifty types of reptiles and amphibians, and is included in Conservation International's global priority list of High Biodiversity Wilderness Areas.[19]

An additional, unique aspect of the El Carmen-Big Bend Corridor initiative is that it is likely the first transboundary protected area owned by a private company and managed to preserve-ecological values. The scope of this vision is vast, potentially involving up to 4 million hectares (10 million acres) of land in a mosaic of ownership including corporate lands, private ranches, *ejidos* (communal lands), lands managed by the U.S. National Park Service, and State of Texas conservation areas. Along a border best known for negative news stories of smuggling and illegal aliens, this is an extremely positive story, with significant implications for conservation, wilderness, and international politics.

Although these South African and Mexican partnerships are initial steps, they have been well received by corporate partners, as well as by the NGO community and government protected areas agencies. Conservation on private lands is not a recent phenomenon. Easements have long proven to be a highly efficient mechanism for conservation around the world, in particular in the United States. But establishing a new corporate wilderness ethic led by corporations on corporate lands has significant potential. We hope to be able to harness this potential to help save the planet's last wild places.

Reid Glacier, Glacier Bay National Park and Preserve, Alaska, U.S.A.
Photo by Melinda Webster, courtesy of the U.S. National Park Service.

Ocean Wilderness

The ocean is a wilderness reaching around the globe, wilder
than a Bengal jungle, and fuller of monsters...
—Henry David Thoreau, Cape Cod[20]

*Mt. Cooper and Lamplugh Glacier, Glacier Bay National Park
and Preserve, Alaska, U.S.A. Photo by Rosemarie Salazar,
courtesy of the U.S. National Park Service.*

The concept of wilderness in the ocean is not by any measure new. Thoreau, in his storied walk along the shores of Cape Cod, found himself recalibrating his perception of wilderness. Could such an elemental and powerful wilderness experience be available to everyone who walks on a deserted beach? Perhaps, but that was in 1865—were he to walk these same beaches again, he would undoubtedly come away with an entirely different perspective.

The idea of ocean wilderness has been rediscovered a number of times: from Wallis[21] (1958), who advocated ocean wilderness stewardship for the U. S. National Park Service; to Eissler[22] (1968), who recommended an "underwater wilderness system"; to Smith and Watson[23] (1979), who posited that "mankind should give serious consideration to underwater wilderness values"; to the more recent, and very thoughtful work of Sloan[24] (2002). Each rediscovery has generated new information and critical thinking. While there are few ocean or coastal areas formally designated as "wilderness," the concept persists.

The concept has also appeared regularly at the World Wilderness Congresses, beginning with a paper by Hance Smith at the 3rd WWC in Scotland in 1984,[25] and as a topic in plenary and special sessions at the 4th WWC in Colorado, where the Congress adopted a resolution to carry forward with ocean wilderness.[26] The recent 8th WWC included two plenary talks and three paper sessions addressing ocean issues. Although more comprehensive, and accompanied by some enthusiasm, it is too early to tell whether this Congress will yield more tangible progress in designation and management of ocean wilderness. However, there are signs of progress.

The 8th WWC provided an unprecedented opportunity to assess the status of ocean wilderness and to examine how to generate traction for applying the wilderness concept to the oceans. The presentations suggest that perhaps a foundation is being laid that can address some lingering questions and assist in identifying ocean wilderness areas once a consensus definition is articulated.

A key session at the 8th Congress provided an overview of the extensive data and information base that can be used to identify ocean wilderness. Jen Molnar of The Nature Conservancy presented their Global Marine Habitat Assessment, which uses available, new, and synthesized data sets on ocean resources to identify areas of conservation importance, evaluate condition and threat, and assess conservation progress. Caterina D'Agrosa then described the Wildlife Conservation Society's Marine Human Footprint Project, mapping the extent and intensity of human impact on the world's oceans. Bill Chandler, on behalf of colleagues Lance Morgan and Fan Tsao of the Marine Conservation Biology Institute, reviewed work on the Baja to Bering Initiative. This initiative uses data on physical and oceanographic features, species distributions, and human uses, and calls on scientists and resource managers from the region to identify and map priorities areas for conservation. Finally, George Shillinger of Conservation International presented CI's work on the Eastern Tropical Pacific Seascape Initiative, a transboundary, multinational program developing a network of marine protected areas in this region.

Other excellent work on this topic includes an initiative by Natalie Ban and Jackie Alder at the University of British Columbia identifying potential coastal and ocean wilderness in British Columbia,[27] and a global analysis entitled "Putting Ocean Wilderness on the Map: Building a Global GIS Atlas of Pristine Marine Environments," conducted by Ben Halpern and colleagues with the support of the National Center for Ecosystem Assessment and Analysis. As a result, there is a growing body of information and analysis that can be used to identify areas that many would agree are "ocean wilderness."

Another session at the 8th WWC reported on the Ocean Wilderness Working Group sessions held at the International Wilderness Law and Policy Roundtable, held in Washington, DC, in 2004 and sponsored by The WILD Foundation. Involving participants from the United States, Canada, Australia, and Chile, this group developed a working definition of "ocean wilderness," identified the key wilderness values preserved under this definition, and identified a number of outstanding questions and issues. This work is a great leap forward in moving toward a consensus definition, an essential precursor to any workable ocean wilderness stewardship program.

The last session at the Congress involved a review of how wilderness waters are managed in U.S. Fish and Wildlife Refuges. Some significant areas in coastal National Wildlife Refuges are designated as wilderness under the U.S. Wilderness Act of 1964, and the USFWS is leading the way in enhancing stewardship and preservation of these waters. While the theoretical data and policy analyses are a necessary element of moving forward, the practical experience of refuge and other resource managers provides a grounding for the more hypothetical and speculative exercises.

Ocean wilderness is an interesting, perhaps even compelling idea, and many over the years have pondered the issue, made contributions to the body of relevant work, and offered impassioned entreaties for designating wilderness in the oceans. But is it an ecological imperative? Only a handful of sites have been formally designated, and of those, few if any are functioning as wilderness[28] (Clifton 2003). The critical question is whether there is real value to ocean wilderness. Are there resources and values that can only be preserved by a wilderness designation? It would seem, on land, that wilderness has undeniable value. Can the oceans be that different?

The views expressed herein are those of the author and do not necessarily reflect the policies, positions, or views of the Department of Commerce, NOAA, or any of its sub-agencies.

Pelican, Everglades National Park, Florida, U.S.A.
Photo by Rodney Cammauf, courtesy of
the U.S. National Park Service.

CHAPTER 19

Conclusion

Cyril F. Kormos[1]

As the preceding chapters indicate, countries around the world have different approaches to wilderness legislation. Some emphasize a more biological approach to wilderness, others a more social and recreational approach, and others give both of these factors roughly equal weight. At the same time, and despite some differences in articulating objectives, a review of the preceding chapters also indicates a significant degree of convergence—wilderness laws around the world tend to be more similar than different, reflecting the fact that the term *wilderness* can be defined with a fair degree of precision and uniformity in a policy context. This final chapter briefly summarizes some of the key conclusions that can be drawn from this review of wilderness legislation.

The Key to Wilderness Legislation is Regulating Human Use, Not Excluding Humans

Wilderness legislation seeks to protect large natural areas in as wild a state as possible and to maintain the biological integrity of these areas into the future. Wilderness legislation in many countries also explicitly seeks to provide opportunities for solitude and to avoid modern industrial infrastructure such as roads, pipelines, and buildings.

However, neither of these factors suggests that wilderness is about excluding people. Rather, the key point is that wilderness legislation regulates human use of certain areas to preserve certain wilderness values, while allowing those uses that are consistent with those values.

Wilderness Legislation Often Operates at Two Levels

Wilderness legislation often operates at two levels. The first level constitutes the ideal—setting the highest standards for biological integrity and wildness. Establishing a clear biological standard at this level is critical because this ensures protection for the wildest lands in the country (or in the state or province). However, in many countries, there may be relatively few places that meet this very high standard. As a result, a second, more pragmatic level is needed. This second level recognizes the fact that certain lands that might not satisfy the highest biological standards today should nonetheless qualify as wilderness because, over time and as a result of restoration efforts, they may be returned to a wilderness state. This tiered approach provides land managers with a realistic policy tool to ensure a long-term strategy for wilderness protection.

Wilderness Can Be Protected Effectively by a Range of Government and Nongovernment Landowners and Managers

Wilderness areas are most frequently protected by governments. However, governments need not be the only protectors of wilderness and wilderness values. In fact, in many cases, local communities, private individuals or organizations, or indigenous groups may be the more appropriate stewards of wilderness. In other cases, partnerships between some or all of the groups mentioned above may the most effective way of protecting a particular wilderness area. However, some degree of government involvement is likely necessary even where nongovernmental entities assume the role of wilderness stewards. This involvement can come in several forms, including incentives to encourage others to take on this land management responsibility, technical assistance with management, coordination to ensure government and nongovernmental land managers are working in concert, and establishment of certification programs to ensure that all land managers meet certain threshold quality standards.

Creating a Dynamic System

Many land management agencies around the world are responsible both for conserving nature and for managing extractive industries. This dual mandate often results in a disincentive to establish new wilderness areas. Several measures can be taken to encourage a dynamic and expanding wilderness resource. One is to legislate for periodic inventories to identify new lands that may be suitable for wilderness designation, as well as assessments of the feasibility of including these lands in wilderness protection systems. Another measure is to empower third parties—individuals or NGOs—to submit proposals to governments for new wilderness areas. While this frequently happens in practice anyway, for example through lobbying efforts and advocacy campaigns by NGOs, creating frameworks for formal submission can facilitate this process.

Wilderness Legislation Is Evolving

Early wilderness statutes emphasized the need for wilderness as an escape from the stresses of modern civilization. However, existing and new wilderness statutes have been evolving in several respects. The first is that governments now recognize that wilderness laws must operate in a context of indigenous land rights. The second is that wilderness laws are recognizing their role not solely as a temporary escape from urban, industrial society, but as an essential component of, and complement to, healthy modern societies. The role of wilderness as a fundamental and universal ingredient in ensuring human well-being across the planet is an important step forward.

The U.S. Wilderness Act of 1964 provides a good example. Although the act as passed in 1964 did not anticipate subsistence use of wilderness areas, the Alaska National Interest Lands Conservation Act (ANILCA), which set aside 22.6 million hectares (56 million acres) of wilderness in Alaska in 1980, recognized that unlike other parts of the United States, subsistence use was still very prevalent in Alaska. As a result, ANILCA explicitly provides for the continuation of these uses. Many other laws and policies (see, for example, the Australian and Canadian chapters) have also given precedence to indigenous or aboriginal rights.

Wilderness Legislation
Often Requires Compromise

Certain political compromises are often necessary to ensure passage of wilderness legislation. For example, allowing certain preexisting uses to continue for a period of time after the law is passed, or simply conceding that certain nonconforming uses are too entrenched to be removed. The challenge is to ensure that the nonconforming uses that are allowed in wilderness areas are not so pervasive as to undermine the fundamental wilderness quality of the protected area.

New Countries
Are Developing Wilderness Legislation

In 1990, there were six countries with some form of wilderness legislation. Today, there are nine countries with laws, at least nine more with wilderness policies or zoning mechanisms, and two countries with laws pending (México, Turkey). In addition, wilderness law and policy is being adopted in countries where the term has no direct translation (e.g. Italy, Ukraine, México, Turkey, etc.), indicating that the concept has strong international and cross-cultural appeal. As the many benefits of wilderness protection become better understood, and as familiarity with the wilderness concept grows, wilderness legislation will likely continue to expand to new countries around the world.

Olympic Wilderness, Olympic
National Park, Washington, U.S.A.
Photo courtesy of the
U.S. National Park Service.

Cradle Mountain—Lake St. Clair National Park,
Tasmanian Wilderness World Heritage Area. Photo by Ian Brown.

Acknowledgments

The WILD Foundation would like to thank CEMEX, Inc. for its support in producing this book, as well as the Interagency Wilderness Policy Council of the U.S. Government for its many contributions to the development of this volume. WILD would also like to thank the Wilderness Society (Australia) for its contributions to this book.

The editor would also like to thank the authors in this volume, many of whom also participated in the Roundtable on International Wilderness Law and Policy organized by WILD in 2004 and chaired by the editor, and in the 8th World Wilderness Congress, both of which were important events in furthering the compilation of this book. Special thanks are also due to the following for providing pictures and graphics for this book: Trausti Baldurrson; Ian Brown; Brian Caouette; Bill Doyle; Evan Ferrari; Patricio Robles Gil; Ian MacNeil; Vance G. Martin; Boyd Norton; Michael Painter; John Reid; Neill Simpson; Keith Springer; and Franco Zunino; as well as the Confederated Salish and Kootenai Tribes; Department of Conservation, New Zealand; Metsahallitus, Finland; Parks Canada; the U.S. National Park Service; the U.S.D.A Forest Service; the Wilderness Leadership School, South Africa; and the Wild Salmon Center.

Finally, the editor would also like to thank his family for their infinite patience and support, particularly in the final stages of compiling this volume.

Cyril F. Kormos, Editor
Vice President for Policy
The WILD Foundation

Notes

PART I

Chapter 1—Introduction

1. Vice President for Policy, The WILD Foundation, member IUCN World Commission on Protected Areas—Wilderness Task Force.

2. Senior Advisor, Conservation to the Canadian Parks and Wilderness Society, Strategic Advisor to the Yellowstone to Yukon Conservation Initiative, member IUCN World Commission on Protected Areas—Wilderness Task Force.

3. Hendee, J. and C. Dawson. 2002. *Wilderness management: stewardship and protection of resources and values, third edition.* Golden, CO: Fulcrum, 57–84.

4. Ibid.

5. Attenborough, David. 1987. *The first eden: Mediterranean world and man.* Boston: Little, Brown.

6. Ibid.

7. Diamond, Jared. 1999. *Guns, germs, and steel: the fates of human societies.* New York: W. W. Norton, 85–113.

8. Vest, Jay Hansford C. 1985. "Will-of-the-land: wilderness among primal Indo-Europeans." *Environmental Review* 9 (4): 324–5.

9. Cantor, Norman F. 1999. *The encyclopaedia of the middle ages.* New York: Viking.

10. IUCN, World Heritage Nomination Summary, Doñana National Park, Spain. 1992. http//whc. unesco.org/archive/advisory_body_evalaution.

11. Player, I. 1973. *Operation Rhino.* New York: Stein and Day, 23.

12. Sanderson E., et al. 2002. The human footprint and the last of the wild (http://www.wcs.org/media/file/human_footprint2.pdf). *BioScience* 52 (10). 891–904; Sanderson, E. 2006. *The human footprint: challenges for wilderness and biodiversity.* CEMEX. 39–59.

13. Millennium Ecosystem Assessment. 2005. *Ecosystems and human well-being: synthesis.* Washington, DC: Island Press, World Resources Institute.

14. Stegner, W. 1990. *It all began with conservation.* Smithsonian 28th Anniversary Issue on the Environment. Washington, DC.

15. Hewitt, C. Gordon 1921. *The conservation of wildlife in Canada.* New York: Scribners.

16. Sullivan, Jerry. 2003. A regional nature reserve: an atlas of biodiversity. Chicago Wilderness. http://www.chicagowilderness.org.

17. Callicott, J. and M. Nelson, eds. 1998. *The great new wilderness debate.* Athens, GA: Univ. of Georgia Press.

18. Judt, T. 2005. *Postwar: A history of Europe since 1945.* London: Penguin, 478–81.

19. Gómez-Pompa, A. and A. Kaus. *Taming the wilderness myth* in Callicott *supra* note 15, 299–300.

20. Cronon, W. 1998. *The trouble with wilderness* in Calicott and Nelson *supra* note 15, 471–499.

21. Phillips, A. 1997. *Landscape approaches to national parks and protected areas. In National parks and protected areas,* eds. J. G. Nelson and A. Serafin. Berlin, Germany: Springer Verlag, 31–37.

22. Alaska National Interest Lands Conservation Act (ANILCA), 16 U.S.C.3101-3233, s.1316; see also Tanner, R. 2004. Subsistence, Inholdings, and ANILCA; The Complexity of Wilderness Stewardship in Alaska, *International Journal of Wilderness* 10 (2): 18–22.

23. Foreman, D. 2000. *The real wilderness idea,* USDA Forest Service Proceedings RMRS-P-15. 33.

24. Mittermeier, R.A., et al. 2002. *Wilderness: Earth's last wild places.* CEMEX, 19–54.

25. Stegner, W. 1961. The wilderness idea. In *Wilderness, America's Living Heritage.* San Francisco: Sierra Club, 97–102.

26. Meier, C.A. 1985. *A Testament to the Wilderness.* Larkspur Landing, CA: Lapis Press.

27. Op. cit. 11.

28. Balmford, A., et al. 2002. Economic reasons for conserving wild nature. *Science* 297: 950–953; Costanza, R., et al. 1997. The value of the world's ecosystem services and natural capital. *Nature* 387: 253–260.

Chapter 2—The Matrix

1. Peter Landres is an ecologist with the Aldo Leopold Wilderness Research Institute, Forest Service, USDA.

2. Brad Barr is Senior Policy Advisor at NOAA's National Marine Sanctuary Program and a member of IUCN's World Commission on Protected Areas.

3. Cyril Kormos is Vice President for Policy at The WILD Foundation and a member of IUCN's World Commission on Protected Area's Wilderness Task Force.

PART II

Chapter 3—Australia

1. James Prest, PhD, Lecturer in Law, Australian Centre for Environmental Law, Australian National University, Canberra, ACT 0200, Australia. E-mail at Prestj@law.anu.edu.au. The author prepared the bulk of this paper as a consultant to the Wilderness Society and acknowledges their input and assistance.

2. Mackey, B., R. Lesslie, D. Lindenmayer, and D. Nix. 1998. Wilderness and its place in nature conservation in Australia. *Pacific Conservation Biology* 4 (3): 182–185.

3. Mackey et al, op. cit.

4. Ibid.

5. For example, both the federal and NSW governments have recently disbanded wilderness units within their environment departments.

6. See *Environment and Heritage Legislation Amendment Bill (No.1) 2006* (Cth).

7. http://www.austlii.edu.au/au/legis/qld/consol_act/wra2005150/.

8. Six rivers were declared under the Wild Rivers Act, including four in Queensland's north-west (Settlement, Gregory, Morning Inlet, and Staaten) as well as rivers on Hinchinbrook and Fraser Islands.

9. Whitehouse, J. 1994. Legislative protection for wilderness in Australia. In *Wilderness: The future*, ed. W. Barton. Sydney, Australia: Envirobook, 97.

10. Muir, K. 2005. Action toward wilderness protection in Australia. In *Science and stewardship to protect and sustain wilderness values: eighth world wilderness congress symposium*, eds. Alan Watson, Liese Dean, Janet Sproull. September 30–October 6; Anchorage, AK. Proceedings RMRS-P-000. Fort Collins, CO: USDA, Forest Service, Rocky Mountain Research Station, 4.

11. *National Parks and Reserves Management Act 2002 (Tas)*.

12. *Wilderness Act 1987* (NSW).

13. Ibid. s.7(1).
14. Ibid. s.7(4).
15. See further, NSW National Parks and Wildlife Service. 2003. *The bioregions of New South Wales: their biodiversity, conservation and history*. Hurstville, NSW: NPWS.
16. *Wilderness Protection Act 1992* (SA).
17. *Wilderness Act 1987* (NSW), s.7.
18. Ibid., s.27(1), *Wilderness Protection Act 1992* (SA), s.34(1).
19. *Environment Protection And Biodiversity Conservation Regulations 2000* (Cth), Schedule 8, Australian IUCN reserve management principles, Parts 1& 2 Principles for each IUCN category. See also Regulation 10.04).
20. *Nature Conservation Act 1992* (Qld), s.24.
21. *Territory Parks and Wildlife Conservation Act* (NT), s.17(7).
22. *Wilderness Act 1987* (NSW) s.9.
23. *Environment Protection and Biodiversity Conservation Regulations 2000* (Cth), 12.11, 12.12, 12.35.
24. *National Parks and Wildlife Act 1974* (NSW), s.81(4).
25. *National Parks and Wildlife Act 1974* (NSW), s.41(2), 47ZA, 54, 58F, 58O, 64.
26. *Wilderness Act 1987* (NSW), s.8(5). The Act protects pre-existing interests including "authority, authorisation, permit, lease, licence or occupancy."
27. *Wilderness Act 1987*, s.2(1).
28. *Environmental Planning and Assessment Act 1979* (NSW), s.78A(7).
29. *Wilderness Act 1987*, s.15.
30. Ibid., s.15(2)(a).
31. *Environmental Planning and Assessment Act 1979* (NSW), s.111(3).
32. *National Parks and Wildlife Act 1974* (NSW), ss.39, 47H, 47ZA, 54, 58F, 64.
33. Ibid., s.41(4), (5);
34. *Wilderness Act 1987* (NSW), s.25.
35. *Wilderness Protection Act 1992* (SA), s.25(1).
36. *Petroleum Act 1998* (Vic), s.137.
37. *Mineral Resources Development Act 1990* (Vic), s.6(1)(b).
38. *National Parks Act 1975* (Vic), s.21C(2),(3).
39. *Nature Conservation Act 1992* (Qld), s.27(1).
40. *Nature Conservation Act 1992* (Qld), s.27(1).
41. *Territory Parks and Conservation Act* s.17.
42. *Mining Act 1980* (NT), s.176A(3).

43. *National Parks and Wildlife Act 1974* (NSW), s.42(1), 47K, 55(1), 58G(1), 58P(1), 64.

44. http://www.racac.nsw.gov.au/rfa/ifoa.shtml; see also http://www.forest.nsw.gov.au/ifoa/default.asp.

45. *Wilderness Act 1987* (NSW), s.12(1)(a).

46. *Wilderness Protection Act 1992* (SA), s.26(1)(a).

47. *National Parks Act 1985* (Vic), s.17C(1)(d).

48. Ibid., s.17C(1)(b).

49. Ibid., s.22C.

50. *Snowy Mountains Cloud Seeding Trial Act 2004*, s.7 excluding Parts 4 and 5 of the *Environmental Planning and Assessment Act 1979* and modifying the operation of the *National Parks and Wildlife Act 1974, Threatened Species Conservation Act 1995, Fisheries Management Act 1994, Protection of the Environment Operations Act 1997*, and the *Local Government Act 1993*.

51. *National Parks Act 1985* (Vic), s.22D.

52. Scott, R. 1994. Mechanised access and wilderness protection. In *Wilderness: the future*, ed. W. Barton. Sydney, Australia: Envirobook, 237–248.

53. *Wilderness Protection Regulations 1992* (SA), r.6(1).

54. *National Parks Act 1975* (VIC), s.17C.

55. Ibid., s.21C(2).

56. *National Parks and Wildlife Act 1974* (NSW), s.81(1),(4).

57. *Wilderness Act 1987* (NSW), s.9.

58. Generally, see *National Parks and Wildlife Regulation 2002* (NSW), Part 3.

59. *Wilderness Act 1987* (NSW), s.12(1)(e).

60. *Nature Conservation Act 1980* (ACT), s.59.

61. *Control of Vehicles (Off-road areas) Act 1978 (WA)*, s.16.

62. *National Parks Act 1975* (Vic), s.17C(1)(c).

63. *Wilderness Protection Regulations 1992* (SA), r.7(1).

64. Ibid., r.8.

65. "Vessel" means a boat, jet-ski, sailboard, raft, pontoon, or any other man-made object capable of floating on water and includes a hovercraft. *Wilderness Protection Regulations 1992* (SA), r.2.

66. *National Parks Act 1975* (Vic), s.17C(1)(d).

67. *Conservation and Land Management Regulations 2002* (WA), r.43.

68. *National Parks and Wildlife (Land Management) Regulations 1995* (NSW), r.6(1).

69. *Wilderness Act 1987* (NSW), s.25.

70. *National Parks Act 1975* (Vic), s.17C(2)(c).

71. *Wilderness Protection Act 1992* (SA), s.41(2)(f).

72. *Wilderness Act 1987* (NSW), s.27(1).

73. For example, under Part 3, *National Parks and Wildlife Regulation 2002* (NSW).

74. In the case of exempt development, s.76(3)(a)(iii) *Environmental Planning and Assessment Act 1979* (NSW); in the case of complying development, s.76A(6) *Environmental Planning and Assessment Act 1979* (NSW).

75. *Plantations and Reafforestation Act 1999* (NSW), s.7(1)(d).

76. *Wilderness Protection Regulations 1992* (SA).

77. *Wilderness Protection Act 1992* (SA), s.25(3).

78. *National Parks and Wildlife Act 1974* (NSW), s.153A.

79. *Land (Planning and Environment) Act 1991* (ACT), s.209.

80. *Wilderness Act 1987* (NSW).

81. *Wilderness Protection Act 1992* (SA), s.12(2)(l).

82. *National Parks Act 1975*, s.4(c).

83. Ibid., s.17(2)(a)(ii).

84. *Nature Conservation Act 1992* (Qld), s.5.

85. Robertson, M., K. Vang, and A. Brown. 1992. *Wilderness in Australia: issues and options: a discussion paper.* Canberra, Australia: Australian Heritage Commission, 183. See Chapter 8, "State and territory legislation for wilderness."

86. Ibid., 128.

87. Whitehouse, J. 1994. Legislative Protection for Wilderness in Australia. In *Wilderness: the future*, ed. W. Barton. Sydney, Australia: Envirobook, 94–126, 121.

88. *Wilderness Act 1987* (NSW), s.27(1); *Wilderness Protection Act 1992* (SA), s.34(1).

89. http://www.wilderness.org.au/campaigns/wildcountry/.

90. The Wilderness Society. 2006. Submission to the Senate Standing Committee on Environment, Communications, Information Technology and the Arts, No. 131. *Inquiry into Australia's National Parks, Conservation Reserves And Marine Protected Areas.* 2. http://www.aph.gov.au/senate/committee/ecita_ctte/nationalparks/su bmissions/sublist.htm.

91. Environmental Law Institute (USA). 1993. *Practical Approaches to Implementing Environmental Laws: Getting to Here from There.* Washington, DC: ELI, 1.

92. For example, *Environment Protection and Biodiversity Conservation Act 1999* (Cth), s.374 et.seq., *National Parks and Wildlife Act 1974* (NSW), Part 4A; *Nature Conservation Act 1992* (Qld), s.18; 40-42; *Parks and Reserves (Framework for the Future) Act 2003* (NT).

93. http://www.deh.gov.au/indigenous/fact-sheets/ipa.html.

94. *Environment Protection and Biodiversity Conservation Regulations 2000* (Cth), Schedule 8, Part 1.

95. "[T]he Aboriginal people of this country had been carefully curating and managing this environment and, in fact, creating it really over the last 50,000 years. So the lie of terra nullius was not only a legal lie that allowed people to take that land, but it's also an environmental lie because it's meant that we can't see that the environment here needs to be managed. I mean, the whole concept of wilderness has come out of terra nullius." Flannery, Tim. 2003. An interview with Tim Flannery, Director of South Australian Museum. *Triple J Morning Show*, April 3, 2003.

96. In 1978, the Queensland Government refused to issue a pastoral lease to an Aboriginal traditional owner, Mr. Koowarta, of the Winchanam people. His subsequent racial discrimination case in the High Court was upheld: *Koowarta v Bjelke Petersen* (1982) 153 CLR 168. However the Queensland Premier, Mr. Joh Bjelke-Petersen created the Archer River Bend National Park as a means of preventing Koowarta from exercising his rights. See: Guy, K. and C. Darlington. 1998. Borbidge flaunts aboriginal rights in Fraser Island plan. Land Rights Queensland, April 1998. http://www.faira.org.au/lrq/archives/199804/stories/borbidge.html.

97. This expansion would seen the diversion of a 5.5-kilometer (3.4-mile) stretch of the McArthur River by the Swiss mining giant XStrata in order to access the remaining rich ore body that presently lies beneath the river bed.

98. Schneiders, W. Lyndon. 2004. Interview. TWS, July 14, 2004; Muir, K. 2005. Action toward wilderness protection in Australia. In *Science and stewardship to protect and sustain wilderness values: eighth world wilderness congress symposium*, eds. Alan Watson, Liese Dean, Janet Sproull. September 30–October 6; Anchorage, AK. Proceedings RMRS-P-000. Fort Collins, CO: USDA, Forest Service, Rocky Mountain Research Station.

Chapter 4—Canada

1. Director, Park Establishment Branch Parks Canada Agency.
2. Leopold, A. 1966. *A Sand County Almanac.* Oxford: Oxford University Press, 268–269.
3. McNamee, K. 2003. Preserving Canada's wilderness legacy: a perspective on protected areas. In *Protected areas and the regional planning imperative in North America,* eds. J. G. Nelson, J.C. Day, Lucy M. Sportz, James Loucky, and Carlos Vasquez. Calgary: University of Calgary Press, 26.
4. Page, R. 1986. *Northern development: the Canadian dilemma.* Toronto: McClelland and Stewart Limited, 33–34.
5. Ibid., 35.
6. World Wildlife Fund Canada. 2003. The nature audit: setting Canada's conservation agenda for the 21st century. Report No. 1. Toronto: World Wildlife Fund Canada, 76.
7. Government of Canada. 1990. Bill C-292—An Act to provide for the protection on wilderness areas and to amend the National Parks Act. Second Session, Thirty-fourth Parliament, 38–39 Elizabeth II, 1989-90, Queen's Printer of Canada.
8. Canadian Environmental Advisory Council. 1991. *A protected areas vision for Canada.* Ottawa: Minister of Supply and Services Canada, 67.
9. Morrison, J. 1995. Aboriginal interests. In *Protecting Canada's endangered spaces: an owner's manual,* ed. Monte Hummel. Toronto: Key Porter Books Limited, 22.
10. McNamee, K. 2002. Protected areas in Canada: The endangered spaces campaign. In *Parks and Protected Areas in Canada: Planning and Management,* 2nd edition, eds. Philip Dearden and Rick Rollins. Ontario: Oxford University Press, Don Mills, 60–61.
11. Warecki, G. M. 2000. *Protecting Ontario's wilderness: a history of changing ideas and preservation politics, 1927–1973.* New York: Peter Lang Publishing, 79.
12. Killan, G. 1993. *Protected places: a history of Ontario's provincial parks system.* Toronto: Dundurn Press, 134–136.
13. McNamee, K. 1993. Preserving Ontario's natural legacy. In *Environment on trial: a guide to Ontario environmental law and policy,* eds. David Estrin and John Swaigen. Canadian Institute for Environmental Law and Policy. Toronto: Emond Montgomery Publications, 288.
14. www.e-laws.gov.on.ca/DBLaws/Statutes/English/06p12_e.htm.

15. May, B. 1989. Newfoundland and Labrador: a special place. In *Endangered spaces: the future for Canada's wilderness,* ed. Monte Hummel. Toronto: Key Porter Books 131.

16. www.hoa.gov.nl.ca/hoa/statutes/w09.htm.

17. Ibid., 131.

18. www.gov.ns.ca/legislature.legc/statutes/wildarea.htm.

19. Berger, T. R. 1988. *Northern frontier, northern homeland: the report of the Mackenzie Valley pipeline inquiry.* Toronto: Minister of Supply and Services Canada, Douglas & McIntyre, 55.

20. Ibid., 56.

21. Ibid., 74.

22. Tennent, C. 1979. Six new national parks in the north? *Park News* 15 (3): 27–29.

23. Fenge, T. 1979. Policy making for northern national parks. *Park News* 15 (4): 12.

24. Parks Canada Agency. 2000. Unimpaired for future generations? Protecting ecological integrity with Canada's national parks, volume 2: Setting a new direction for Canada's national parks. Report of the Panel on the Ecological Integrity of Canada's National Parks. Ottawa: Minister of Public Works and Government Services, 3–13.

25. http://laws.justice.gc.ca/en/showtdm/cs/N-14.01.

26. Parks Canada Agency. 2000. Action plan for the declaration of wilderness areas. Unpublished. October 12, 2000, 4.

Chapter 5—The Mission Mountains Tribal Wilderness Area

1. Rudzitis, G. and R. Johnson. 2000. The impact of wilderness and other wildlands on local economies and regional development trends. USDA Forest Service Proceedings, RMRS-P-15-Vol-2.2000.

2. Power, T. M. 1988. *The economic pursuit of quality.* New York: M. E. Sharpe Publishers.

Chapter 6—Finland

1. Senior Advisor, Metsähallitus.

2. Veijola, P. 2002. Metsähallituksen kokemuksia erämaa-alueiden hoidosta ja suunnittelusta. In Erämaapolitiikka: Pohjoiset erämaat arjen, hallinnan ja tutkimuksen kohteena, ed. J. Saarinen. Metsäntutkimuslaitoksen tiedonantoja 827, 13-20. ISBN 951-40-1807-9.

3. Erämaakomitean mietintö. 1988. Komiteanmietintö. 1988: 39.Valtion painatuskeskus. ISBN 951-47-1225-0.

4. Erämaalaki: Act on Wilderness Reserves, No. 62. January 17, 1991
5. Hallikainen, V. 1998. The Finnish Wilderness Experience. Metsäntutkimuslaitoksen tiedonantoja 711. Finnish Forest Research Institute, Research Papers 711. Rovaniemi Research Station. 288 p. Hakapaino Oy, Helsinki. ISBN 951-40-1656-4.

Additional References:
Hallikainen, V. 2000. The Finnish Social Wilderness, U.S.D.A. Forest Service Proceedings RMRS-P-15-Vol-2.
Saarinen, J. Ed.) Erämaapolitiikka: Pohjoiset erämaat arjen, hallinnan ja tutkimuksen kohteena. Metsäntutkimuslaitoksen tiedonantoja 827. 160 p. ISBN 951-40-1807-9.
Wildernesses in Finland. Metsähallitus. Brochure.

Chapter 7—Iceland

1. Trausti Baldursson is Manager for Ecology and Rangers, Environment Agency of Iceland, Nature Conservation Division.

Chapter 8—Japan

1. Japan Program Coordinator, Wild Salmon Center.
2. Population Reference Bureau 2006. http://www.prb.org/Countries/Japan.aspx.
3. Biodiversity Hotspots, www.biodiversityhotspots.org/xp/Hotspots/japan/biodiversity.xml.
4. Birdlife International. 2004. *Important bird areas in Asia: key sites for conservation.* Cambridge, UK: Birdlife International.
5. Totman, C. 1990. *The green archipelago.* New Haven, CT: Yale University Press.
6. Ibid.
7. Forrest, R. 1998. Japan. In *The north Pacific frontier: an overview of natural resources and strategies to conserve them: China, Japan; the Koreas; Siberia and the Russian far east.* Oakland, CA: Pacific Environment and Resources Center.
8. Ministry of Environment. 2002. *Living with nature: the national biodiversity strategy of Japan.* Tokyo: Ministry of Environment.
9. Kerr, A. 2002. *Dogs and demons: tales from the dark side of Japan.* New York: Hill and Wang.
10. Ministry of Land, Infrastructure, and Transport Japan, www.mlit.go.jp/yosan/yosan06/yosan/000331/01.pdf.

11. Executive Office of the President of the United States, http://www. gpoaccess.gov/usbudget/fy06/browse.html .

12. Op. cit., 9.

13. The Japan Dam Foundation. 2003. Dam Almanac 2003. (In Japanese.) Tokyo: Nihon Dam Kyoukai.

14. Fukushima, M. 2006. Modeling the effects of dams on freshwater fish distributions in Hokkaido, Japan. *Freshwater Biology.*

15. Ministry of Environment, www.env.go.jp/en/nature/npr/ncj/section5. html.

16. Ibid.

17. Ministry of Environment. 2000. *Wildlife conservation in Japan.* Tokyo: Ministry of Environment

18. Ibid.

19. Ibid.

20. Birdlife International 2004. *Important bird areas in Asia: key sites for conservation.* Cambridge, UK: Birdlife International.

21. Ministry of Environment, www.env.go.jp/en/nature/npr/ncj/section5. html.

22. Yamanaka, M. 2006. Social and political problems related to wildlife and park management in Shiretoko National Park. In *Wildlife in Shiretoko and Yellowstone National Parks: lessons in wildlife conservation from two world heritage sites.* Hokkaido, Japan: Shiretoko Nature Foundation.

23. Ibid.

24. Ibid.

25. Ibid.

26. Ministry of Environment, www.env.gov.jp/en/nature/nps/wanca. html.

27. Ministry of Environment. 2000. *Wildlife conservation in Japan.* Tokyo: Ministry of Environment.

28. Shiretoko World Heritage Site, http://whc.unesco.org/en/list/1193.

29. Ibid.

30. Kuwahara, T., et al. 2005. The current inventory of dams in Shiretoko Peninsula, Hokkaido Island, Japan. *Bulletin of the Shiretoko museum* 26:1–8. (In Japanese.) Hokkaido, Japan: Shiretoko Nature Foundation.

31. Op. cit., 14.

32. Personal observations and communications, June 2005 and October 2006.

33. Yoshinaka A. 2006. Conservation and management policy in

Shiretoko National Park. In *Wildlife in Shiretoko and Yellowstone National Parks: lessons in wildlife conservation from two world heritage sites.* Hokkaido, Japan: Shiretoko Nature Foundation.

34. Shiretoko World Heritage Site, http://whc.unesco.org/en/list/1193.
35. Ministry of Environment, http://www.env.go.jp/en/.
36. Ministry of Environment, http://www.env.go.jp/en/.
37. Ramsar Sites, www.ramsar.org/wn/w.n.japan_20sites.htm.
38. http://wwwsoc.nii.ac.jp/jdf/Dambinran/binran/Syuukei/Syuukei Soukatu.html.
39. http://www.rinya.maff.go.jp/puresu/h179gatu/0916jyukyuhyou.html.
40. BBC News. 2005) *Japan Population starts to shrink,* http://news.bbc.co.uk/2/hi/asia-pacific/4552010.stm.
41. http://www.vill.sarufutsu.hokkaido.jp/web/PD_Cont.nsf/0/D646E0CA8F84341249256E3E0023FDAB?OpenDocument.

Chapter 9—México

1. Director, Environmental Policy, The Nature Conservancy—Mexico Program.
2. Primer Seminario Nacional sobre Tierras Silvestres, October 24, 2005.
3. Adapted from: Bezaury-Creel J. 2005. Protected areas and coastal and ocean management in Mexico. Pages 1016–1046. In *Ocean & Coastal Management.* Integrated MPA Management with coastal and ocean governance: principles and practices 48 (11–12): 2005, 843–1046.
4. CONABIO. 2006. Capital Natural y Bienestar Social. Comisión Nacional para el Conocimiento de la Biodiversidad.
5. Article 45. Ley General del Equilibrio Ecológico y la Protección al Ambiente. Published January 28, 1988, modified December 13, 2006.
6. 8th World Wilderness Congress. 2005. 8th World wilderness congress generates conservation results! New Wilderness and Protected Areas. http://www.8wwc.org/.
7. Bezaury-Creel, J. in prep. [Assembled with data from: Instituto Nacional de Estadística, Geografía e Informática (INEGI), protected area management programs published by the Instituto Nacional de Ecología (INE) or CONANP, pre establishment of protected areas studies by CONANP, Vargas Márquez, 1997 and other documents].
8. Bezaury-Creel, J. in prep. [Assembled with data from: Registro Agrario Nacional (RAN), Procuraduría Agraria, Programa de Certificación de Derechos Ejidales y Titulación de Solares (PRO-CEDE), INEGI, Secretarías de Medio Ambiente y Recursos Naturales

(SEMARNAT) y de Desarrollo Social (SEDESOL)].

9. Ley Agraria, Agrarian Law, Article 119.

10. Ley Agraria, Article 120. As defined by a grazing coefficient established by the Secretary of Agriculture, Livestock and Fisheries (SAGARPA).

11. Ley Agraria, Article 119 Sociedades Propietarias de Tierras Agrícolas, Ganaderas o Forestales

12. Ley de Inversiones Extranjeras, Article 2.

13. Area of land and/or sea possessing some outstanding or representative ecosystems, geological or physiological features and/or species, available primarily for scientific research and/or environmental monitoring. IUCN. 2004. Speaking a Common Language. Cardiff University, IUCN—The World Conservation Union and UNEP—World Conservation Monitoring Centre.

14. Large area of unmodified or slightly modified land, and/or sea, retaining its natural character and influence, without permanent or significant habitation, which is protected and managed so as to preserve its natural condition. IUCN. 2004. Speaking a Common Language. Cardiff University, IUCN – The World Conservation Union and UNEP—World Conservation Monitoring Centre.

15. Ley General del Equilibrio Ecológico y la Protección al Ambiente, Article 59, second paragraph.

16. Initiated in 2002, currently a total of 139,683 hectares/345,017 acres (as of November 2006), have been certified by CONANP.

17. Zonas Silvestres.

18. Tierras Silvestres.

19. Reglamento de la Ley General del Equilibrio Ecológico y la Protección al Ambiente en Materia de Areas Naturales Protegidas.

20. Consejo Nacional de Areas Naturales Protegidas. The "Council" represents a plural and independent body, that provides advice to the Secretary of the Environment and Natural Resources (where CONANP is ascribed) on its protected area management functions, as stipulated by the Ecology Law.

21. Both prerequisites are expected to be fulfilled and finalized in 2007, in order to legally recognize the Cañón del Diablo Wilderness Zone, within the Maderas del Carmen Flora and Fauna Protection Zone.

22. Currently present only in biosphere reserves, but due to the February 23, 2005 modifications of the Ecology Law, core zones will now be included in protected areas of all categories.

Chapter 10—New Zealand

1. Chief Legal Adviser, Department of Conservation, New Zealand.
2. Section 2 Conservation Act 1987 defines a conservation area to mean "any land or foreshore that is:
   a. land or foreshore for the time being held under this Act for conservation purposes; or
   b. land in respect of which an interest is held under this Act for conservation purposes." "Conservation" is defined by the same section to mean "the preservation and protection of natural and historic resources for the purpose of maintaining their intrinsic values, providing for their appreciation and recreational enjoyment by the public and safeguarding the options of future generations."
3. The term *reserve* is defined in section 2 Reserves Act 1977.
4. Section 2 National Parks Act 1980 defines a national park or park to mean a national park constituted under the National Parks Act.
5. Established as a department of State by section 5 Conservation Act 1987.
6. See section 20 Conservation Act 1987, section 47 Reserves Act 1977, and section 14 National Parks Act 1980.
7. The system covers recreation reserves (section 17), historic reserves (section 18), scenic reserves (section 19), nature reserves (section 20), scientific reserves (section 21), government purpose reserves (section 22) and local purpose reserves (section 23).
8. Section 47 Reserves Act 1977.
9. Section 14 National Parks Act 1980.
10. Ibid.
11. See section 20 Conservation Act 1987, section 47 Reserves Act 1977 and section 14 National Parks Act 1980.
12. See section 103(1)(h) Reserves Act 1977; and section 56(1)(i) National Parks Act 1980.
13. General Policies, Conservation Management Strategies, and National Park Management Plans.
14. The office of Director-General of Conservation was created by section 52 Conservation Act 1987.
15. Section 53 Conservation Act 1987.
16. The Wilderness Policy can be found in Appendix 2 of The State of Wilderness in New Zealand, edited by Gordon Cessford, published by Department of Conservation, 2001.
17. Section 44 National Parks Act 1980.

18. Section 17B Conservation Act 1987.

19. Section 15A Reserves Act 1977.

20. Section 40A Reserves Act 1977; and section 17D Conservation Act 1987.

21. Section 44A National Parks Act 1980.

22. Section 17D(4) Conservation Act.

23. Although some Conservancies have more than one.

24. Section 45 National Parks Act 1980.

25. Id., Section 44A(2).

26. Section 18(2) Conservation Act 1987.

27. Id., Section 49(2).

28. Id., Section 49(2)(c).

29. Id., Section 49(2)(d).

30. Id., Section 49(2)(e).

31. Id., Section 18(1).

32. Id., Section 18(3).

33. Id., Section 18(5) .

34. Sections 26 & 26A Reserves Act 1977 provide for vesting of reserves in administering bodies.

35. Sections 28, 29 & 30 Reserves Act 1977 provide for the appointment of administering bodies to control and manage reserves.

36. Id., Section 47(1).

37. Id., Section 47(2).

38. Id., Section 120(1)(c).

39. Id., Section 120(1)(d) .

40. Section 14(1) National Parks Act 1980.

41. Section 18(7) Conservation Act 1987; section 47(1) Reserves Act 1977; section 14(1) National Parks Act 1980.

42. Section 18(8) Conservation Act 1987. Neither the Reserves Act 1977, nor the National Parks Act 1980 specifically requires public notification and a proposal to revoke would be raised in the context of a draft conservation management strategy or national park management plan which must undergo public notification.

43. Section 20 Conservation Act 1987; section 47 Reserves Act 1977; section 14 National Parks Act 1980.

44. Sections 39 and 44 Conservation Act 1987. But see also sections 94 and 103 Reserves Act 1977 (maximum of one month's imprisonment and $500 for an individual and maximum daily fine of $10 while offence continues, and a maximum of $1,000 for a corporation with a maximum daily fine of $10 while offence continues); and sections 60

and 70 National Parks Act 1980 (maximum of 3 months imprisonment or fine not exceeding $2,500 for individual and maximum daily fine of $250, and a maximum fine not exceeding $25,000 for a corporation and a maximum daily fine of $2,500).

45. Recreation Opportunity Spectrum.
46. Section 20(2) Conservation Act 1987; section 47(5) Reserves Act 1977; section 14(4) National Parks Act 1980.
47. Section 20(2) and (4) Conservation Act 1987; section 47(5) and () Reserves Act; section 14(4) and (6) National Parks Act 1980.
48. Section 29A Civil Aviation Act 1990.
49. Section 30 Resource Management Act 1991.
50. Section 17Q Conservation Act 1987; section 59A Reserves Act 1977; section 49 National Parks Act 1980
51. Section 17T(2) Conservation Act 1987.
52. Id., Section 17U(3).
53. Section 20(1)(d) Conservation Act 1987; section 47(4)(d) Reserves Act 1977; section 14(2)(d) National Parks Act 1980.
54. Section 20(2) Conservation Act 1980; section 47(5) Reserves Act 1977; section 14(4) National Parks Act 1980.
55. Section 20(1)(b) and (c) Conservation Act 1987; section 47(4)(b) and (c) Reserves Act 1977; section 14(2)(b) and (c) National Parks Act 1980.
56. Section 20(2)(b) Conservation Act 1987; section 47(5)(b) Reserves Act 1977; section 14(4)(b) National Parks Act 1980. Although where Maori own particular minerals then the taking of samples by hand could potentially be authorised.
57. Section 20 Reserves Act 1977.

Chapter 11—The Russian Federation

1. BP Russia, HSE Manager, IUCN CEL Member.
2. DLK Inc., Environmental Specialist, IUCN WCPA Member.
3. When this chapter was in final editing, new Forest Code (in effect since 1 January 2007) and the corresponding law on the Code's enactment had been adopted in Russia. Both substantially changed a number of provisions related to i) classification and reclassification of forests including new approach to nomination of protective/protected forests, ii) logging rules, including within protected areas, iii) organization of forest management and control systems, iv) new rules of permitting for logging and use of forests and etc. Most of changes one

or another way affect PA management.

4. New Water Code (adopted in 2006 and coming into force from January 1, 2007) introduced new system of classification, identification and delineation (identification of boundaries) of water protection zones. It also introduced private property rights for some specific water bodies (ponds and watered quarries and pits).

5. Unfortunately the draft amendments to the protected areas law proposed in December 2006 were developed by the economic ministry and seek to remove buffer zone provisions from Russian legislation and to abolish existing buffer zones. If adopted, they will destroy substantial areas of currently protected natural and wilderness areas in the country.

6. Changes in the specific types of logging regimes were introduced by the new Forest Code and are active as of January 1, 2007.

7. In exceptional cases, sport fishing may be allowed for local residents in allocated places.

8. New amendments to the Federal Law on Protected Areas (Federal Law on Enactment of the Forest Code of 4 December 2006) and specifically to article 15 were adopted in Russia to allow for construction activities, sport development and activities in the national parks in preparation for the winter Olympic games in 2014 (Western Northern Caucasus). These plans seriously affect the Sochi National Park and the Caucasus *Zapovednik*. The new amendments change the definition and regime of recreational zones of national parks allowing for mass sport activities, including "construction, reconstruction and exploitation of sport and sport-technical facilities and objects, and objects of engineering, transportation and social infrastructure." A special article was included on regulation of recreational activities in national parks.

9. The list is open: other kinds of zones may also be established by the statute of a national park.

10. See note 6 *supra*.

11. See note 6 *supra*.

12. See note 6 *supra*.

Chapter 12—South Africa

1. The authors are members of the Wilderness Action Group, South Africa.

2. Geddes-Page. 1979.

3. Department of Environmental Affairs and Tourism. 2002.
4. Bainbridge. 2001, 2002.
5. Department of Environmental Affairs and Tourism. 2002.
6. Ibid.
7. NEM:PAA, Chapter 3, Sect. 17 (a).
8. Cowling & Hilton-Taylor. 1994; Bainbridge. 2001.
9. Myers. 2000.
10. van Wyk. 1994.
11. Ibid.
12. NEM:PAA Section 26.
13. Chapter 2, Section 24.
14. Id., section 2.
15. Id., section 5.
16. Id., section 9.
17. Id., section 35.
18. Id., section 36.
19. WHCA section 4(1).
20. Id., section 4(1)(a) to (p).
21. Id., section 22.
22. NEM:PAA section 13.
23. NHRA section 3(1).
24. Id., section 3(2).
25. NFA section 3.
26. Id., section 8.
27. NEM:PAA section 15.
28. NFA section 11.
29. Id., section 10.
30. NEM:PAA section 20.
31. Id., section 22.
32. Ibid.
33. NEM:PAA section 26.
34. Id., section 27.
35. Id., section 18.
36. Id., section 28.
37. Id., section 13.
38. Id., section 14.
39. Id., section 15.
40. Id., section 16.
41. Id., section 38.

42. Id., section 39(1).
43. Id., section 39(2).
44. Id., section 41(1).
45. Id., section 41(2).
46. Id., section 41(3).
47. Id., section 42(1).
48. Id., section 43.
49. Id., section 44.
50. Id., sections 45 and 46.
51. Id., section 47.
52. Id., section 48.
53. Id., section 49.
54. Id., section 50.
55. Freitag-Ronaldson, et al. 2003.
56. F. Venter and S. Freitag-Ronaldson. 2006.
57. A. Skownow. 2006 Personal communication.
58. Ramsar Convention Bureau. 1990; and ed. K. N. Barnes. 1998.
59. Clark and Stankey. 1979.
60. Haas, et al. 1987.
61. Kreuger, S. 2006. Personal communication.
62. Ramsar Convention Bureau and ed. K. N. Barnes. 1998.
63. Hartley, P. 2006 Personal communication.
64. van Riet, W. 2004.
65. NEM:PAA section 53 (1)(a).

Chapter 13—Sri Lanka

1. Vice President for Policy, The WILD Foundation, member IUCN World Commission on Protected Areas—Wilderness Task Force.
2. 1992 Protected Areas of the World: A review of national systems—Sri Lanka Country Sheet, United Nations Environment Programme—World Conservation and Monitoring Centre http://www. unep-wcmc. org/protected_areas/data/countrysheets/lka.htm. See also Alwis, L. 1999. Origins, evolution, and present status of the protected areas of Sri Lanka. *International Journal of Wilderness* 5 (2): 37.
3. Ibid., 3.
4. National Wilderness Heritage Areas Act, No. 3 of 1988, Certified 4th March, 1988. Sinharaja was notified a national wilderness heritage area on October 21, 1988, Gazette No. 528/14.
5. CIA Factbook, https://www.cia.gov/cia/publications/factbook/geos/

ce.html.

6. Mittermeier, R.A., et al. 2004. *Hotspots Revisited.* Cemex, Inc., 152.

7. Environment Sri Lanka—Sinharaja Forest at http://www.environ-mentlanka.com/sinharaja.html.

8. United Nations Environment Programme—World Conservation and Monitoring Centre at http://www.unep-wcmc.org/protected_areas/data/wh/sinharaj.html.

9. The only other country in Asia that designates wilderness protected areas is Japan. The Philippines previously used the term for the Palanan Wilderness Area, but that protected area has been incorporated into the Northern Sierra Madre Natural Park. The law governing protected areas in the Philippines (Republic Act No.7586, An Act Providing for the Establishment of a National Integrated Protected Areas System, Defining its Scope and Coverage, and for Other Purposes Act of 1992) does not list wilderness as a protected category (though the definition of a National Park in Section 4(e) refers to "a forest reservation of natural wilderness character").

Chapter 14—The United States

1. Policy Director for the Campaign for America's Wilderness.

2. Group Manager, Wilderness, Rivers, and National Trails, Bureau of Land Management, U.S. Department of the Interior.

4. Except where noted, all acreage data in this paper are from www.wilderness.net, accessed February 15, 2007. This is the definitive source for statistics about the NWPS and each of the 702 areas protected by the Wilderness Act.

4. Subsection 2(a), Wilderness Act; 16 U.S.C. 1131 (a). The full text of the Act can be found at http://leaveitwild.org/psapp/view_art.asp?PEB_ART_ID=55.

5. Scott, Doug. 2004. *The enduring wilderness: protecting our natural heritage through the wilderness act.* Golden, CO: Fulcrum Publishing, 27–40.

6. Reid, Kenneth A. 1939. Let them alone! *Outdoor America* 5 (1): 6.

7. Leopold, Aldo. 1949. *A Sand County Almanac* New York: Oxford University Press, 189.

8. Wilderness Act, subsection 2(c); 16 U.S.C. 1132 (c).

9. Statement of Senator Clinton P. Anderson, in Senate Committee on Interior and Insular Affairs, *Wilderness Act,* Hearings before the Senate Committee on Interior and Insular Affairs, U.S. Senate (87th

Congress, 1st session), February 27–28, 1961, page 2.

10. Supplementary Statement of Howard Zahniser, Executive Director of the Wilderness Society, in *National Wilderness Preservation Act*, Hearings before the Committee on Interior and Insular Affairs, U.S. Senate (88th Congress, 1st session), February 28 and March 1, 1963, page 68.

11. Op. cit. 5, pages 66–72, 126–129.

12. Howard Zahniser. 1964. The people and wilderness. *The Living Wilderness* 28 (86 Spring/Summer): 39.

13. The way in which this requirement of passing a new law to alter wilderness area boundaries or protections serves to strongly guarantee that preservation will be sustained may not apply as strongly in parliamentary systems, where a change of government by the election of a new legislative majority can result in rapid and wholesale revision of earlier statutes.

14. George Marshall. 1969. *Wilderness and the quality of life*. Introduction. Eds. Maxine E. McCloskey and James P. Gilligan. San Francisco: Sierra Club, 13–15.

15. Subsection 4(b), Wilderness Act; 16 U.S.C. 1133 (a).

16. This is explored in detail in Douglas W. Scott, 'Untrammeled,' 'Wilderness Character,' and the Challenges of Wilderness Preservation, *Wild Earth*, Fall/Winter 2001–2002, pages 72–79, http://www.leaveitwild.org/reports/Untrammeled_Article.pdf.

17. Subsection 4(c), Wilderness Act; U.S.C. 1133 (c).

18. *Preservation of Wilderness Areas*, Hearing before the Subcommittee on Public Lands, Committee on Interior and Insular Affairs, U.S. Senate (92nd Congress, 2nd session), May 5, 1972, pages 61–62.

19. http://www.wilderness.net/index.cfm?fuse=MRDG.

20. Dave Foreman summarizes the etymology of the word *wilderness* as traced by historians and philosophers: "According to historian Roderick Nash, the word wilderness comes from the Old English *Wil-deor-ness*, which he defined in 1967 as "place of wild beasts." *Wil*: Wild, or willed. *Deor*: Beast, or deer. *Ness*: Place, or quality. In a 1983 talk at the Third World Wilderness Conference in Scotland, philosopher Jay Hansford Vest also sought the meaning of wilderness in Old English and further back in Old Gothic languages. He showed that wilderness means "'self-willed land' … with an emphasis on its own intrinsic volition." He interpreted *der* as of the, not as coming from *deor*. "Hence, in *wil-der-ness*, there is a 'will-of-the-land'; and in *wildeor*, there is 'will of the animal.' A wild animal is a 'self-willed animal'—an

undomesticated animal—similarly, wildland is 'self-willed land.'" Vest shows that this willfulness is opposed to the "controlled and ordered environment which is characteristic of the notion of civilization."

21. Leopold, Aldo. 1925. The last stand of the wilderness. *American Forests and Forest Life* 31 (382): 603.

22. Marshall, Robert. 1930. The problem of the wilderness. *The Scientific Monthly* (February 1930): 146.

23. Zahniser, Howard Zahniser. 1949. A statement on wilderness preservation in reply to a questionnaire [submitted to the Legislative Reference Service, Library of Congress]. March 1, 1949. Reprinted in *National Wilderness Preservation Act*, Hearings before the Committee on Interior and Insular Affairs, U.S. Senate (85th Congress, 1st session), June 19–20, 1957, page 192.

24. Senator Hubert H. Humphrey, Wilderness Preservation, *Congressional Record*, June 7, 1956.

25. No President has ever used this authority.

26. Special Use Provisions in Wilderness Legislation, Natural Resources Law Center, University of Colorado School of Law, 2004; www.colorado.edu/law/centers/nrlc/projects/wilderness/SpecialUse Provisions.pdf (accessed January 25, 2006).

27. Alaska National Interest Lands Conservation Act of 1980, 43. U.S.C. 1602.

28. Federal Land Policy and Management Act of 1976, 43 U.S.C. 1701.

29. Zahniser, Howard. 1963. Guardians not gardeners. Editorial. *The Living Wilderness* (Spring/Summer 1963): 1.

PART III

Chapter 15—Southern and Eastern Africa

1. Vice President for Policy, The WILD Foundation, member IUCN World Commission on Protected Areas—Wilderness Task Force.

2. President, The WILD Foundation, member IUCN World Commission on Protected Areas—Wilderness Task Force.

3. Mittermeier et al., 2005. *Transboundary Conservation: A New Vision for Protected Areas*, Cemex, S.A. de C.V., pp. 247–275.

4. The Role of National Parks at http://www.tanzaniaparks.com/role.htm.

5. Ibid.

6. Gereta, E.J. 1998. Serengeti shall not die—national parks in Tanzania.

National Parks Journal (December 1998): 6.

7. Mtahiko, M.G.G. 2004. Wilderness in the Ruaha national park, Tanzania. International Journal of Wilderness 10 (3): 41.

8. Serengeti National Park (SENAPA), General Management Plan 2005-2015, TANAPA, August 2005.

9. Op. cit. 6, p. 12.

10. Loc. cit.

11. Op. cit. 5, p. 43.

12. Stolberger, S. 2005. The Ruaha national park, Tanzania. *International Journal of Wilderness* 11 (1): 33.

13. Hendee, J. and C. Dawson. 2002. *Wilderness management: stewardship and protection of resources and values, third edition.* Golden, CO: Fulcrum, 82.

14. Iain Jarvis, Executive Director, Wilderness Africa Trust, March 2, 2007.

15. Ibid.

16. Op. cit., 11.

17. http://wildernsessafricatrust.org/index.cfm?id=22.

Chapter 16—Italy

1. Co-founder and Secretary General of the Associazione Italiana per la Wilderness (AIW).

2. Italian Ministry for the Environment and territory 2005. 5 Years to Make a Difference, Italy launches countdown 2010 initiative to halt the loss of biodiversity.

3. Ministry of the Environment, Nature Conservation Service 1998. Italian National Report on the Implementation of the Convention on Biological Diversity, p. 5.

4. Zunino, F. 1980. Wilderness, a new necessity for the preservation of natural areas. (In Italian.) Italy: National Department of Agriculture and Forests.

5. Zunino, F. 1984. A wilderness concept for Europe. In *Wilderness the way ahead: proceedings of the 3rd world wilderness congress,* eds. V. Martin and M. Inglis. Finhorn Press and Lorian Press, 61–65.

6. For more information on particular areas designated as wilderness in Italy please see Zunino, F. 1995. The wilderness movement in Italy—a wilderness model for Europe. *International Journal of Wilderness* 1 (2).

7. Friuli Venezia Giulia Region, Regional Executive Board (Delibera della Giunta Regionale) Decree no. 3117/2006.

8. Leopold, A. 1921. The wilderness and its place in forest recreation policy. *Journal of Forestry. Reprinted in The River of the Mother of God*

and other Essays by Aldo Leopold, S. Flader and J. B. Callicott. University of Wisconsin Press 1991, 78.

Chapter 17—Ukraine

1. National Taras Shevchenko University of Kiev, Kiev Ecological and Cultural Center.
2. University of Idaho, Environmental Science Program.
3. Verhovna Rada of USSR N 1264-XII 1991.
4. Verhovna Rada of Ukraine N 2456-XII 1992.
5. Verhovna Rada of Ukraine N 2768-III 2001.
6. Parliament of Ukraine.
7. Verhovna Rada of Ukraine 280/97 VR 1997.
8. Governing body of an administrative region. Ukraine is subdivided into 27 administrative regions: 24 provinces, 2 municipalities and 1 autonomous republic.

PART IV

Chapter 18—New Directions

1. Vice President for Policy at The WILD Foundation and a member of the IUCN-WCPA Wilderness Task Force.
2. President of The WILD Foundation, and Co-Chair of the IUCN-WCPA Wilderness Task Force.
3. Senior Policy Advisor at NOAA's National Marine Sanctuary Program and a member of IUCN's World Commission on Protected Areas.
4. Respect for the Land: The Dehcho Land Use Plan, The Dehcho Land Use Planning Committee, Final Draft Plan May 2006.
5. See http://www.conservation.org/xp/frontlines/2006/08090602.xml.
6. Aragon, D. 2007. The Wind River Indian Tribes. In *Wilderness, wildlands and people: a partnership for the planet, proceedings of 8th world wilderness congress,* eds. V. Martin and C. Kormos. Golden, CO: Fulcrum Publishing.
7. Tribal Wilderness Management Tool Box, Section D, Management of Tribal Wilderness, Primitive Areas, and Wilderness Lands Re-classified to Tribal Jurisdiction at http://www.wilderness.net/index.cfm?fuse=toolboxes&sec=IFST.
8. Tlingit and Haida Indian Tribes of Alaska, Tribal Statutes and Administrative Code, Title 11, Land and Natural Resources, Chapter 02, Land Uses, Section 11.02.002 (A)(3), (B)(2), April 1995 at http://www.ccthita.org/statutes.html.

9. Confederated Tribes of Warm Springs, Tribal Code, Chapter 411 Zoning and Land Use Code, Section 411.215 7 enacted by Ordinance 56 (7-29-87) at http://www.warmsprings.com/Warmsprings/Tribal_ Community/Tribal_Government/Current_Governing_Body/Tribal_ Code_Book/.

10. Tribal Wildernessess, Tribal Research Natural Areas, and Tribal Vehicle Permit Areas on National Forests, Great Lakes Indian Fish and Wildlife Commission, Version 1.1, June 2004.

11. Tribal Wilderness Management Toolbox, Part D., Management of Tribal Wilderness, Primitive Areas, and Wilderness Lands Re-Classified to Tribal Jurisdiction, 6–10 at http://www.wilderness.net/ index.cfm?fuse=toolboxes&sec=IFST.

12. Alaska National Interest Lands Conservation Act (ANILCA), 16 U.S.C.3101-3233, s.1316; see also Tanner, R. 2004. Subsistence, Inholdings, and ANILCA; The Complexity of Wilderness Stewardship in Alaska. *International Journal of Wilderness* 10 (2) August 2004: 18–22.

13. Tomkins, D. 2007. How things got started. In *Wilderness, wildlands and people: a partnership for the planet, proceedings of 8th world wilderness congress*, eds. V. Martin and C. Kormos. Golden, CO: Fulcrum Publishing. See also Foundation for Deep Ecology, The First Ten Years 1990–1999 and The Conservation Land Trust, The First Ten Years 1992–2002. http://www.deepecology.org/.

14. http://www.africanparks-conservation.com/.

15. Chittenden, Maurice. 2006. It's my forest now. no logging. *The Sunday Times*, March 19, 2006.

16. See http://www.wcs.org/353624/4556203.

17. http://www.apa.state.ny.us/About_Park/index.html.

18. Butler, T. 2007. Wildlands philanthropy: an American tradition. In *Wilderness, wildlands and people: a partnership for the planet, proceedings of 8th world wilderness congress*, eds. V. Martin and C. Kormos. Golden, CO: Fulcrum Publishing.

19. CEMEX, Inc. *El Carmen: Cemex in the Conservation of Biodiversity.* Undated brochure.

20. Thoreau, H. D. 1865. *Cape Cod.* http://thoreau.eserver.org/capecd00. html.

21. Wallis, O.L. 1958. Research and interpretation of marine areas of the U.S. National Park Service. *Proceedings of the Gulf and Caribbean Fisheries Institute* 11: 134–138.

22. Eissler, F. 1968. Toward an underwater wilderness system. Sierra Club

Bulletin 53: 26.

23. Smith, P.M. and R.A. Watson. 1979. New wilderness boundaries. *Environmental Ethics* 1(1): 61–64.

24. Sloan, N. A. 2002. *History and Application of the Wilderness Concept in Marine Conservation. Conservation Biology* 16(2): 294–305.

25. Smith, H. 1983. Marine wilderness areas and multiple use management. In *Wilderness: the way ahead,* eds. Vance G. Martin and Mary Inglis. 1984. Forres, Scotland: Findhorn Press and Middleton, WI: Lorian Press, 99–103.

26. Foster, N. and M.H. Lemay. 1988. Oceanic wilderness—myth, challenge or opportunity? In *For the Conservation of Earth,* ed. Vance G. Martin. Golden, CO: Fulcrum, 71–74.

27. Ban, Natalie. 2005. Personal communication. September 19.

28. Clifton, J. 2003. Prospects for co-management in Indonesia's marine protected areas. *Marine Policy* 27: 389–395.

Chapter 19—Conclusion

1. Vice President for Policy, The WILD Foundation, member IUCN World Commission on Protected Areas—Wilderness Task Force.

Index